BETTE

THE LIFE OF BETTE DAVIS

"Vivid . . . as close to an ideal biography as we've had in some time. . . . she's presented as a whole person who, in numerous situations, is paradoxically sympathetic and difficult, wretched and mistreated, hilarious and infuriating. . . . *Bette* presents a very human being—unvarnished and likeable." —*The Pittsburgh Press*

"Captures the magic. . . . like Davis, when the book is good, it is very, very good . . . the story of a winner." —*Columbus Citizen-Journal*

"Higham attempts to reconcile Ms. Davis's Jekyll-Hyde images: the highly intelligent, down-to-earth, witty professional we see on talk shows, and the rampaging harpy who has brought disaster—personal and professional—upon all heads, especially her own. It is the honorable persistence of Higham's search into the mystery of personality, and the complexity and fascination of the personality he probes, that make this the best book so far that says what it has to say about Bette Davis." —*Dallas Times Herald*

OTHER BOOKS BY CHARLES HIGHAM:

Kate: The Life of Katharine Hepburn
Errol Flynn
Marlene Dietrich
Starmaker: The Autobiography of Hal Wallis

BETTE

THE LIFE OF BETTE DAVIS

Charles Higham

A DELL BOOK

Published by
Dell Publishing Co., Inc.
1 Dag Hammarskjold Plaza
New York, New York 10017

Dell ® TM 681510, Dell Publishing Co., Inc.

ISBN: 0-440-10662-1

Reprinted by arrangement with Macmillan Publishing Co., Inc.

Printed in the United States of America

First Dell printing—December 1982

For Toni Lopopolo,
my editor

BETTE

CALIFORNIA PROLOGUE: 1963

The road winds upward through Bel-Air, passing banks of Algerian ivy, magnolia trees, pink and purple flamboyants. Here is a French château, there a British witch's cottage, and there again a building that looks like a small Gothic tomb. The vegetation has a surrealist absurdity: Canadian pencil pines frame a doorway that suggests eighteenth-century Brazil; palms, cut down to stumps, are stuck in authentic Italian Renaissance pots; daffodils flank five plump green cacti. In one of these houses recently, I saw the parchment text of a Gregorian chant used as a lampshade.

We arrive at our destination. Don Prince, crew-cut movie-publicity man, who once splashed naked in a fountain with singer Helen Morgan, and whose favorite phrase summarizing Hollywood is "They eat their young," points out the house. Beyond a black-painted iron gate, two jockey ornamental hitching posts stand on the lawn, the jockeys' hands outstretched for nonexistent reins. We might be in the South—in Margaret Mitchell territory—but the cottage itself is quasi-New England: primly cozy and formalized, with self-assured red bricks.

A woman dashes out, full-breasted and wide-hipped in shirt and slacks, arms flapping at her sides, reddish hair tossed in bangs. Of course, it couldn't be anyone else. The voice seems, like so many voices, younger than its owner.

11

The energy is all in the movements and gestures; the fiercely intelligent face is lined, deeply marked with suffering.

It is nice that, unlike most stars, Bette Davis doesn't lurk at the top of a regal staircase, to descend only when the guest has been kept waiting long enough. It is as though she is herself a quarter of a century ago in *The Great Lie*, running out to greet George Brent as he flies back from some South American mission to the bride he had left behind.

She pumps my hand. Her grip is as tight as a boxer's. "Come indoors, *for Christ's sake!*" she cheerfully commands, grinning and grabbing my arm.

Looking for clues to her personality, I enter the cottage. What I had taken to be the front door turns out instead to be a back door. We walk through the kitchen. It is spanking clean, as neat and organized as a model kitchen in a department store, with everything, from blue china dishes to brass cooking implements to glass jars of cookies, set out so conscientiously that they might be for sale.

A strange couple materializes. The more striking of the pair is the woman. She is thin, pale, excessively nervous, dressed in a sad range of grays. Her eyes seem incorrectly aligned, the portions of her face oddly ill-matched, but she may have been almost pretty at one time. The man is dressed like a servant, in a black coat and striped pants with pegged bottoms over black patent-leather shoes. Both husband and wife (for that, transparently, are what they are) look rather miserable. They are not introduced. They stand smiling crookedly like servants in a Charles Addams drawing. I feel a sense of discomfort when, after much dipping into my memory bank, I come up with a bonus: The woman is Bette Davis's sister, Bobby; the man is Bobby's husband.

Now we are in the living room. It exudes an atmosphere of Hollywood–New England snugness, and looks as though it has been put together by a set designer for one of Bette Davis's 1940s movies. A round mahogany table, polished to a fault, boasts a lazy Susan that offers salt, pepper, nutmeg, and a half-dozen other spices and condiments. On a wall is a gilt-framed picture of the star done in pastels; she is dressed as Jezebel in somebody's idea of an antebellum lace gown. I know stars who order wooden books to match the wallpaper. Her books are real, and they have been read. They are for the most part novels of thirties vintage. The covers are designed to look like parchment, with heavy, red-and-black classical lettering and pictures of the hero and heroine framed against Gothic sunsets. They have top-stained pages—rare in our austere age—heavy-stitched bindings that would defy a wrestler to tear them apart, thick luxurious paper, reliable lending-library names like Bromfield, Ferber, Marquand, Frances Parkinson Keyes. And nearby are prints of hunting or fishing scenes, family pictures in silver frames, and a photograph of a girl with distracted, haunted eyes: the star's adopted daughter.

I notice in one frame a handsome, clean-cut, all-American boy with hair as bleached as a gull's wing: surely her son Michael. A tall, rather serious-looking blond girl: her daughter Barbara. Only the latest of her four husbands is on display: the actor Gary Merrill, whose film career reached its zenith in *All About Eve*. Later on, he will run a lighthouse and appear in a Broadway play. He looks strongly masculine, with the hands of a lumberjack and thick black hairs sprouting from his chest through a checked open shirt.

The star fixes us Scotches; she sinks into an antique rocking chair. With a characteristic gesture, she strikes a wooden kitchen match under the table. She lights up a Philip Morris plucked from a pewter mug, sucking in her cheeks, but not inhaling. Now I know why, after smoking a zillion cigarettes, she hasn't so much as a smoker's cough. She looks at me hard, in the eyes, challenging me. "Shoot!" she snaps. Yet I, not she, have to face this particular firing squad. I begin by asking about her mother, known to showbiz people as Ruthie. Bette holds the cigarette between her thumb and forefinger; clearly, the cigarette is a prop in both senses.

"*Ruthie!*" She rises, pacing about the room like the villainess of *The Letter* lying about a murder. "Oh, my *God*, how I miss her! I owe *everything* to her. People called her

13

the typical show business mother. But she *wasn't*. She over-protected me and coddled me rather than pushing me out in the spotlight. It was *I* and *I alone* who decided to be a star. *She*, it is true, wanted to be an actress. But *she* would never have made it. *I* had to be the monster for both of us! I knew from the beginning I was good and I also knew how to act the poor, woebegone little *wren*! Nobody knew what I was up to. They all thought, 'She's impossible. She has two left feet and she wouldn't say "boo" to a goose.' How wrong they were! I would have said 'boo' to a *bison*!"

I don't have the courage to mention that she is being excessively kind to Ruthie, who drained Bette of her money and lived in a house three times larger than Bette's own.

Bette continues: "Why don't you ask me about *Father*? He walked out on us when I was eight. I missed him like *hell*. He was a *brain. Brilliant!* He was *tremendously* proud of my career, even though he thought I was *mad* to under-take it. He came backstage one night when I was on Broad-way. I *ached* for his words of praise. But he was far too reticent to do anything except express admiration for every-body in the cast except me. I wanted to shake him and say, 'I was good, too!' But I loved him dearly just the same, and his death was a *horrible* shock to me." As she says these words, she looks up at herself in the *Jezebel* portrait, and I recall something I once read—that Harlow Morrell Davis died when she was in the middle of making that picture.

I take a plunge. What about her husbands? She screams. "My *God*! You reporters nowadays want to know *every-thing*, don't you? Aren't you going to ask me about my pickshaws?" (She rhymes the word with "rickshaws.") I sit silent, not knowing what to say—even if I had the chance. She pours another Scotch and throws it down, visibly irri-tated that I have turned in desperation to 7-Up. Like all stars who enjoy a drink in the middle of the afternoon, she regards interviewers who don't as incorrigibly weird. But she's still not going to give up her performance, even if it kills both of us. She paces around the room, hands flapping like a seal's flippers, smoke rising in small mushroom clouds over her head, all temperament and talent and teeth. And fire and music.

"My *husbands*!" She pronounces the word with the same inflection most people use when they mention Adolf Hitler. "My first, as I'm sure you know, was called *Ham*. Ham Nelson! He suited the *Ham* but not the *Nelson*! I named the Oscar after him. He had a middle initial O, like David Selznick. He had a fat, epicene bottom. It made *mine* look like Charles Atlas's! Did I say *had*?" She explodes into a burst of laughter. "I should have said, '*Has*'! I saw him the other day. And first thing up, I looked at his fanny. It hadn't improved. So when I got hold of that statuette when I won it for *Dangerous*, I said to myself as I turned it around, 'Oh, *God*, its fanny's a dead ringer for Ham's!' Now I couldn't call the greatest acting award in the world a *Ham*, could I? So it *had* to be an Oscar!"

I think about Ham Nelson for a minute. A weak charmer, who conducted a dance band at the Hollywood Roosevelt Hotel, getting home at four o'clock every morning when Bette had to rise at six to drive to Warner Brothers studio. When she talks of him, all those sepia movie magazines of the thirties in which they were seen like two figures in a valentine now seem sadder than ever. But she *did*, she said, love her second husband, Arthur Farnsworth, who oddly combined the jobs of flier and night manager at an inn where she once stayed. She said, "When his mother buried him, the blasting kept me awake all night. He was in rocks—in the family crypt back East. How I longed to blast him out again! He should be waiting for me in Forest Lawn. But now I'll never have the courage to bring him West again."

Recalling Farnsworth, whom she felt she would have stayed with forever had he lived, doesn't seem to provoke tenderness or warmth in Bette. One sees her tragedy; she had to fight so hard in a world of men, she was afraid to seem feminine or sensitive, and finally her natural vulnerability was hidden behind fierceness and a tough, down-to-earth charm.

15

As for her third husband, William Grant Sherry: "He was a painter of marine landscapes, and *I* was supposed to be a patron of the arts. Actually, I liked the way he looked on the beach in a pair of shorts. If you think you see a fool sitting before you, well—" (this with a new stroke of a kitchen match under the table), "I've got news for you. You do. But I'll always be grateful for one thing. *Mr. William Grant Sherry gave me a daughter!*"

She was silent about Gary Merrill. ("Please don't ask me.")

I turn to Miss Davis's movies. *Of Human Bondage*? "The studio—Warners—*fought* my doing that picture. But I loved Somerset Maugham's book, and I begged them to let me go to RKO. They finally agreed. I knew they were thinking. 'All right, let her sink herself; we're tired of her anyway. Nobody will believe her as a Cockney waitress.' Well, they *did* believe me. I decided there could be no middle way, no glamour. Mildred *had* to be a bitch. And *God*, what a bitch! I was *disgustingly* good. I looked, as you British would say, a *fright*. My *hair*! I wouldn't let them take me within a hundred *miles* of a beauty parlor. Mildred was poor; she was making maybe two bucks a week. She was on her feet all day; she was dog-tired at night. She was serving food, cheap English food, the worst on earth, and dragging filthy, dirty dishes, and she hated people as a result. Oh, if Mildred was going to have a man in her life he had better be exciting, strong; he had better make her feel wanted. And then she meets this weak sister, this *writer*, for God's sake!"

She stops a minute, realizing she is talking to one, and then continues. "You've seen *Of Human Bondage*?" I reluctantly confess I have not. She lets out a cry. "Oh-h-h! I'll take care of that!" She rushes to a closet, drags out a print of the picture, and stands it up against my chair. "Call me when you've seen it! And in the meantime, let's talk about something else!"

She rushes on to another picture, *Old Acquaintance*. She surprises me by saying that the part of the novelist she played in that picture was closer to herself than any other character she had portrayed. The novelist was a picture of

16

brisk, healthy, outgoing good cheer, with a balanced, shrewd mind and a cool absence of temperament. But the woman I am looking at is more like the temperamental popular writer played by Miriam Hopkins in the same picture. "John Van Druten wrote *Old Acquaintance* with someone like me in mind!" Bette Davis exclaims. I'm not courageous enough to tell her that she was the last choice for the part.

Instead, I change the subject and move over to *The Letter,* the excellent picture in which she played a memsahib in Malaya who murdered her lover while apparently under the influence of the moon. I ask her about the opening sequence in which she shoots her lover to death outside the plantation house at night. "The director, William Wyler, made me do that scene *thirty-three* times! I kept running out of ammunition and that poor man who played my victim had to have a constant supply of white tuxedos! They were endlessly rushing up and brushing off his poor dirty face. And then the producer, Hal Wallis, printed the first take! To keep Willie happy, he told him it was take thirty-three."

I ask her how it felt to play a murderess. She looks me straight in the eye, and I feel as though I've just stepped into the ring with Muhammad Ali. "I *know* why you ask me that question. I'll say this—actresses hate playing murderesses more than anything. Even when Loretta Young hit someone over the head with a blunt instrument to save herself from rape in a picture, she cried and *cried.* But I've *never* worried about my image being dented. There are quite a few people I'd like to kill right now. I'll kill *you,* for instance, if you ever print the name of a man who dropped his *Communist party card* on my living-room floor, directed several of my pictures, exposed everybody in the Unfriendly Ten, and fled to Mexico to escape trial!"

And what about *The Little Foxes,* in which Bette was exceptionally fine as Lillian Hellman's vicious southern woman, Regina Giddens? "I *hated* every minute of that picture. Willie Wyler kept saying, 'Play Regina charming. Let her kill with a smile. Remember Tallulah.' Well, I didn't *want* to remember Tallulah. Bankhead was far

17

greater than I in the part—I made the horrible mistake of seeing her on the stage—and I couldn't easily play a woman as charming who tells her own husband she wants him to die—and die soon. *Who lets him die!*"

My attention wanders for a minute as I recall the picture. "Are you listening to me?" Miss Davis's voice snaps. I reply that I don't have an alternative, and she slaps her thigh and bellows with laughter. "I am talking, in case you're lying, about *All About Eve*! That picture saved my life. Professionally and personally. When I made it, I had been hit by a truck—the same truck that hit Margo Channing, that great bloody ham I played. Oh, I don't mean a *real* truck. I mean, I had been hit by the knowledge, which is heavier than a truck for most women, that I was *forty*. And I knew Margo felt *every one of those years* hitting her and I felt down here in my gut every word she said when she told her lover, 'I hate men!' She hated them for staying attractive forever. From the day I was forty, I *screamed* every time I saw a mirror. It wasn't as though I was Hepburn. She could look great at a *hundred*. Sometimes I see my face in a shop window and I want to *die*."

I feel like saying that if she looked at other people's faces instead, it might help.

"And then—" (a puff of her fifth cigarette and a third Scotch down the hatch), "I did *Another Man's Poison*. Right after *All About Eve*! I must have been out of my mind—a murderess in riding breeches?"

It's time to go. We have talked all afternoon. She signs her autobiography—I had brought it with me—with a flourish, in a large, round, bold hand, surprisingly in green ink. She writes, "I so enjoyed my interview with you." How odd she should put it that way, as though she had conducted the interview herself.

Of course, I realize, she has. As I rise to leave, I can see she isn't just that bold, hard-hitting, feisty dame she likes to be. I look into the pale blue eyes, alive with humor and intelligence, and see another, hypersensitive, thin-skinned self, full of insecurity, vulnerability, bad nerves. She has given the same interview for over thirty years. The same sort of lively interview all stars cook up in different ways

18

to pacify the press, to keep their secrets. I hold a thought of her as Don Prince and I drive back to the hotel. The nervous, retiring girl who forced herself to be a demon to make it in show business. The picture of health who was edgy and frightened; the thrifty New Englander who damaged herself financially to help a mentally sick sister and a devouring, emotionally blackmailing mother. She wants to be a monster, I tell myself, so people will fear her; she knows what it takes to claw the way to the top. But scrape away the greasepaint and there is an almost-too-honest, still-unfulfilled woman, whose fierceness is a cover for terror, sadness, and loneliness. I feel a wave of melancholy as we go off downhill—then recover quickly. I remember that Bette Davis is a supreme actress of our time, that in her tormented life her career is—has had to be—reward enough for her in place of comfort and happiness.

It scarcely needs saying that only Katharine Hepburn has matched Bette Davis's range and achievement as a screen actress. The essence of Davis's genius is not merely that she has given us an unforgettable personality, expressed in a striking array of theatrical mannerisms that identify her the moment her name is mentioned. Underneath the battery of technique, of sheer adroitness, there is the extraordinary truthfulness, the uncompromising realism. Whereas most stars have remained static, relying on a fixed, immutable personality that fades with the passing of fashion, she has survived because she has been able to adapt herself to successive decades, to become "modern" again as each new decade is born. Today, in 1981, she is as imposing as ever. Under the rugged conditions of television, with no time for rehearsal, for preparation, even for several takes, she is back in the kind of pressure-cooker atmosphere she knew in the early days of the talkies. And the pressure suits her, supremely practiced as she is; she is among the few "names" the television chiefs automatically think of when they need a star in her age group to appear in a television movie-of-the-week.

She has never, of course, been "beautiful" in the conven-

19

tional sense; but her face is better than beautiful. It is mysterious, intriguing, capable of an extraordinary expressiveness. She has the star's knack of imposing herself on every part, making it her own, and yet discovering unexpected depths in it, "becoming" it so that she is able to convert herself, with striking intensity, into someone unlike herself. She has often said in interviews that her unease with the human being called "Bette Davis," her discomfort with her challenging personality, has made her want to lose herself in others by acting parts to the full; yet her ego could not have managed these hiding places in imagined personalities unless it were itself possessed of great power. She has always had to impose herself in order to escape from herself. She acquired by forcefulness a control over producers and directors that once bent the motion picture industry to her will. Only great popular acceptance could have made the exercise of that will possible. In the 1950s and 1960s, when her public acceptance faded, she was extremely frustrated. She rejoices in her comeback in the 1980s.

Her first screen self was slender, vulnerable, eager, and trembling with nervous excitement. Despite her lack of conventional good looks, her face, even at the beginning of her career, was mesmerizing. Young people today who were born long after she reached her zenith can identify with her when they see her movies. She has great individuality; a kind of fresh, anticipatory energy and sweetness. There is a feeling of courage about her, as though she would dare anything; her real-life fear of so much of life was consumed in the audacity of her screen presence.

She was at her best under strong directors who controlled her and sought out the best she had to give. The great William Wyler, who was in love with her, managed to use her fierceness and nervous mannerisms with great creativity. The results are seen in her finest performances. As the frustrated Regina Giddens in *The Little Foxes* she suggested in every taut, strained gesture the anger of a heartless, ambitious woman living in a world run by men. In *The Letter*, as Leslie Crosbie, a murderess, she was no less striking; in an early scene she lies about the circumstances of her lover's death, with simulated tears, a damp handkerchief twisted in her palm, her words tumbling out in a stream of carefully rehearsed sentences. When she finally tells the truth—that she has killed the man deliberately—she speaks with a more mechanical, repressed emotional severity, making us see how she has willed both falsehood and truth in her life. And in *Jezebel*, she rises above a rambling, novelettish script to fashion a real character out of the selfish southern belle, Julie Marsden. Spoiled, defiant, petulant, and destructive, Julie is a fully rounded creation.

Only one other director besides Wyler brought Davis to this level—Joseph L. Mankiewicz, in *All About Eve*. She has, of course, become more famous for this movie than for any other, and it is a sorrow that the Academy Award vote was split between her and Anne Baxter, depriving her of an Oscar for what was perhaps her best performance. As Margo Channing, a theatrical star in the Bankhead mold, the full range of her talent can be seen and enjoyed. It is, as she has always said, a dream of a part. Margo— unhappy, vulnerable, absurdly generous, extravagant in all her feelings, insecure and afraid of the future yet capable of bold, transcendent bitchery—is a role "made" for Davis, and she brings it gorgeously to life.

Davis dominated her pictures completely. Having conquered Hollywood, she tended to have weak directors, sometimes effectively, sometimes fatally, controlling them. Her tendency toward inventive makeup rivaled that of Kabuki actors, so that, aided by her friend, the makeup artist Perc Westmore, who enabled her to look any age she chose, she sometimes allowed exaggeration; the bushy-browed face of the spinster aunt in the early scenes of *Now, Voyager*, the hag that Fanny Skeffington becomes in *Mr. Skeffington*, the carnival-mask countenance of Baby Jane, seem altogether too extreme. It is well known that she often plunged into self-parody, out-parodying the parodists themselves—who were legion. Yet she could be capable of restraint, control, and subtle makeups, as in the neglected *Winter Meeting*, in which she touchingly played a worn, virginal New York poet; or in *Dark Victory*, in which she triumphed over soap operatics in a sensitive, subdued performance as an heiress with a terminal brain disease.

The gestures, the hip-swinging stride, cigarette puffing, widening of the eyes at moments of stress or humor, turning on a heel with arms whirling, the hand brushing back a wing of hair, the fingers nervously clenching and loosening, the "Broadway-British" voice with its heavy emphases on final consonants—all these are part of our popular culture. But too often her quieter talents have been overlooked. Everyone remembers "What a dumppp!" and "Fasten your seatbelts, it's going to be a bumpppy night!" But one would do better perhaps to recall the moment in *Dark Victory* when the heiress finds the "prognosis negative" medical report that tells her she has only a short time to live; Miss Moffat's examination scene in *The Corn Is Green*; or her farewell to the miner-writer Morgan Evans in the same picture when her face is blurred with tears at the window. One can't overlook her crippled wife in *Phone Call from a Stranger*, hoisting herself up, in a perfect simulation of a paraplegic, to express love for her humdrum husband who has devoted himself to her following a swimming accident. Or her plump and unhappy Bronx housewife, in shapeless summer dreses, winding up her hair in a tight, defiant coil, in *The Catered Affair*. The weight of the gesture, the heavy movement of the arms, the smudged expression in the mirror, are proofs of an actress at the peak of her powers.

These exquisite performances completely invalidate any claims made by Davis's detractors that theatricality is her only stock-in-trade. More importantly, they justify the unshakable belief in her own talent that carried her, often over some very rough roads, from the staid and repressive New England world of her childhood to the top.

ONE

Ruth Elizabeth Davis was cheerlessly conceived. Hers were stark and stony New England origins. In *Now, Voyager*, she takes out a picture of aunts and uncles, all of whom face the camera as though they are facing a firing squad. It is an almost autobiographical moment. "Respect" and "honor" were words used more often by the Davises than "affection" and "love." The Davis family line ran like a fine-meshed chain from the sturdy anchor of early Welsh Puritan settlers in Massachusetts. Wintry Davis faces and bony figures, complacent with self-denial, devoted to good works and the building of churches and wooden villages, gaze at us from early paintings of the time. They founded Massachusetts on good, New World bedrock. They sailed clippers up and down the coast looking for whale. They founded their dynasty earnestly.

On the other side of the family were the Keyeses. English, they sailed from Britain to Watertown in 1634, and later settled in Lowell. Bette's uncle, Rev. Paul G. Favor, discussed her ancestry in a family memoir. Levi Keyes was Bette's great-great-grandfather. Levi was the father of Harriet Keyes Thompson, who raised her granddaughter Eugenia from infancy, after the baby's mother died.

In 1878 Eugenia married William A. Favor, of French Huguenot descent; their second child was Bette's mother, Ruth.

The Keyeses, the Reverend Favor tells us, were driven by a motor that propelled them, an engine of ruthless ambition. Favor describes Bette when he describes her mother, grandmother, and great-grandmother: "This elemental driving force of the Keyes [womenfolk] was a double power, the power of vision to see what they would accomplish, and the power to release an uncommon degree of energy which recognized no obstacle strong enough to deter them from achieving their ends."

Bette's grandmother Eugenia was the most formidable of powers. She managed the family as though all of its members composed a Sunday school class. Paul Favor adds: "She was not tyrannical or violent, but she was as persistent as a flowing river and as irresistible. To escape from that river was as impossible as for logs to swim upstream. . . . She sought, by precept and example, to inculcate lessons of industry, studiousness, morality, and religion." Each day was laid out with the aid of a large, ruled, black book, in which everything performed was predicted and willed at the exact hours appointed.

At mealtimes, a gong rang and the children—and later the grandchildren—had to appear that instant or they were forbidden their food. They were not to speak in the presence of adults, even to indicate a stomachache or headache. Music lessons were conducted with metronomic precision. The smaller children had a half hour of practice, fixed to the second; the larger boys and girls, exactly one hour and a half. Piano and voice would be interrupted even in the middle of a bar of music when the clock struck, announcing the appointed time.

It is scarcely surprising that the children called grandmother "Madam." Madam Eugenia Favor or Grandmother Favor were the terms used, not of endearment exactly, but of military recognition. Favor says, "She had decided the kind of family she would have. And have it she did."

It is significant that Grandfather Favor barely appeared on the scene. He would materialize briefly and then vanish, mostly to his club, while the women dominated the family picture.

24

Bette's mother, Ruth, known to everybody as Ruthie, was as driving as Madam Eugenia. She was, Paul Favor tells us, no intellectual at school. But she was senior commanding officer of the Girls' Battalion: "Short and broad-shouldered, like her father and her paternal grandparents, attractive in feature, magnetic and executive, Ruthie was the very soul of efficiency and leadership." She pushed her way up to the position of editor of Lowell High's monthly magazine. She wrote a series for the magazine; starred in plays, upstaging everyone; painted and sketched with expertise and created every poster hung on the school's green-painted walls. Ruthie was an "artist," Paul Favor tells us; she painted cups, saucers, bowls, and pitchers with great industry and some expertise. Ruthie's gifts for decoration, ambitious but tasteful, continued to flourish when Bette became famous. Her "physical strength and perpetual motion" were felt in Bette's houses—she chose the antiques, selected and hung the wallpaper, ripped out walls and remodeled rooms from top to bottom. She was very much Madam Favor's daughter.

Ruthie was a tomboy. She liked to be called "Fred," and wore her brother's pants and work shirts. She dreamed of being an actor, and joined the Chautauqua classes run by Sadie Porter, daughter of the Baptist pastor of Lowell, Massachusetts, where she learned acting, calisthenics, dancing, and elocution. She emoted in plays in the family attic, with herself as the heroes, and local girls as the wilting heroines. When she turned villain—as the Wolf in *Little Red Riding Hood*—she terrified Ms. Antoinette Birch into a fainting fit. As Tamerlane, in General Lew Wallace's *The Prince of India*, she excited the audience at the Chautauqua auditorium in Ocean Park, Maine. Favor tells us that "through her, the great audience was transported to distant Persia . . . and brought face-to-face with one of history's thrilling moments. Her performance was followed by a storm of applause seldom equaled in Ocean Park's Chautauqua Assembly Hall."

But these were childish exhibitions in the eyes of the stern Baptist Madam Favor and her stiff-necked brood.

Madam Favor decided that the sooner this young lady found a husband, the better. The stage represented moral evil: the poison of greasepaint, the lure of dangerous men.

Madam's approach to life had a melodramatic exaggeration—like the melodramas she despised.

After considerable research, examining pedigrees and photographs, and doing everything except applying a tape measure and a pair of calipers, Madam Favor finally settled on an appropriate husband for her far-from-willing daughter. His name was Harlow Morrell Davis, and at the time he passed muster, he was approximately twenty-two years old. He was skinny, with a bulbous forehead and a humorless, cold, efficient look. The bespectacled young man was bedrock Boston down to the soles of his black patent-leather shoes. A churchman's son, he was a male chauvinist Baptist who had been brought up to believe that women were an inferior breed, fit only to cook, sew, and mother children. His brother, in an imitative spirit, dated Ruthie's sister Mildred—and also arranged a match.

After a regulation courtship, Harlow and Ruthie were married in a wedding ceremony that was solemn and cheerless. It took place at the family home in Lowell one month to the day after Harlow had graduated in law from Bates College in Lewiston, Maine, and had secured a position with a shoe company, where he remained a patent lawyer for the rest of his life. The couple was not encouraged to live anywhere but in Lowell. They were to make their home on a maple-shaded street in a somber, three-storied clapboard house with frowning eaves and blind windows that stared blankly out at the world.

After the small and formal wedding party, attended only by a static array of Davis and Favor relatives—no one as insignificant as a mere friend was invited—the young couple (after Harlow Morrell had shouted angrily at those who threw rice) went off on the honeymoon. Ruthie was miserable, but she was sufficiently puritanical to be pleased by her state of mind.

The wedding night must have been an unpleasant experience for both of them; certainly, its aftermath was sordid and depressing. Harlow Morrell had no intention of becoming a father right away; he wanted to rise to eminence in his profession before he allowed his wife the indulgence of having a child. On the night, Ruthie neglected the chance to prevent Bette's conception. Harlow was furious when he found out. When, a month later, Ruthie missed a period, Harlow Morrell lashed out viciously at her, blaming her for this catastrophe to his career. This monster then asked his young bride whether the child could be given away. She burst into tears, too appalled by his question to bring herself to answer it.

It is easy to understand Bette Davis's character when one knows that she was born of a father who hadn't wanted her. Aware that she had been born against obstacles, she regarded the rest of her life as an obstacle course. If she wasn't confronted by major problems, life seemed unnatural, so she invented problems for herself. Peace and quiet, love and wanting—the consolations of most people's lives when confronted with the prospects of physical decline and death—were no appeasements to her spirit. Since her father hadn't intended her to exist, she must therefore make an overwhelming mark on the world; indeed, she must become one of the most famous people in it. Her whole life was a thrust toward glory, and heaven help anybody who stood in her way. It wasn't that she was cruel or crushing. She was generous and honest and giving. But she was still fighting the battle against oblivion and infinity of darkness that she had been fighting from the moment her father reluctantly penetrated her mother's body.

She has spent her lifetime remembering she was born in a violent flash of lightning and clap of thunder. Actually, weather reports show Ruth Elizabeth was born not with a bang but a whimper—in a low whine of breeze and a sprinkling of rain on April 5, 1908.*

Bette's first awarenesses were of the imposing house, with its static collection of ornaments and furnishings, swept and dusted over decades until the very wood seemed

* The name by which she was later called, Bette, was suggested by a friend of her mother's who had read Balzac's *Cousin Bette*.

27

to groan. She learned to dread the brisk, precise footsteps of her father coming home, the cold slam of a door, and the steely voice that needled and humiliated her mother. She grew to feel an overwhelming love for Ruthie, who was theater-mad, gushing, fond of pretty dresses and fancy hairdos, soft and sweet, subject to fits of tears and outbursts of helpless rage.

Lowell was not a beautiful place to grow up in. It was a mill town: Theodore Dreiser territory. Years later, Lowell gave birth to another kind of rebel—Jack Kerouac. Bette, who often expressed violence in her personality, was born in violent times. Lowell was torn by strikes and riots, lootings and burnings in those dark years after the turn of the century. Smoke smeared the chill porcelain blue of the New England sky. There was scarcely a fancy window in the better parts of town that did not look out on the dark, satanic textile mills built of gray stone. High-hat Yankees such as the Favors were in the minority in Lowell. They lived far above the common herd on wide, lawn-fringed streets, shaded with maple and elm and oak.

Eighteen months after Bette was born, Harlow Morrell Davis more willingly fathered another child. He and Ruthie, in one of their rare judicious moments, had decided that having only one child in the family was insufficient and unfair. Indeed, Harlow also knew that there might be criticism of his marriage within his company and even doubts cast on his virility. The second child, Barbara, known as Bobby, lived her life in the fantasy that her father had wanted her to be born for her own sake. But she learned early that Bette was in every way more remarkable than she, and the knowledge crushed and ultimately destroyed her.

There was a symbolic moment at the beginning. Bette, who at first welcomed her sister as a kind of doll, quickly asserted her power. She came back one time from a toddle into another room to discover that Bobby had climbed into Bette's playpen and was sitting there with a complacent look on her face. Bette picked up the child and carried her the full length of the room, depositing her firmly on their parents' bed. "And there you stay!" she is reported to have said, thus setting the tone of her personality and her career from the outset.

Bette despised dolls; she flatly refused to play with any such childish object, even though she went through a performance of cuddling one for a baby picture. She had no interest whatsoever in collecting anything. She was devoid of infantile mischief. Neighbor women shook their heads over her, as she stared at them glumly from her baby carriage, and announced that she was "an old soul." Although she became appealing later, she was an ugly duckling at first, with her maternal grandmother's slightly bulging forehead, small nose, and uneven teeth that had to be fixed in a brace and still wouldn't set properly. She had a habit of bringing worms, beetles, snails, and other disagreeable creatures into the house. On one occasion, Ruthie was giving an elaborate party with tea and cakes. Someone was heard at the door. Bette, aged six, marched in with great ceremony, carried something up to the table, and placed it on the lace cloth. The women screamed. It was a dead field mouse.

Because her mother overprotected her, sheltered her from the world, Bette suffered for the rest of her life from physical cowardice. Under her seeming toughness and precocity, she was shy and frightened of everything. And then would come sudden unexpected outbursts of savage temper.

She had a mania for orderliness. Her mother wrote: "Her passion for neatness began very young. One day when I was dressing her, she saw a tiny spot and quite a few wrinkles on her dress. She began to cry and would not be appeased. Finally I took out a fresh dress as an experiment and she became all smiles."

She was endlessly plumping up pillows and fixing drapes. A crooked curtain, a flickering light bulb, or a speck of dust on a table exasperated her. She liked to smooth out rugs, rearrange candlesticks on the table, and fix crooked paintings on the walls. She would have straightened shadows if she could.

Bette's first school was the Wingate Private Kindergarten, which she attended at the age of five. "She trudged off to school in the snow or rain or sunshine with equal eagerness," Mrs. Davis wrote. She was a good student and made friends easily, but she never let her fellow pupils get too close to her. She always seemed to be at a distance from them; perhaps they sensed that her destiny would lead her far beyond them.

If there was one deep influence upon Bette's life apart from her mother, it was Madam Favor's. Madam grew mellower and kinder with the passage of time. She taught Bette Bible stories. In a family-authorized, long-since-forgotten newspaper series on Bette buried in the pages of the defunct *Boston Herald American,* George W. Clark wrote:

> Grandmother Favor knew all the sweet secret places in cool marshlands where could be found the first violets of spring. She knew the best grassy hilltops in New Hampshire, drenched in sun and whipped by the west wind, where one could live for long hours watching the march of white billowy clouds. She knew where the far-off hills were bluest and where the salt sea spray whipped off the whitecaps at the seashore. And in drowsy summer days, she knew exactly how to help one pass the long hours in the orchard beside the old house in Lowell. But winter was the most fun when, before the roar of a fire, she'd read *Snowbound* out loud to Bette to the beat of a nor'easter against the clapboards.
>
> Like a bird she was. Always in movement. She seemed to ripple rather than walk and to be with her was to be strangely content, but no one could ever reason why. And if Bette Davis seems to flutter like a lovely bird sometimes now in her world of shadows, it is because of Grandmother Favor. And if on occasion she stamps her little feet, her eyes flashing, her throaty voice strident in rage, it is because of Grandmother Favor, too, because she was one of many moods, of many fancies.

Madam Favor tried to break a certain dog-in-the-manger attitude of her granddaughter. Ruthie wrote: "What is hers is hers. She loves her possessions. She is generous to a fault in giving money, but not her things. She hates to lend anything, especially her books. She hates this in herself I think, but it is a deep-seated characteristic. When she is for some reason forced to lend something, she ends by saying, 'Keep it.' "

War broke out in Europe in 1914 when Bette was six. She dressed up in a converted bedsheet her mother had turned into a nurse's uniform, and acted out scenes of being in the Red Cross on the western front, with Bobby as her assistant or patient.

This was her first show of theatrical skill. At an alarmingly early age, she could recite the first verse of "The Midnight Ride of Paul Revere." All attempts to discourage her proved futile. One day, when the other children in the neighborhood were playing, Ruthie found Bette sitting on the steps in the drifting flakes of an early snow, reading favorite passages of verse by Longfellow to an audience of starving sparrows.

Bette saw her first motion picture at the age of eight: a Mary Pickford romance. She loved it, weeping happily at its purple situations. She was fascinated by the horrors of *Grimm's Fairy Tales,* which contained dire warnings to the proper through the punishments that were meted out to the wicked. She was intrigued by the novels of Louisa May Alcott, with their sober woodcut illustrations and poised, puritanical prose. She had an almost boyish interest in the historical romances of Sir Walter Scott and the rich, fustian sagas of Bulwer-Lytton.

In summer, Bette and her sister were often in Maine at camp, enjoying canoeing, swimming, and plucking wildflowers on nature-study walks in the forest. Theirs were innocent days of berry-picking and pea-shelling, and clambakes. It was hard to go back to the family home at summer's end. As soon as Harlow Morrell's step was heard each evening, the laughter faded and the merry running up and down the stairs stopped cold. He sat at a separate table during meals every night except Saturdays, when he condescended to join his family. Meals were conducted in silence. If the children cried or asked for anything, his face grew pale with fury.

Yet Bette's childhood was not as uniformly stark as Harlow Morrell might have wished it. As he rose in importance during the years of World War I, the family moved from Lowell to nearby Winchester, a more pleasant town. Against the wooden buildings painted gray, as if to deprive the eye of pleasure, there were woods and rock climbs and an abundance of flowering shrubs. God-fearing womenfolk even went so far as to loosen their stays a little during the warm summers.

Nineteen-eighteen finally brought the rift in the relationship between Harlow Morrell and Ruthie out into the open. They hadn't been talking for months, and at last were forced to admit they could no longer keep up the pretense of marriage. The family's world was shaken as though by a minor earthquake. Divorce was as unheard of in the Welsh Baptist Davis and Episcopalian Favor families as in any Roman Catholic one. Madam Favor held a family conference. Decisions were made in order to avoid the slightest hint of scandal. Harlow Morrell would simply announce that his wife had left him. Even though he had, in effect, left her already by refusing her sexual communion, in those days the woman had to bear the brunt of the calumny.

Ruthie moved out and took Bette and Bobby to Florida with an Irish nursemaid. After the children were relaxed and softened by weeks of sun, sand, and surf, Ruthie sat them down, took a deep breath, and told them she and their father had separated. Bette burst into delighted laughter. Bobby's reaction was different; she cried miserably and, in a sense, for the rest of her life never recovered from her father's disappearance from the family scene. Unlike Bette, she knew instinctively that her father had wanted her to be born, and despite evidence to the contrary, she clung to her fantasy that he was a kind and generous man. Further, knowing how close Bette was to Ruthie, she felt cut out of that relationship. From that early moment, her tragic life—dogged by mental and physical illness, shattered marriages, breakdowns, a position as

32

Bette's shadow or servant—was laid out for that unhappy child.

Even at the age of ten, Bette seemed to know that, much as she would miss her father, his loosening of the bonds that he had so religiously assumed helped to ensure her future. She probably would never have gone on the stage if he had remained in charge. He would have forbidden any such whorish, frivolous indulgence. She would have been married off to a Boston banker or lawyer and grown fat raising a brood.

The next few years were marked by restlessness of movement. In 1930, Ruthie wrote: "We lived in something like eighty houses: a record I believe. If there are those who take this with a grain of salt, I have a list of addresses and pictures of every place."

After the divorce, Ruthie became estranged from the upright family, but in view of her plight they gradually softened and made small gestures of help. In 1919, mother and daughters were all stricken with the "black flu." When they recovered, Madam Favor copied out a list of schools advertised in *The Atlantic Monthly* and wrote to each of them in turn. She selected from the replies a letter written by a Miss Marjorie Whiting of the Crestalban School in the Berkshires, located between the Hoosic and Housatonic rivers.

Crestalban was a very proper place: a boarding school with an emphasis on vigorous outdoor living. It gave Bette the lifelong physical constitution that withstood the demands of her fierce and nervous nature. The first arrival of mother and daughters at Crestalban was unforgettable. It was a profound New England winter. The schoolhouse was a converted white-clapboard farmhouse, with red barns and a brown-shingled cottage that served as a classroom for some lessons. Snow was falling on the roof, making a picture fit for a Christmas card. Miss Whiting greeted the arrivals in a small sleigh. The new arrivals traveled over crisp, linen-smooth, whitened roads to their destination.

Twinkling and apple-cheeked, Marjorie Whiting, a niece of the artist Abbott Thayer, ran the school with her brother and three sisters, while the Whiting parents were the cooks.

There were only thirteen students. Ruthie wrote: "Miss Whiting's brother Harry ran the farm . . . there the children learned the miracle of birth, watching the cows, the pigs, and lambs, and here they learned the art of home-making, as well as French and the three R's."

Mrs. Davis recalled that eighteen out of every twenty-four hours were spent out of doors; that the children, including Bette and Bobby, took nude snow baths before breakfast and dried themselves off before a roaring fire; that they slept on a porch with snow for a top blanket; took classes on that porch, wearing mittens and sitting in woolen bags with a steam pipe under their desks on which they warmed their feet. The children reveled in every moment—and soon learned sewing, mending, and cooking.

Bette played hockey and tennis with enthusiasm but little skill; she was better at swimming. She was a good, but not brilliant, pupil, who managed history and languages but was hopeless at mathematics, chemistry, and botany.

At the age of eleven, she was at Crestalban on Christmas Eve while Ruthie was working as housemother at Miss Bennett's School for Girls, Millbrook, New York. There was a Christmas party and Bette was Santa Claus. She wore the traditional red flannel cap and coat, cotton hair and beard, and cotton lining. Because Crestalban did not have the luxury of electricity, the branches of the tree were decorated with red candles. When Bette reached out to fetch presents for the children, she noticed one of the candles had gone out and relit it with a match. The flame rose suddenly and caught the cotton of her sleeve. A moment later her costume was on fire. She screamed and snatched it off, but the flames rushed up to her beard. Somebody threw a rug over her and stifled the flames.

It was then that she made her debut as an actress. Her teacher shrieked, looking at her as she lay badly burned on the floor, "She's blind! *Oh, my God, she's blind!*" Bette stood up, her eyes tightly closed, groping around the room and touching the pupils' faces one by one to tremendous effect—before at last revealing to everyone's intense relief and annoyance that she was able to see perfectly.

Her face *was* severely blistered; but after her playacting,

34

nobody took her seriously enough to take her to the hospital. Instead, she was packed off on Christmas morning with the other students for a trip to New York. Cinders from the engine funnel embedded themselves in her face, and she screamed alarmingly during most of the journey. She was hugely enjoying her "stardom," and didn't care if her face ever healed up again.

Ruthie, at the station to meet her children, became hysterical when she saw Bette. She screamed abuse at the teacher, only to be argued with by a staunch if damaged daughter, who drew herself up to her full height and said, with the virtuous hauteur of the Boy on the Burning Deck, "It was my fault, Mother! Don't blame Teacher! They told me not to go near the Christmas tree. I disobeyed!" While her fellow pupils groaned, Bette's teachers smiled at her display of saintliness.

Bette, basking in celebrity, was taken to the doctor. For fifteen days and nights her mother treated the eleven-year-old's face with boric acid. An alarm clock was set to go off every fifteen minutes, at which times fresh applications were made. The treatment left Ruthie exhausted and Bette almost a beauty. Bette screamed punctually around the clock. Mother dizzily told a reporter some years later, "I think that's when Bette's eyes got big. It had something to do with the boric acid. The irises were enlarged. The eyes the world knows! Isn't that amazing?"* Bette's face lost the top layer of skin following the accident and it never grew back. This gave her the strange "bald" look that became famous; it also gave her extreme sensitivity to sun and windburn, and to the toxic properties in makeup.

Bette's fiery accident not only made her identify with Joan of Arc, but made her supremely conscious of her face. She was at once fascinated and repelled by it—as though it were someone else's. Drawn to it and yet terrified of mirrors. In later years, she often felt uneasy if she saw herself on the screen.

* Actually, her eyes are normal size; her actress's trick is to dilate them.

Bette returned to Crestalban and soon became just another kid. She grew as Alice in Wonderland had after swallowing the contents of the Drink Me bottle. Her neck was elongated and her arms and legs grew skinny. She was so nervous with boys that in her own words, she "couldn't get out even a bleat when I was with one. Oh, *awful!*"

When she left Crestalban to start high school, she quickly discovered that fierce intelligence and drive were no substitute for glamour or ease of manner. She was in peril of being branded a bluestocking—not good for a girl. Skirts were going up and waistlines were going down. Girls started to smoke behind the gymnasium. Lips were "beestung." Colleen Moore was all the rage; her picture *Flaming Youth* would index a generation. Bette preferred the prim "Victorian" romances of Mary Pickford. She read books when other girls were off flirting with boys under Chinese lanterns after dances or when sitting around campfires listening to tunes played on Victrolas under harvest moons.

For a while, she hung back from romantic invitations. She never thought of herself as attractive, yet she was: her infectious laughter, her stylish, swinging walk, her trick of balancing herself on her heels and turning unexpectedly, her quick wit, and her wide blue eyes started to draw the attention of young bloods in their raccoon coats. She began to feel a flicker of encouragement at sixteen; boys, with their slicked-down hair, swarmed through the house, took lemonade with her on the porch from jugs clinking with ice chunks, and gave her a spin on their bicycles. Her confidence grew; maybe she could fascinate. Looking in the mirror one morning, she was surprised to find she was a woman. Her teeth had been straightened by years in metal braces, her eyes could probe like a hypnotist's when she chose. She was still skinny, but she had heavy, voluptuous breasts. Life had seemed horrific at twelve. Now it seemed almost promising.

Ruthie dominated everything. She was "psychic" and carted Bette off to a fortune-teller who predicted a great future for her. Ruthie and Bette were very close. One night

36

Ruthie was at the movies when she had an overpowering feeling that Bette was in danger. She spotted one of Bette's beaux in the theater and urged him to drive over and pick up Bette from a dance. A bribe ensured his cooperation. Bette arrived home in a blaze of temper asking Ruthie what she meant by ruining her evening. The telephone rang. Bette heard the news: The boy she had intended driving home with had run off a cliff and been killed.

One evening Bette had a date with a young, gangling boy named Henry Fonda. A friend of his dated Bobby. Hank's friend drove the Model T, and Bette and Hank sat in the back seat. She firmly insists he kissed her; he insists with equal vehemence that he did not. She was very attracted to him, but he says that he was not attracted to her. The story has clearly gotten mixed up in both their minds. They never dated each other again.

Then this small but intense girl fell in love with the theater. Her most overpowering experience was seeing Blanche Yurka and Peg Entwistle in Ibsen's *The Wild Duck*. Peg Entwistle's performance as the fragile and touching Hedvig moved Bette to tears. She told Ruthie: "If I don't play Hedvig very soon, I'll die!"

Years later, Bette was shocked when she learned that Miss Entwistle had thrown herself off the top of the Hollywood sign to her death because of her failure to succeed in movies.

The Wild Duck gave Bette her first intoxicating dream of stardom. She pestered Ruthie with her visions. Soon, she said, she would enjoy a country home, a Packard car, diamonds, enough money so that Ruthie would never lack for anything, three strands of pearls, lots of clothes, world travel, the chance to be tall and dignified; she would become an expert horsewoman and learn to laugh like a lady. Her chief longing to be an actress was based on a dislike of "herself": her high, sharp laughter; her pinched face; her bulbous forehead; her quickness to anger; her fear of anything unknown; her mania for perfection; and the way that, though fanatically clean, she always covered herself with ink when she wrote letters.

37

Mother and daughters continued moving constantly in those years. The family gave little help financially and it seems that Madam Favor was less than generous. From Lowell to Winchester to Ashburnham in Massachusetts; from Ashburnham to Peterboro, New Hampshire; from Peterboro to the Maine towns of Southwest Harbor, Ogunquit, and Ocean Park—the moves went on.

In 1924 Bette enrolled in the Cushing Academy in Ashburnham. There she experienced First Love. Her fellow student, Harmon ("Ham") O. Nelson, was her beau.

Ham was not one of the Scott Fitzgerald boys, with patent-leather hair and brisk clothes. He was awkward, weak, nervously charming, retiring, and not very bright. He had no talent for sports, so in a college where athletics were the certified cause of acceptance, Ham was an outsider. But he was tall and slender and quite nice-looking, with dreamy, romantically liquid dark eyes. His chief advantage was that he was a musician. He played several instruments, and also sang and composed. Because he was a leading light in the college band and ran various productions, he retained a fragile form of popularity. He seemed to have little interest in girls.

Bette was the first sophomore to attract him. When they first met he said, "Miss Davis, would you like to sing in the minstrel show?" She would, and did. She had a crush on him. But, despite his interest, he was insecure with her and Bette felt challenged. She told Ruthie, "I'm going to get him if it's the last thing I ever do!"

It was uphill work. They sang in the Glee Club together; they went to dances. But Ham seemed too wrapped up in his music to think about romance, and Bette was still waiting for their first kiss. She begged Ruthie for pretty dresses. Ruthie stretched the budget. Bette did and redid her hair. She wanted to be alone with Ham, but in those days dances and parties were chaperoned like prison benefits. On Sundays, during the coed hour when the students were allowed to fraternize in a brief stroll through the grounds, she prayed for rain. Maybe then she could achieve her objective under an umbrella. There was a drought.

38

At eighteen, Bette and Ham drifted apart, and she now devoted all her energy to playacting. She wasn't expert; she performed like a sparrow, but she acted obsessively in everything she could—in theaters in Maine during summer vacation, in pageants, in every school play. She had to be an actress. Could she be one?

Ruthie wrote in her unpublished memoir:

> As I look back on this part of my life I wonder what drove me on. Was it that through my daughter I would realize all of the many ambitions that were hidden within me? Whatever it was, my belief in Bette's ability certainly came true. Whether this driving desire to make her an actress . . . made her happy, I don't know; but at this point nothing could have stopped either of us.

Even before she went to Cushing, Bette had studied dancing. She was a pupil of "Roshanara," who taught at the Mariarden Dance School in Peterboro, New Hampshire. Bette worshipped this English girl with the pretentious Indian name. Ruthie worked hard as a photograph retoucher to pay for Bette's lessons. She also made extra money working as a freelance photographer.

Through Roshanara, with her training in Indian dance, Bette learned the physical discipline and control that later marked her best work. The classes were held in the musty basement of a church, from which, like moths from a chrysalis, the pupils emerged to perform in the summer on smooth green lawns.

Bette enjoyed the discipline of the work. She rehearsed a full eight hours each day. She learned Roshanara's specialty, "The Moth," and costumed in white silk, danced on a special glass floor with lights illuminating her body. The audience applauded her wildly. Ruthie wrote: "Bobby sat close to me as we watched Bette and we could not believe it was true. I've sat through many opening nights, but this was the most thrilling."

While Ruthie took wedding and school pictures, Bette

emerged as a star pupil at Mariarden. The summer vacations, with their dancing lessons and weekly performances, were not to be forgotten. Roshanara's early death came as a shock, terminating a period of joy.

Bette returned to Cushing for the fall term in 1925. The day she left Mariarden for the last time, the actor Frank Conroy made a remark without which no biography of a star is complete: "Mrs. Davis, if you don't put that child on the stage, it will be a crime. She has something that you can't buy, something that makes your eyes follow her even when she doesn't speak. And when she does, it is just added excitement."

Bette graduated with honors from Cushing. She made her way through her final year by working as a waitress at the college. Before taking the job, she had called her mother to ask if she, Bette, could help out the family finances by waiting tables, and had been shocked when her mother unhesitatingly agreed! It was hard work, and by the time Bette dragged herself off to the cottage in Ogunquit, where Ruthie and Bobby were staying that summer, she was totally exhausted and cried for two days.

That post-college vacation in Ogunquit was the last joyous time of Bette's life. It was a golden summer, without a day of rain. Bette became a lifeguard and started to look much healthier. She and her sister ran about the rocks and small beach and teased the painter Stanley Woodward who was living there. Years later, Stanley Woodward said: "I'll never forget Bette and Bobby Davis. Bobby was still at high school, and those two years definitely meant a great deal to her. She was nervous and shy. . . . Bette was the exact opposite. You never saw such energy! She did everything head-on. You could see what she would become. Her eyes were not really big, but she knew how to make them enormous when she wanted to win an argument. I think she fancied herself as a hypnotist. It took a painter to notice that!"

The consuming ambition of every young girl with dramatic aspirations in those days was to be admitted to the severe discipline of the Eva Le Gallienne drama school in New York City. So that Bette could enter the school, she,

Ruthie, and Bobby came to Manhattan and rented a modest apartment.

Eva Le Gallienne was a remarkable woman. A great actress, she was diffident and detached on the surface but wholly committed to her art. There are several versions of what took place when the nervous, long-necked girl and her desperate mother arrived at Miss Le Gallienne's offices. Ruthie wrote that "this first experience was very humiliating and we never did see Miss Le Gallienne." But that was untrue. While Ruthie sat in the outer office, Miss Le Gallienne's secretary questioned Bette in an atmosphere of somber austerity. Bette was not invited to sit down. She was asked the names of books she had read on the theater and was then handed a play to read to Miss Le Gallienne. She was astonished to discover that she was supposed to deliver a speech by an ancient Dutch woman in a Dutch accent.

She entered the sanctum sanctorum. Wispy but authoritative, Miss Le Gallienne had no interest in this awkward pale girl who seemed utterly lacking in the promise of style or presence. She did her best to discourage her by first bombarding her with questions about her sources of income. When it came time to deliver the speech, Bette stumbled through it, and giggled nervously. "Miss Davis," Miss Le Gallienne said icily, "I can see that your attitude toward the theater is not sincere enough to warrant my taking you as a pupil. You are a frivolous little girl. Good day."

Asked about this occasion recently, Miss Le Gallienne said she could not recall it: "There were so many young girls who came in looking for a break."

Bette burst into tears and ran from the office. For days she was hysterical with rage and grief. She paced the New York streets, talking to herself, convinced she was going mad. She said later: "I really was out of my mind. I had to be an actress. I wasn't an actress. I *had* to be an actress. Like a crazy pendulum, my mind swung from nauseating discouragement to furious rebellion. I would end it all. I would show the world, show Eva Le Gallienne, Ruthie, the whole family. I would stun, startle, astound; give performances and become history!"

With her mother and sister, Bette went back to Massachusetts, but Ruthie saw how she fretted constantly about not being in New York. One morning, while Bette was still sleeping, Ruthie made up her mind. The only way to save Bette's sanity was to get her on the stage and keep her there. Shaking her daughter, she said sharply: "Wake up, Bette! We're off to New York again!"

"You're mad, Mother!" Bette replied.

"Fix your hair!" Mother snapped.

Once Ruthie's mind was made up, there was no stopping her. If she couldn't get Bette into Eva Le Gallienne's class, the next best thing was the John Murray Anderson–Robert Milton Dramatic School. After their arrival back in New York, that was where Ruthie, with Bette in tow, headed.

Hugh Anderson, the school's executive director, was astounded by the determined little woman and her edgy, skinny, pop-eyed daughter who swept past his secretary into his office. Ruthie put all her cards on the table. She said, "My daughter wants to be an actress. You've got to make her one!" She took a deep breath. "And I haven't a nickel. I'll have to pay on the installment plan." Hugh Anderson was so overpowered by Ruthie's determination that he nodded weakly and agreed to Bette's admission.

Ruthie returned to Massachusetts and continued to work as a retoucher. Bette rented a single room in a cold-water walk-up on East 58th Street with a girl, also from Massachusetts, named Virginia Conroy. The two became fast friends. They cooked on a hot plate or ate at the Automat; they did their own laundry, and hung it to dry on a line strung across the room; they learned the trick of drying handkerchiefs wrinkle-free by sticking them against the sunny windowpane. One night, Ruthie came for a visit. She declined to bunk with Bette and, instead, rigged up a bed out of two wooden chairs, with her upright suitcase between them. In the early hours of the morning Bette and Virginia were awakened by a crash. The chairs of the improvised bed had slid away from the suitcase and Ruthie was on the floor, arms and legs flailing.

The Anderson school was a wonderful training ground for Bette. Arthur Hornblow, the legendary dean, was very helpful, as was the great star, George Arliss, who taught diction there. He told Bette (advice she did not always heed): "Remain simple in your diction. Never adopt that exaggerated English speech you often hear on the stage."

Bette became friendly with a fellow pupil named Joan Blondell, who recalled later that Bette, all eyes and talent, "was consumed with ambition day and night." Bette appeared with Joan in an Anderson school production of an obscure eighteenth-century play written by Susanna Centlivre—actress, dramatist, and wife of the chief cook to Queen Anne of England—which Arthur Hornblow unearthed in an English attic. Titled *The Wonder! A Woman Keeps a Secret*, it was an outrageous farce which involved plenty of scampering through bedrooms. Bette and Joan were cast as saucy Restoration girls, looking like Watteau milkmaids in their billowing dresses. The audience on the first night was dismayed by the racy dialogue and numerous goosings and wild escapes through windows. After the initial shock of seeing this kind of play being produced in such a soberly distinguished school, everyone relaxed and enjoyed the evening. The production cost just forty-seven dollars. It would have run more than three nights if, as John Murray Anderson recalled in his memoirs, "some busybody hadn't come in and attached one of the draw curtains that belonged to the theater."

Among Anderson's other pupils were Lucille Ball, Cesar Romero (known as "Butch"), Paul Muni, and Anita Page. It was a joyous atmosphere. The school lasted for only three years, but they were three years that made history in the American theater. Among the lecturers were Don Marquis, creator of archy and mehitabel; Robert Edmond Jones; Channing Pollock; and Willy Pogany. It was a galaxy that shone a hard light on the students.

Bette had good teachers. In addition to studying with Arthur Hornblow, she was taught dancing by Martha Graham. Miss Graham gave her understanding of the use of her body, how to "center" her emotions in a way that made her so magnetic in pictures later on. Miss Graham says of

Bette as a student: "She had control, discipline, and at the same time, electricity. I knew she would be something."

Her mother fueled Bette's drive. Armed with a deserved scholarship, Bette decided to apply for work in the professional theater. She had made a hit in *The Famous Mrs. Fair*, her examination play, in which she had to change from a delicate ingenue to a tough society woman. Despite laryngitis, she had triumphed; and Frank Conroy, still an admirer of hers, gave her a letter to George Cukor, who was operating a summer stock theater in Rochester, New York.

TWO

Before Bette Davis leaves for her assignment in Rochester, let us pause a minute and consider her at the age of twenty, standing on the edge of her great career. Physically, she still has an odd, unfinished look. The mousy hair, the bald, burned-through face, the pale blue eyes that widen constantly to emphasize a point, the small mouth, long neck, and gawky figure do not add up to a picture of conventional prettiness. But she is nevertheless immensely attractive. She exudes vitality, energy, wit, and style. Instinctively, without forcing it, she projects a kind of ice-cold sexuality, intelligence combined with passion, sheer nerves coupled with pointed reason. She is a picture of humorous aggression, with her vulnerability and terror of life, her obvious virginity, making her irresistible. Her movements, crucial to an actress's individuality, are already those of an original. She walks very quickly, very impatiently, with an odd combination of the feminine, in the looseness in the hips, the thrust of the large breasts; and the masculine, in the firmness of step, the athletic resolution in the well-shaped legs. She is hampered by the long, heavy dresses of the time; she will look better in the severely tailored clothes of the late thirties and forties.

Her colossal, all-consuming ego is formed. She has rushed into a theatrical career, not merely because of a mother who would have wanted to herself and couldn't, or because she herself could think of no other way for a bachelor girl to make a living except by becoming a schoolteacher or secretary. The theater is a means of escape from her great inner tensions and strains and from the harsh realization that (a disaster for some girls) she isn't a beauty. In the theater she can work out her inherited stormy power without making her mother's life unbearable and she can tuck away her cowardice—the weakness that lies under the violent temper. Aside from a superior talent, she has all the attributes necessary to become a great actress—she is a perfectionist, self-obsessed, temperamental, warm, outgoing, and gifted with a prodigious memory. An audience, if halfway interested, inspires her; audiences love her. Whereas most people would dread facing a crowd, she is a typical actress in that she finds life intolerable without applause; it is as necessary to her as a blood transfusion to a child with pernicious anemia. She feeds on handclapping, laughter, tears. It is lucky for her that she has emerged in an uncool period when unbridled romances and melodramas filled the stage. Like Sarah Bernhardt, Bette needs big emotions and big scenes. She will soon prove that a comparison of herself with that great artist is quite justified.

She is still without the experience of sharing herself fully with a man. Ham Nelson, with his weak sexuality and insecure masculinity, has been an ideal companion for her. There has been no one else who mattered.

When Bette left for Rochester on April 27, 1928, shortly after her birthday, it was to be her first long separation from Ruthie. Ruthie, tied to one of a drab succession of depressing jobs that were paying for Bette's career, could not accompany her on this occasion. The extent of Ruthie's emotional involvement with her daughter can be seen in an immensely long letter she gave her to take along on the journey. It contained not only minute instructions on how to conduct herself on the trip, but a precise breakdown of everything that could happen. The note makes clear that Ruthie was, in spirit, on the train herself, sitting beside Bette, fussing lovingly over everything. The letter begins:

46

Take twice, darling, to read all of this and check your things off as you pack—then read it over after you go to bed—the instruction part! [There follows a crude drawing of a smiling face like the moon: Mother watching over her child.]

I'll be with you every step of the way. And I'll pray to God to watch over my little girl as I can't—*but you help there*!

The memorandum continues with a complete list of everything in the suitcases, including pink and orange pajamas, towel ("do not use washcloth in train unless you purchase little rubber case for it"), raincoat and rubbers ("may be pouring in Rochester"), pink kimono ("you should go to wash before donning dress"), and, rather oddly, "black suede gloves in case of rain."

There is a list of underwear, with instructions not to use the laundry in hotels but to wash the clothing herself at night; also listed were stockings, handkerchiefs, hairpins, safety pins, blue evening dress and green [one] ("but I doubt if you could get into it alive"), black satin hat, black velvet hat, white felt hat for raincoat, gray hat, old sport hat, bathing suit, red practice dress, slippers, lavender-silk and green-chiffon hangers, "and must look immaculate for breakfast on train!"

The letter contains instructions on how to unpack in the train compartment, how to repack, and how to hang everything. There are warnings of men who make passes at girls *without* glasses, and advice on correct deportment around older people. One doubts that even a duchess in Jane Austen's world would have gone into such detail to cover the movements of a virginal daughter by carriage from the family mansion to a lady's finishing school in Bath.

Not content with all this, Ruthie gives Bette directions on life itself:

When in Rochester (or anywhere) be *sure* to be your simple self—especially quiet and reserved at all times in public. This is *very* important, as you are alone and

47

so young, dear—people are ready to believe a girl—bright and young and alive—gay unless she is *very* conservative.

The effect of this comprehensive list of dos and don'ts was overpowering. Bette was to arrive at the train exactly fifteen minutes to the second before it left; she was to get settled before the train whistled to announce its departure; she mustn't disturb other passengers by talking in the sleeping car; she mustn't undress and go to sleep until she has laid out her clothes for the next morning; the porter must wake her exactly half an hour before breakfast; she is to eat it from 8:00 to 9:00 A.M. and no longer, so that others would not be kept waiting; she was to tip ten cents on a dollar for meals, ten cents to each porter for carrying her bags upstairs, and if any of these were fresh, "be sure to resent politely if possible, but if not—not!"

Buried in this Tolstoyan missive is the most revealing instruction of all: "Always keep fruit or crackers in your room—being hungry keeps me awake." So there it is, spelled out in neon lights: She *is* Bette, and "being hungry keeps *me* awake."

Rochester was, as it is today, a bleak and depressing city, with square, brown office buildings, streets lined with starved trees, and winds that prowled angrily down the thoroughfares. But the Cukor-Kondolf Stock Company, as it was known, provided a chance for a budding artist.

The plump, dynamic George Cukor was about thirty at the time; he had not yet emerged as a famous figure. In later life he would become the director of such pictures as *The Philadelphia Story*, *A Star Is Born*, and *Gaslight*. He was witty and shrewd and tasteful, and very skilled with performers—a master of delicate details of gesture. He had the ego, the temperament, the drive, the love of his own opinions, that made him a natural success in the theater.

Bette was cast immediately. Using her "psychic" powers, Ruthie had predicted that the girl who played the chorine, Pearl, in George Abbott's play *Broadway* would have an accident and Bette would be needed to replace her. So bent

48

was Ruthie on Bette's success that, if the original actress had not fallen down, Ruthie would have made her way to Rochester to push her. Bette even wondered if she had.

Broadway was a concoction about New York gangsters and their chorus-girl molls. Bette played Pearl, one of the dancers who shoots her lover in the back. Marlene Dietrich, a lifelong fan of Bette's, began her career in the same part.

It was a small role, but a good one. George Cukor described Bette's appearance years later:

> The girl came down the stairs, delivered her speech, and fired her gun. Davis seemed to know this was her big chance and she took hold from the first moment. I was worried she might be overdoing it. The other girl had played it toughly, coldly, but Bette had a mind of maniacal fierceness, and even seemed to be *willing* the actor to die. The audience was stunned. I realized that Bette had the same "white heat" that Jeanne Eagels had—though I wasn't as impressed with Eagels as many people were. I was delighted with Miss Davis. I hired her to play right through the next season. But somehow she got it into her head that I sacked her on the spot as a reward for her efforts. She has talked about it for years! It's become boring!

The engagement in Rochester lasted only a week. Bette got her next job with the Cape Playhouse in Dennis, Massachusetts, where she had been promised a job by a smooth-talking youth in New York who had claimed to be the Playhouse's manager in order to get a date with her. When she arrived, there was no job. Fortunately, the director of the Playhouse hired her as a theater usher to save her from starving. It was not until Ruthie arrived and rented a small cottage (Bobby came along too) that life became tolerable.

Trying to contain Bette Davis as a theater usher was like trying to bottle thunder. She spent every moment during the performances of the Cape players studying all the parts within her age range. Everyone noticed her. While the other girls who were acting as ushers chatted about dresses, makeup, hair, and boyfriends, she stood in the darkness at the back of the theater staring intently at the stage. If she had had to, she probably could have acted every part in every play perfectly. She badgered the director Raymond Moore to give her the chance to appear in something—anything. In her own words, "I would willingly have been a deaf-and-dumb maid or a hunchbacked cousin locked in an attic room with meals left at the door, if necessary."

One of the producers of the repertory season was Laura Hope Crews, a snappish pudding of a woman who is best known for her role as Aunt Pittypat in *Gone With the Wind*. Suddenly Miss Crews found herself without a girl to play the part of Dinah in A. A. Milne's play, *Mr. Pim Passes By*. The part called for the actress to play a song entitled "I Passed by Your Window" on the piano and to sing it at the same time. Miss Crews snapped at Bette: "You want to be in this play, don't you?"

Bette's smile was more eloquent than words. "I have one question," Miss Crews said. "Can you play and sing 'I Passed by Your Window' by tomorrow morning at eight o'clock?"

"Of course!" Bette snapped back. Her thoughts raced. She hadn't the remotest idea what "I Passed by Your Window" was. What was she going to do?

She ran home and told Ruthie, "I've got to play and sing 'I Passed by Your Window' by tomorrow morning." Ruthie panicked. She took off in a beat-up Ford—an ancient Model T she had bought secondhand—and drove frantically to the only music shop in Dennis. They had never heard of the song. In desperation, she rushed off to Hyannis. There was a larger store there, but they had never heard of the song, either. Ruthie's desperation deepened. She drove at a mile-an-hour pace along every street in Hyannis, peeking through windows to see which of the occupants had a piano. With astonishing boldness, she then rapped on the doors to ask if any of the sheet music lying on the pianos might happen to be the elusive song. One or two people had heard of it; nobody owned it.

By nightfall, she was at the end of her tether. She resigned herself to the fact that she'd have to return to Dennis and inform her theater-usher daughter that her chances of appearing in *Mr. Pim Passes By* were virtually hopeless. But as she turned a corner, "inspiration" seized her at the sight of a church: Church organists usually stocked up on tunes so that they could play medleys at benefits. She invaded the church, discussed the matter with a parson, obtained the address of the organist, interrupted him while he was weeding his garden—and, to her unrestrained delight, discovered that he had the precious score. He couldn't have been more amazed when a woman he had never met before flung her arms around him, kissed him, whooped with joy, and swept headlong into his house to pick up the music and make off with it to Dennis in a cloud of dust.

Bette sat up until 3:00 A.M. studying the music. The next day she walked onstage at the first rehearsal and performed it perfectly. Unfortunately, once she started acting she waved her arms about like windmill sails. Laura Hope Crews told her to imagine she had lead weights in her hands; otherwise, her mannerisms (later to become famous) would distract attention from the rest of the cast. That may have been what was intended. But Bette did her best to obey. "I stood," she said later, "like a figure in a Rembrandt." At the dress rehearsal, when the lead weights disappeared and the windmill sails revolved, Laura Hope Crews hauled back and struck her across the face. Bette said: "My face burned and I counted to ninety-five." The lead weights returned. She was triumphant in *Mr. Pim*.

A great pleasure of that summer was running into Ham again. She and Ruthie had gone to see Norma Shearer in a movie melodrama and Bette was astounded to notice Ham seated nearby. She screamed like an ambulance siren and the whole audience shushed her. Ruthie kicked her in the shins.

She began dating Ham again. He was playing in a band at the Old Mill Tavern in Amherst, on the other side of the Cape. On the days when there was no matinee of *Mr. Pim Passes By* and Ham wasn't giving a daytime performance, they whizzed about in his Ford and went swimming together. They lay chastely on the sand, scarcely touching, and talked their hearts out about everything. They knew they were right for each other. Only one thing bothered Bette. Ham was unwilling to see her in the play. His excuse was that he feared he would distract her, but she always suspected he was not interested in the theater.

The earliest surviving printed notice of a Bette Davis stage performance appeared in the Dennis *Times* on July 21, 1928. It was a review of a performance of a drama called *The Charm School,* given as a Methodist church benefit at East Dennis's Sears Memorial Hall. The review read:

> The junior players presented their first drama of the summer season and Miss Betty [sic] Davis was totally charming in the leading role . . . her comedy was delightful and the applause that greeted her dramatic exit in the second act confirmed our opinion. . . . In this play, Miss Davis' sister, Barbara, also took part as one of the pupils of the "Charm School," who were all overflowing with vivacity.

At the end of the season at the Cape, after a glorious summer of theater, romance, and long, warm, beach afternoons, she and Ham had to part. Despite the fact that he was not the kind of strong and virile man she wanted, she loved his sensitivity, and she was grateful to him all her life for teaching her to love music. His long, narrow dark face, half-sad, half-humorous eyes, and compact, smoothly muscled body made a deep impression on her. But she had to think of her career, so there could be no question of "seriousness." Ham had engagements elsewhere and she had to return to Rochester for the next Cukor season.

She was cast in a show that was oddly named *Excess Baggage.* The local *Times* printed the following item:

> Among the fifty actors and actresses who arrived in this city from New York in preparation for presenta-

'tion of *Excess Baggage*, a Broadway production, at the opening night of the season at the Temple Theater, were Frank McHugh, the leading man, Charlotte Wynters, the leading woman, Wallace Ford, and Bette Davis, the ingenue, a pretty blonde slip of a miss.

Bette's part in *Excess Baggage* was a much larger one than that in *Broadway*. She played Frank McHugh's wife. Wallace Ford told me years later: "I got the impression Bette had been told to be shy, subdued in the part she played. But she didn't fool any of us for a minute. She was afraid to say 'boo' to a goose, butter wouldn't melt in her mouth—*for exactly five minutes.* After that, I took one look at her and said as she walked onto the stage, with her long goosey neck and her big eyes, 'Miss Ruth Elizabeth Davis, you're no goody-goody who's scared of her own shadow; you're thunder and stage lightning and goddamn greasepaint. You're going to be a *tiger* on the boards. Look out, world!' "

Charlotte Wynters, the star of *Excess Baggage*, became excess baggage herself when she broke her ankle. The talk in the company was that her understudy, Miriam Hopkins, had sawed through the heel of Miss Wynters' left shoe.

Miriam was certainly capable of it. It gnawed into her far-from-tender spirit in later years that she had to play second fiddle to Bette in pictures—after all, as she insisted on telling her friends to their barely concealed amusement, *she* had been the star of *Excess Baggage*, and Bette a mere bag!

Miriam Hopkins was a pretty, blond, ruthless young woman—hard-bitten, mean-tempered, a "card," and a caution. She hated to have anybody in the cast receive even minimum attention from the audience while she was onstage. If an actress threatened to take over a scene, Miriam would rearrange flowers, wind a clock, straighten a picture, or even take out a book and read it to distract everybody's attention from the lines being spoken. Few could, in fact, upstage her. With her cat's eyes, her mischievous, sexy, crinkly stare, and her tricky, swooping southern voice, she had a captivating theatrical presence. She would fling herself into a chair with complete abandonment and throw down martinis as though they were lemonades. She could also be, if the mood suited her, the epitome of elegance, using her beautifully curved back as expertly as a question mark. She was jealous, consumed with hatred, petulant, self-pitying, coarse. And she was an actress of actresses, as Bette, who despised every bone in Miriam's body, had the common sense to admit.

Wallace Ford said: "Even *then* Miriam was afraid of Bette. She knew Bette was at least as talented as she, and that although she wasn't nearly as attractive, she suggested a feminine, sexy, 'touch-me-not' quality that Miriam, with her bull-like aggression and tired, experienced bedroom look couldn't match. She dreaded every moment Bette was on stage. The men were looking at Bette, not her. I'll bet my bottom dollar some of the young guys got erections looking at Bette. Miriam challenged them; they might have been looking at another man. When Miriam sat down she spread her legs wide. She wanted the men to look up her skirt—a lady she wasn't! But they didn't like the gesture, it turned them off, it was too brutal. Bette crossed her legs daintily, hiding everything, and they had to have her. You should have *seen* the beaux at the dressing-room door!"

Bette went on to appear in *Cradle Snatchers, The Man Who Came Back, Laff That Off* (in which she played a slave), and *The Squall,* among other plays. The Rochester *Times* wrote of Bette's performance in the last production: "The sweetheart was done with quite a bit of demure charm by Bette Davis, who gave us further evidence that she is likely to be a good actress in the making."

Her co-star in another play, *Yellow,* was the tall and imperious Louis Calhern. Asked years later why, during the production of *Yellow,* Bette was suddenly dismissed from the company by George Cukor, Calhern said: "The trouble was that she wasn't too popular. She refused dates with the young men (I could have understood her attitude toward the older ones), and that wasn't considered kosher. She wasn't supposed to sleep around, but she wasn't supposed to be Saint Theresa of Avila either. After the performance at night, she seemed very uppity and Cinderella-like. She didn't drink or (incredible as it may seem) even *smoke* in those days! She simply fled back to her lodging house. She was so grimly dedicated to work that it became boring. Of course, that dedication took her further than any of us. But it didn't make for comfort in an incestuous company like that. She was a terrific team *player* but she wasn't a team *person*. I think Cukor yielded to pressure in getting rid of her. She was *very* unpopular!"

Bette, however, landed on her feet. She went to New York and joined the respected James Light at his Province-town Playhouse, located near Washington Square. She was cast in a play called *The Earth Between*, a drama of incest set on a farmstead in Nebraska, and she was so innocent she played the part of a girl in love with her father without beginning to understand the nature of the relationship.

It was her first real chance. For, though it wasn't Broadway, but only Greenwich Village, it *was* Bette's debut in New York, and most important the critics were present at the opening night. It was also a big occasion for the unknown playwright, a Nebraska boy named Virgil Geddes.

Bette's Uncle Paul was part of the first-night audience. He wrote:

> I well recall the mixed rain and snow in MacDougal Street "where a man may call his soul his own and see who cares." I sat with my sister Mrs. Davis, Bobby, and several close friends of our family. We were really excited. Despite the weather the little theater was well filled. A stuffy, rather forbidding little barn of a place, yet full of dramatic memories of bygone stars. It was a halcyon night for Bette. Telegrams, letters, flowers poured in.

By all accounts, Bette flung herself into the part of the daughter with great intensity, suggesting a delicate, vulnerable, fragile quality. The applause was tremendous. The only flaw in the evening, and it was a deep one, was the

55

absence of Bette's father. She was in anguish when she noticed he hadn't come, but partly consoled by the fact that he sent her a wicker basket of flowers.

She tossed and turned all night, the expected bad notices whirling around in her brain. But soon after dawn, Ruthie burst into her room in ecstasy and flung Brooks Atkinson's review at her.

Bette sat up, rubbed her eyes, and snatched up the paper, the all-important *New York Times*. Atkinson had written: "Miss Davis, who is making her first professional appearance, is an entrancing creature who plays in a soft, unassertive style." Atkinson wasn't exactly calling her Sarah Bernhardt, but Bette could make do with "entrancing."

The Daily News reviewer wrote: "The performances are good, particularly that of Miss Davis, a wraith of a child with true emotional insight." St. John Ervine wrote in the *World:* "Miss Bette Davis and William Challee ably suggest the disturbed minds of Floy and Jake."

She was launched. No doubt about it, she was *launched*! And a dream came true: her dream of appearing in the company of Blanche Yurka. During one evening performance a penciled note on the back of a blank form for ticket applications was pushed under Bette's dressing-room door. It read:

Bette Davis is asked to be at the Bijou Theater at 11 A.M. tomorrow. Miss Blanche Yurka wants to see her.

It was a command which Bette Davis had to obey. Blanche Yurka, with her great mournful eyes, scraggly dynamic body, and unkempt look was an empress among actresses. Entrée to her charmed circle was as treasured as entrée to Joseph Papp's is today. Bette had never forgotten the impact made on her by Yurka's production of *The Wild Duck,* with the ill-fated Peg Entwistle. If it killed her, Bette had to work for Yurka.

Fortunately, Bette was committed to only four weeks in *The Earth Between,* because the play was set for a limited run. She dashed over to the Bijou Theater in a state bordering on ecstasy. Blanche Yurka swept up to her like a great ragged eagle and embraced her in the wings of her dress. Bette almost broke into tears when the great star offered her the part of Hedvig in *The Wild Duck*.

It was almost too good to be true. The part of Hedvig had an intense meaning for her: the child whose father had not wanted her. Her joy was only slightly dented when she heard that she was a replacement for the talented Linda Watkins who, feigning illness, had announced she could not go on tour.

Bette rushed home and studied the part all night long, with Ruthie taking the other parts. She finally went to sleep in the morning, only to wake with a violent fever and headache. Every effort she made to get out of bed was useless. In those blessed days, doctors still made house calls. A physician pronounced her the victim of measles, which she had somehow skirted in childhood and adolescence.

One of the toughest phone calls Ruthie ever made in her life was to tell Miss Yurka that Bette, who was sobbing helplessly in the background, would have to give up the part. Astonishingly, Yurka said in her typically abrupt manner, "Mrs. Davis, we'll wait."

Years later, Blanche Yurka told me: "Bette Davis was by no means an accomplished actress at the time. Her mother, frankly, was a pain in the neck, and it's a miracle she didn't sink Bette's career from the outset. She was endlessly and sentimentally fussing over her. She was a weak, silly creature and, despite Miss Davis's loyal demurs then and later, she was the show-biz mother to end all! Even Bette, overeager and full of tears and tantrums, was a maddening handful. But one gets an instinct in this business. I knew Bette would be a great Hedvig. She would attack the part, not with technique, but with her nerves and with her heart."

It was true. Bette struggled out of her measles-induced condition and sweated her way through rehearsals, despite two relapses during her convalescence. Nothing was going to stop her from going on tour.

The opening in New York was very successful, and in April 1929, the company moved to Philadelphia. Bette's vibrant, heartbreakingly intense performance moved audiences to tears. The *Philadelphian* said:

> The strikingly effective portrayal in the production is that by Bette Davis in the role of the daughter suddenly brought to the knowledge that she is an unwanted child and that her supposed father had never been more to her than a provider. Miss Davis—wan, sickly, yet cheerful as a child should be—thrills us in the poignant grief that comes with the revelation of the child's great tragedy. Such grief could hardly be more helpless.

The tour proceeded to Washington. *The Washington Post* said:

> Especially commendable was the selection of Bette Davis, a talented ingénue with a native sweetness and spiritual wholesomeness that blend ideally into a loveable character. Bette Davis is a young woman who is going to advance far in her stage endeavors. She was a profoundly sympathetic and appealing Hedvig and gained more by her simple natural charms than a more experienced actor could ever have hoped to do.

In Boston, Bette played at her most intense in front of an audience filled with her personal friends and relatives. Her father came backstage but, inhibited and incapable of expressing praise to her face, that miserable man lauded all of the other players and made no reference whatsoever to her performance. He told her, "You would make a very competent secretary." When he left her dressing room, she felt utterly desolate and empty.

He evidently relented when he got home. He wrote her a letter saying that he got a big kick out of seeing her in the show; that he was proud of her fine debut, and was most awfully tickled that she had the "so-nice Ibsen uptown engagements." He fretted that she hadn't seen him for any length of time in the dressing room, that she wasn't up to taking supper with him, and that his suitcase had been swiped at the depot. And he added, "By the way, you looked sorta peaked to me. Take care of yourself so you won't crack up just when things are going so nicely. You need lots and lots of cream, milk, eggs, fruit, green vegetables—you ought to build yourself up. I was glad to see my so-accomplished daughter do so well."

She enjoyed a storm of applause that night, the chance (seldom allowed by Miss Yurka) to take a solo curtain, and the opportunity to show those who had doubted her ability that she had the stuff of greatness. The *Boston Traveler* led the local papers in a chorus of praise: "Miss Davis manages to wring this emotional part dry of its dramatic content without lessening Miss Yurka's role, and what a feat that is!" It was generally agreed that Bette had surpassed the fabled Nazimova in the role.

It was in every way a triumphant tour that probably meant as much to her as anything else in her career. Although Blanche Yurka was a disagreeable presence, with a repulsive body odor when she sweated, and had a habit of forgetting lines at rehearsal—which threw the rest of the cast off-balance—she was a good and noble tutor. Bette learned much from Blanche Yurka: her use of stillness after great whirls around the stage, the sudden break in her voice in a moment of emotion, and above all the way she had of concentrating all of her power into her huge and brilliant eyes.

When the tour ended, Bette was already established as an actress of promise. This was no mean accomplishment in a period when, unlike today, Broadway boasted a galaxy of great stars and was a showcase for some of the greatest dramatists of the age. In that year, 1929, there was a giant's feast of pleasures. New plays by George Bernard Shaw, Noel Coward, and Eugene O'Neill played with brilliant casts to audiences that savored every word. Shakespeare flourished on Broadway, along with Ibsen, Strindberg, and Pirandello.

It was a fine time for an actress to emerge. Bette could cut her teeth on the harsh perfectionism of rehearsals under commanding, demanding tutors. Given her New England love of discipline and taste for torture, she relished the hard work and slaved like a salt miner in front of an audience. At the end of a performance, she collapsed, wrung out, into Ruthie's arms. Miss Yurka's chief memory of her was that she would "gear herself up to such a pitch that at times in the middle of a line I would almost freeze, thinking she was going mad right in front of me. She seemed so small and so frail. She and her mother ate the most dreadful food, probably because of the wretched money I paid her. She would leave the magical world of Ibsen, and I'd see her and Mrs. Davis at a hamburger stand in the rain. They seemed to be happy, laughing. I've never seen such love between a mother and daughter. Much as I hated that dreadful Ruthie, I was often on the verge of tears at the sight of them."

During the Yurka tour, Bette had played briefly as one of the young, spirited, laughing sisters in Ibsen's *The Lady from the Sea*. Among the audience in Philadelphia was a successful young director saddled with the name of Marion Gering. He told me in Japan years later: "I was very taken with her, and when I was casting a rather bad play called *Broken Dishes* by Martin Flavin, I thought she would be good in the show as the daughter. I asked to have her come in for a reading, and this frail, awkward girl kind of *sidled* into my office holding her mother's hand as though she were a child of eight. I realized that she had not been Hedvig for nothing, that she was *still* a baby—eager, tearful, spoiled, virginal, and subject to wild shifts of mood.

"She stood there looking at me, clumsily poised on her high heels and wearing an ugly little hat. Her impossibly long neck made me itch to fetch an axe. She was very pale, and trembled, while Ruthie looked at her as though she had just given birth to her. The whole thing was totally insane but I told myself, 'My God, she's impossible! She's neurotic; she looks at once intellectual and emotionally backward; but she's got "actress" written all over her. She's *made of lightning.*' I had to have her, but I was frightened. Wouldn't she be too strong for the play?"

When Gering gave her the part, Bette hugged Ruthie ecstatically. The show was essentially a vehicle for that perfect Milquetoast, Donald Meek, who was as nervous and virginally middle-aged as any tiny, bald, put-upon man he ever played in the theater. It was the story of a revolt among the Bumpsteads, a fairly typical midwestern family. Like *The Earth Between,* the play was authentic Americana. It dealt with small-town life in a mood of great sympathy and conviction, and was (the critics agreed) very well played by Meek as the drudge who rebels against his family, and by Bette as the daughter who aids and abets him and discovers true love in the process. It was generally conceded that Bette was triumphant in the final scene in which she denounced, in a powerful speech, her tyrannical mother and the matriarch's hypocritical relatives. Brooks Atkinson praised her warmly.

Even the Wall Street crash could not affect the success of *Broken Dishes,* and despite the fact that Donald Meek lost his life's savings, he came onstage the night the market plunged and gave a brilliant performance. Bette adored him for it.

A great thrill for Bette was when Madam Favor descended from her rarefied sphere in Boston to attend a performance. It was the first time she had agreed to see Bette on a professional stage. At first she sat in her orchestra seat primly upright in black silk, while gales of laughter swept around her. But she soon gave in and smiled a little. After Bette's big speech at the end, she joined the crowd in a standing ovation. It was one of the great moments of Bette's life to see her grandmother there, tiny, self-contained, and commanding.

Madam Favor visited Bette backstage before proceeding to the Davises' apartment on East 53rd Street, where she was to spend the night. Bette went on to a theater party, and when she got home at 2:30 A.M. was astonished to find Madam still sitting up, waiting to congratulate her once again.

Broken Dishes ran for 178 performances. Bette was the toast of the town. She won the admiration of girls who identified with her part, wishing that they, too, could rebel against their families. It was a stroke of luck that she began her career with a role that excited sympathy in the young. Soon young women would be her largest audience.

Hollywood movie producer Samuel Goldwyn sent a talent scout to watch her performance and she was given a screen test in New York for the film *Raffles*. But with her irregular features and awkward stance she looked impossible, and Goldwyn threw up his hands in horror. She was not upset. In common with all other theater people, she thought Hollywood was an absurdly vulgar place where no one in his right mind would want to go.

Early in 1930, Bette went on the road tour of *Broken Dishes*. She was in Washington when she was offered a chance to return to Broadway in *Solid South*. The play opened on October 14, 1930, under the direction of Rouben Mamoulian.

Bette was fascinated by Mamoulian, a gifted and sophisticated Armenian just beginning to make a major name in the theater. He directed her meticulously. *Solid South* was an uproarious farce of the Deep South, dominated by the great Richard Bennett (father of movie stars Constance and Joan), who was overpowering as a grandiose army major careening headlong through his mansion and living out all the outrageous fantasies of the traditional southerner in flowery speeches. Bette played a sweet young girl in love with Owen Davis, Jr., in a style of tender anticipation and joy. When comedy was called for, she played up expertly. It was Richard Bennett's play from start to finish, but she made a small, certain impression.

When she came to New York for the production, she had shown her true spirit. Richard Bennett had said to her with freezing disdain, "I suppose you're another of these young ham actresses."

Bette replied, "I've been up all night on a train. Unless you show me more consideration than this, I'll go home and we'll forget the matter."

As a result, she was hired.

There were curious incidents during the production. During one performance, finding a prop missing, Bennett broke off in the middle of a line and called out, "Stagehand, where's my cigar?" Bette, in her memoirs, recalled another incident in which he turned directly to the audience and, glaring at it, said, "I suppose I'll have to tell you a dirty story to get you to laugh!"

Her reviews in *Solid South* earned Bette a chance for another screen test. She had the choice of continuing in *Solid South* or going to Hollywood. She was still hesitating when *Solid South* abruptly folded.

Though dubious about the screen test, she decided to make it anyway. It was a freezing late-November day, and she had to take a train to a remote suburb of New York. She was distraught with fear, knowing she wasn't photogenic. By the time she reached the stage to play a brief scene in Preston Sturges's *Strictly Dishonorable,* her nerves were unbearably taut. When the director screamed, "Action!" she fainted.

At last she came round—and delivered the now-classic remark: "Don't worry! I do this quite often!"

Despite the shaky start, the test was a success and she was offered a contract. But she didn't want to go to Hollywood. She tried hard to obtain a role in another play, and when that effort failed, she and Ruthie decided to take the big chance and go West for six months to see what would happen. Hollywood still seemed to be the end of the world. And there was another problem. They had a year-long lease on their apartment and the landlord refused to allow them to leave without paying the balance of the rent. This was out of the question, since they had only a hundred dollars between them. Finally, after their persistent begging to be allowed to sublease the place, the landlord relented. But two weeks later they still had not succeeded in finding someone to take over the flat and they were afraid they would have to be separated—a quite unthinkable possibility.

They were due to leave for the Coast on December 8,

1930. On the 7th, while they were clinging together in a chair, crying with despair, the bell rang. The flat was on the main floor. Ruthie ran out and flung open the door so rapidly that she forgot to dry the tears on her face. A tall, gray, sinister-looking man stood there. *"Show the apartment!"* he ordered.

Ruthie acted up a storm as she introduced the man to her famous daughter, extravagantly praised everything in her dismal home, and watched his face intently for a reaction. Finally he said, in a harsh, eerie near-whisper, *"Is there a closet that can be locked up and not easily reopened?"* Ruthie looked at Bette. Was the man a murderer? Was he hiding stolen jewelry? What did it matter!

"Yes!" Ruthie answered triumphantly.

The man silently extracted a number of twenty-dollar bills from his wallet and gave them to Ruthie with the words, delivered in an icy monotone, "The maid must come and leave at twelve. Here's a hundred dollars for her. Leave your name on the bell and mailbox. Write the name and address of the person who will receive the rent, whether that's you or somebody else." Mrs. Davis later commented, "I wrote the name of a friend who had been kind, fearing if I gave the man a Hollywood address, he'd never send the money."

As it turned out, the man paid his rent punctually and there was never any word of an arrest. On the morning of December 8, mother and daughter and their wire-haired terrier, Boogum, set out on their adventure to Hollywood, where she now had a Universal Studios picture contract.

THREE

Bette and Ruthie now had exactly fifty-seven dollars between them. Bette's earnings on the stage had been swallowed up by the cost of dressing properly for the role of an up-and-coming actress. Forty-three dollars had gone for meals and preparing things for the new tenant. Ruthie allowed ten dollars a day for the trip, which would take five days.

The journey seemed endless. Mother and daughter had finished reading their magazines within hours after leaving New York. Most of the time they gazed blankly out the sooty windows. The parlor car was full of cigarette smoke and barroom conversation unfit for a young lady's ears. The elegant first-class section, with its Art Deco dining room, mahogany fittings, traveling bookstore, barbershop, and swarms of handsomely uniformed black attendants, was several worlds away from the crowded, swaying day coaches, the snack bar, and the long lines at the bathroom in the morning. And it was very cold. The heating system was temperamental and frequently gave out. In places along the tracks there were snowdrifts, which had to be cleared away before the train could proceed. Sitting up in the day coach at night meant that sleep was virtually impossible.

There was a brief stopover in Chicago, where they were to change trains. The chilly, echoing station, in those days before central heating, provided a bleak interlude. The papers there were full of shootings, and the people were rude and pushy.

By the time the train had chugged through the rolling wheat fields of Kansas, the parched deserts of New Mexico, and the small farms, deserts, and mountains of southeastern California, Bette felt numb. She felt she had been on the train for five years. Much as she loved her mother, she wished her sister Bobby, now at college, had been with her to exchange the funny, silly small talk that sisters enjoy. She felt desolate at the prospect of living in Hollywood, but mindful at the same time that she was going to prove herself out there, along with all the other young Broadway actresses who were being enlisted for the new age of talkies. So she played with Boogum, chatted with her mother about childhood days, and hoped things wouldn't be too bad at the end of the rainbow.

Bette and her mother were fascinated by the fact that their three-thousand-mile journey from the winds and sleet of the eastern states had brought them to a subtropical climate. They stepped down on a gravel platform next to a waiting-room office roofed with red tiles like dragon scales. A few wind-bent palm trees relieved the dusty shimmer of this strange place.

Bette had been swept up in a fantasy of her own making: that a press corps would greet her with cameras and notebooks and eager questions about her love life. Instead, there was only one photographer, who disappeared quickly after snapping her and her mother poised on the steps of the railroad car, both looking decidedly awkward in their slanting hats, ankle-length dresses, and loose, ill-fitting coats.

They had been promised that a press agent would meet them and drive them to the Hollywood Plaza Hotel on Vine Street, where Universal Pictures had booked them. But no one turned up; they weren't considered worthy of such special treatment. They were forced to spend most of their remaining seven dollars on the cab fare.

Their arrival in Hollywood was at a time of upheaval in the motion-picture industry. Only three years earlier, the

66

success of *The Jazz Singer* had rendered silent pictures virtually obsolete. By 1930, silent stars without the speaking voices that are acquired through stage-training or those with unintelligible foreign accents had been driven ignominiously from the screen. Bette was an insignificant speck in a dust cloud of obscure performers that had blown in from the East. She realized she amounted to little, that she wasn't even remotely as attractive as the gorgeous girls she saw driving roadsters past her on the wide highway through the hills.

Her vision of Hollywood had been formed by the fan magazines, with their sepia-toned pages of purple prose and photographs of handsome men and women swimming, playing tennis, and bouncing balls along a beach. She was soon to learn that Hollywood was worse than she had imagined it would be. As Robert Benchley described it in the year of Bette's arrival:

> Hollywood [was] a flat, unlovely plain, inhabited by a group of highly ordinary people, all of them quite at sea and usually in a mild state of panic in their chosen work, turning out a product which, except for certain mechanical excellences, was as unimportant and undistinguished as the product of any plant grinding out rubber novelties or automobile accessories.

It was a town that knew little of theatrical entertainment or culture. There were no nightclubs, and the only place where food was served after midnight was a lunch wagon on Hollywood and Vine that offered egg sandwiches every other night. There were no speakeasies—nor even a cocktail bar. It was a long time since people gathered to, in Benchley's words, "swap cocaine and pistol shots."

For anyone used to New York, the distances between one place and another were daunting. It invariably took almost an hour to get anywhere, driving at a thirty-mile-per-hour speed limit and often having to negotiate a steep climb in second gear up the sides of crumbling hills. New Yorkers who were uninterested in tennis, swimming, bed at ten o'clock, and buckets of orange juice frequently turned into grumbling alcoholics.

Fear ruled everything: the fear of dismissal if the box-office results on a picture were not satisfactory; fear of not having a voice that the microphone would flatteringly register; fear of gaining an ounce of weight or a single gray hair; fear of being named in a scandal that might offend the women's clubs; fear, above all, that talking pictures might be just a temporary phase and that those who had committed themselves to them would go all the way from millionaires to paupers in no time at all.

And beyond the fear there was the dream of fabulous incomes—former gas-station attendants and waitresses were suddenly the occupants of pseudo-eighteenth-century French châteaux. But the tumbril was always waiting.

Hollywood itself was a suburb of beige-colored office buildings, pepper and banana trees, and apartments furnished in early Pullman. The Hollywood Plaza Hotel was a far cry from the Plaza in New York. Its drab lobby offered speckled mirrors and pink lamps that looked like outsized pepper shakers. Mrs. Davis and her daughter walked into it on December 13, 1930. The room they were given overlooked the wide, traffic-filled street.

The heat was amazing; already, Bette's skin, with its burned-off outer layer, was drying and freckling badly. There was, as there is today, nothing quite as desolating for a stranger as a first day in Hollywood; even in hard-bitten New York, people were more warm and welcoming. Perhaps because of the distances between people's homes and the snobbery of property and money, the penniless visitor tended to feel that he had been dropped on the surface of the moon. People were brusque and even downright rude to those who were neither rich nor handsome, nor in the possession of a costly and ostentatious automobile. Even a dog, which would have evoked affection and pleasure in the East, was given an icy glance because it might soil a sidewalk or a fake marble lobby.

Ruthie testified that Bette cried from terror at the blankness and impersonal hardness of the environment. Her friends were left far behind—along with the theater she loved. She didn't dare tell her mother outright of her disappointment; that was the worst part. Mrs. Davis wrote:

> Three years of praise and applause in the theaters of the East meant nothing here. Here you were guilty from the start until you could prove your worth. If we could have talked to each other (about our unhappiness in Hollywood), things would have been easier. But Bette retired into herself, hating it all. And I spent a period of trying to bolster up her flagging spirits.

The first day in Hollywood was tedious. Ray Jones, the photographer who had met the Davises at the station, turned up at the hotel to drive them to Universal Studios.

The journey took them over a canyon, past pink stucco bungalows and "Moorish" mansions clinging to the edge of precipices. Universal Studios was not the empire it is today, with its black glass tower, sprawl of enormous sound stages, and its commissary, where the diners are gazed down upon by giant blowups of the stars. It was a disorganized scattering of wooden, verandaed buildings and rambling palm-lined streets. Purple mountains loomed over foothills that resembled giant sand dunes covered irregularly in scrub.

Universal had weathered the transition to talkies largely by rereleasing some of its silent classics with musical scores and sound effects. Its first part-talkie, *Lonesome,* was not the overpowering success hoped for, and instead of following that picture with more delicate love stories, the studio made a futile stab at *Show Boat,* with mixed sound and silent sequences, and began trying to make it into the big time with the ambitious and powerful *All Quiet on the Western Front* and the horror films *Dracula* and *Frankenstein.* Bette knew from the first that Universal wasn't in the same league as MGM, Paramount, or the up-and-coming, feisty young Warner Brothers Studio. Aside from *All Quiet,* there was little to indicate the greatness of Universal in the silent period.

As an obscure beginner, all she was asked to do was spend the morning posing for photographs in her street clothes, including (incongruously in the Hollywood sunshine) two silver foxes that had cost her her last nickel the winter before. She held Boogum high, embraced her mother, and smiled obediently, all the time wishing she were thousands of miles away.

Ray Jones recalled an example of Bette's wit some years later. As they were leaving the photographic studio, he said to her, "Who is your favorite actress?"

"Garbo," Bette replied.

"Oh," Ray Jones said, "there's a letter in *Photoplay* this week in which a woman says she believes in Garbo in the same sense she believes in God."

"That must keep Miss Garbo awake at night!" Bette retorted.

On the next day, a Saturday, Bette looked at Ruthie, and Ruthie looked at Bette. If they were going to tolerate this place at all they had better get out of the hotel fast. Only a house would make the situation tolerable. They walked along Hollywood Boulevard until they found a real estate office. A Mrs. Mary Carr took them on a long drive through the hills looking at different homes. Although they had no idea how they would pay the first and last month's rent, since by now they had only a dollar and a half between them, they were sufficiently good actresses to convince Mary Carr of their affluence.

At last they found a place they liked: 4435 Alta Loma Terrace, a Grimm's fairy-tale cottage with redwood door and eaves. They fell in love with it at once. But the rent was $80 a month. How could they afford it? Bette's salary was $450 a month but she wouldn't receive the money for several weeks, probably not until after the Christmas holidays.

Neither Ruthie nor Bette slept well that night. They had to have the house. They couldn't afford the house. They had to have the house. And how were they going to pay the hotel bill when they checked out?

They talked of asking the mean Harlow Morrell Davis for money. But Ruthie knew that an old friend of the family, Carl Milliken, lived at the Hollywood Roosevelt Hotel, a fifteen-minute walk from the Plaza. Maybe, she figured, he could supply the cash.

Early that morning, while Bette was still asleep, exhausted from a flood of tears shed the night before, Ruthie got up, dressed silently, and walked to the Roosevelt. She found Milliken on the tennis court in white flannels, playing with a Japanese coach. She walked straight up to him, looked him in the eye, and without even bidding him a good morning, took a deep breath and said very fast, *"It is absolutely essential that I have four hundred dollars!"* Then she reminded him who she was!

Milliken instantly produced four hundred-dollar bills! Ruthie gabbled that she was going to obtain a house and car and then she ran off, very embarrassed, while Milliken called after her: "You must be frugal, you know. This town is a fickle mistress!"

Unwilling to disclose to Bette that she had turned herself into a beggar, Ruthie ventured on a complicated theatrical ruse. She walked over to the Western Union office on Cahuenga Boulevard and wrote on a telegram form: AM SENDING THE MONEY YOUR MOTHER ASKED TO BORROW. DAD. She had restricted the message to ten words in order to make it seem convincingly like one sent by a miser. When she returned to their room at the Plaza, she found it locked. She slipped the telegram and the money under the door and heard Bette scream with delight.

Bette flung open the door, grabbed Ruthie, and ran with her headlong to Western Avenue, where they snapped up a brand-new Ford on the spot. Bette never let on that she knew Ruthie had forged the telegram.

Once mother and daughter had moved into their pretty house in the hills, their spirits began to brighten. But they were dampened again soon after when they were confronted with a Christmas without friends or relatives, without snow or sleigh bells, without carol singers and children's laughter. Bobby came out by train, stayed for a week, and hated everything. Hollywood Boulevard was decorated with silver tinsel and papier-mâché figures of Santa Claus, reindeers, and figures from fairy tales illuminated by bulbs in their stomachs. Wind-up phonographs in stores played carols through loudspeakers.

The Davises braved out the holiday season with Mother's favorite dishes of roast stuffed goose and mince pie. They began to buy little things that reminded them of home: brass ornaments (which Bette always refused to polish), a print of a New England snow scene, flowered plates. Boogum frisked about happily, chasing chipmunks and raccoons, and skunks which frequently added their unique aroma to nights filled with the scent of jasmine. At least the New Year lay ahead. Until then, life was perhaps just bearable.

Bette was to experience a rude shock when she reported for work after the holidays. Although "Uncle" Carl Laemmle was the ostensible head of the studio, this shrewd German-Jewish emigré had handed over the reins of power to his singularly uninspired son, known as "Junior." At the age of twenty-one, Junior was a depressing example of the results of nepotism. His sausage-machine-like approach to making pictures based on second-rate novels or plays resulted in work of surpassing mediocrity. As an executive, he had about as much skill as the average janitor.

Inevitably, for such were the macho demands of Hollywood executives, new starlets were subjected to a minute physical analysis, often followed by a private "screen test," conducted horizontally. Perhaps fortunately, Bette failed to pass muster when Junior had her to his office. He opened his door, looked her up and down, and closed it again. The prospective "audition" was canceled.

She went through the motions of an official test. The director told her that her legs must be shown or she wouldn't succeed in Hollywood. He trained a camera on her and threw a powerful light on her face that made her squint. She raised her skirt nervously, even though her legs were in fact very shapely. Some claim that she saw the test, cried out, and fled in horror from the screening room; but in Hollywood young actresses were never allowed to see their tests.

She was put in the hands of makeup man Jack Pierce, who specialized in monster movies and whose next achievement would be the horrific creature played by Boris Karloff in *Frankenstein.* Pierce did his best to turn Bette Davis into Jean Harlow. He dyed her hair a garish blond; he plucked her eyebrows and penciled in artificial ones. He shadowed her cheeks to make them seem intriguingly hollow. When the makeup session ended, she was handed over to wardrobe and then given further tests in clinging satin dresses with large bows, in bathing suits, and in afternoon outfits with eyeshadowing hats. Bette found the whole routine insufferable. Ultraserious and used to the commitment and intelligence of the Broadway stage, she found all this dyeing, reshaping, and refashioning of her into a reliable sexy image utterly nonsensical.

In her dramatic tests, she played with her head and not with her emotions or any of the expected eroticism and coyness of the time. She acted with an edgy, uneasy, almost neurotic gaiety and sharpness. Clearly, she was too brainy; she exemplified Wilde's dictum that intellect destroys the beauty of any face. People began to feel she wouldn't last in Hollywood. She was too high-hat, too "Manhattan." It was a relief for Bette to come home at night after these grueling sessions and put her feet up and talk to her mother about the good old days in New England before they had made the horrible mistake of coming to California. Another consolation was that she and Ruthie began to make one or two friends. Reginald Denny was a well-setup young Englishman who had been a great success as a comedian in silent pictures and now, in the talkie era, was setting out on a career of being the tweedy, pipe-smoking, reliable friend of the heroine in countless pictures with "British" settings.

Denny met Bette in the Universal commissary. He told me years later: "Bette and I were good friends. There was no question of a romance. I was happily married, with children and that rarest thing in Hollywood—a secure and comfortable home life. I knew Bette was hating it in Hollywood. She longed to go back to the theater. But I encouraged her to stay. I knew that although she wasn't conventionally pretty, she would outlive all the platinum blondes who were walking around trying to be noticed. Her face

73

was 'made' for the camera. It was amazingly open. The emotions weren't hidden by deceit. You could read all her feelings in those hauntingly expressive eyes. I suggested to her that, instead of fretting over lost theater, she should immerse herself in good movies. She should see the stars who counted—Garbo especially. Garbo had done very little in the theater yet her face told millions about her most secret feelings. Bette, I felt, could do the same."

Bette heeded Denny's advice. She began to go with Ruthie to Garbo pictures, sitting in the balcony and gazing transfixed at the luminous face of the Swedish actress, watching Garbo's instinctive, totally uncalculated style and grace. But it was clear to her from the start that she wasn't a phenomenon of nature as Garbo was. She would have to will herself, force herself, into success. Sheer brains and toughness would have to get her there.

At about the same time, Denny introduced Bette to a remarkable, sweet-natured woman, Bridget Price, who would later become Bette's indispensable secretary, adviser, and friend. Bridget seemed to know that Bette would soon be prominent. She waited around for the chance to be the righthand woman of a star.

Bette missed Ham acutely during those first weeks in Hollywood. She wrote to him frequently in her bold, round hand in green ink on extraordinarily flimsy stationery. Ham had been promised a job as a trumpeter in the official band of the Olympics that were to be held in Los Angeles in 1932. He wrote that he would come out there the following year to set up the arrangements; meantime, he was very busy playing trumpet with a band in the East.

Bette was in a constant state of longing to be married and to become a mother. But Ruthie kept the pressure on her to stay in Hollywood; already, in her mind, Ruthie was counting the future dollars.

Just after New Year's Day, 1931, Bette was suddenly asked to report to work for *Bad Sister*, a screenplay based on *The Flirt*, by Booth Tarkington. Her first delight at appearing in a screen version of a story by a writer she admired was dashed when she discovered that the script was a travesty of the author's whimsical Hoosier tragedy.

She was to appear in the movie with a mediocre British actress, Sidney Fox. Bette's part as Laura Madison called for her to be an unhappy girl whose sister is the town flirt and gadabout. While Laura clings to the hearth with her knitting and her books, Marianne whirls about parties with gay young blades. The young Humphrey Bogart was cast as Valentine Corliss, a con man who degrades Marianne.

Bette found herself confronted with an uninspired director, Hobart Henley; poor dialogue; and the stationary cameras that were sealed in telephone-boothlike boxes so airless the operators tended to faint in them. The sound stage was completely sealed off, even down to the ventilators, to prevent outside sound from being heard. Even so, a backfiring truck or automobile, or a biplane flying overhead, could penetrate the silence and ruin a whole sequence. The microphones were the size and shape of corncobs and were concealed in bellpulls, in cigarette boxes, or uncomfortably between an actress's breasts. Bette had to wear one in her bodice, with a large, black, insulated wire attached to the wall that made it impossible for her to move in any direction. If she turned her face toward the leading actor, her voice would fade; she had to address most of her lines in the approximate direction of her stomach.

It is scarcely surprising, in view of these conditions of shooting, that Bette played the whole part in a whining, complaining manner that only too clearly revealed her dissatisfaction with the absurd mechanics of motion-picture making. She was also far from happy with the presence of Humphrey Bogart on the scene. In later years, she failed to agree with the enduring public adulation of him. She found him bad-mannered, ill-tempered, heavy-drinking, and downright boring. She also told Reginald Denny that someone should have told Sidney Fox she shouldn't play a Booth Tarkington story in a voice that reeked of Mayfair.

The New York Times correctly observed upon *Bad Sister*'s release at the beginning of April 1931: "Miss Davis's interpretation of Laura is too lugubrious and tends to destroy the sympathy the audience is expected to feel for the young woman." Bette acknowledged the truth of the verdict.

Junior Laemmle, speaking about *Bad Sister*, told me: "Bette Davis has spent a lifetime saying that . . . I told someone in my office while she was outside the door that she was 'about as sexy as Slim Summerville.' First, I don't know what she was doing eavesdropping at my office door! Eavesdroppers never do hear good of themselves! But I never said anything of the kind. I said she could have changed parts with cornball Slim Summerville and nobody would have known the difference. That was closer to the mark.

"She was very bad in *Bad Sister*. When I was at the sneak preview in San Bernardino, I saw her slipping out with her mother about halfway through. I'll take an even bet they were both in tears."

Laemmle, though much criticized by Bette, renewed her option despite the bad reviews of her performance and cast her in a more ambitious picture, *Seed*, which flopped quickly after its release a mere six weeks after *Bad Sister*. It was directed by John Stahl, a manic sadist who, paradoxically, sentimentalized everything he touched.

Seed was a family story, with a plot so complex that it filled an entire column of *The New York Times* and still remains totally incomprehensible. Bette was reduced to a very subsidiary role as one of five children of John Boles, an actor who was only about six years her senior. Much of the story consisted of the mother's problems with the father, who is trying to get off the ground as a writer. There is endless discussion of royalty checks and manuscripts, none of which was of the slightest interest to an audience. Bette's chief contribution to the picture was in one scene, where, with forgivable relish, she cut her father's novel into strips.

Shortly after *Seed* was released, Ham came out to visit. During his stay, he deepened still further her love and knowledge of music. She was upset when he had to return to New York, and didn't like working in *Waterloo Bridge*, a genteel, romantic fantasy about lovers in World War I London, in which she played an insignificant supporting part, with her name mentioned just above "Old Woman" in the printed cast list.

Doris Lloyd, a British actress who appeared in the picture, said: "I liked Bette. I could see her staying back after she'd finished her work for the day to watch the other players, widening her big eyes and trying to overcompensate for her miserable part by vicariously living with the characters. Such ambition! Such hunger!"

Bette was miserable with the director, James Whale, whom she found indifferent, cold, rude and quite unimpressed by her talent. She was unaware of the fact that he was a fastidious artist whose British background in the theater brought a striking authority to the evocation of London. He insisted that even a chamber pot under a bed or a wallpaper pattern be scrupulously correct. *Waterloo Bridge* was a shadowy, haunting, poetic work reflecting Whale's almost feminine sensibility. Bette was lovely and fragile in the very minor role of the hero's sister. Whale, despite her disclaimers, directed her with considerable skill, bringing out her vulnerability in the same way Marion Gering had done in the theater.

The lease on Alta Loma Terrace ran out, and Bette and Ruthie began a series of moves, with eventual brief stays at Zuma Beach, Canyon Drive and Havenhurst Avenue in Hollywood, and San Vicente Boulevard in Brentwood. It was part of Ruthie's nature that she was unable to settle anywhere for long before becoming restive and irritable. A place that seemed a dream house one day would present innumerable imaginary problems the next.

Bette had gained a little recognition in movies, but she still didn't have a "name." She had to borrow constantly on her salary to make ends meet and to support her mother and sister. She gave an early interview to W. E. Oliver of the *Los Angeles Examiner* in 1931, saying: "It is an ordeal in pictures after you've made a name on the stage. I can walk into any New York agent's office and they know me. Here I'm back where I was three years ago, getting a first foothold."

Junior Laemmle confirmed that he felt he had made a mistake in increasing Bette's first option to twelve months at $450 a week. He immediately started lending her out: to Columbia for *The Menace*, a melodrama set in a gloomy old mansion in which she screamed and ran about; to an independent group for *Hell's House*, an undistinguished offering co-starring Pat O'Brien; and to RKO for a pleasant rural comedy, *Way Back Home*. She was happiest at RKO, presided over by the benign Pandro S. Berman, who gave all of his productions a special quality. She also became a friend of the Pat O'Brien's, and she and her mother often visited with them. She liked the bluff, outgoing Irishman, with his big genial face, tremendous energy, and rapid line of talk.

With her career at Universal seemingly aborted, Bette became convinced that she should return to New York for good. Ruthie was beginning to feel the same way, when suddenly an opportunity arose.

George Arliss was at the time at the peak of his success as a Hollywood star. He specialized in portraits of a Rembrandtesque realism. Skeletal and round-shouldered, with a beaked nose, darting, alarming eyes, and an affected, high-pitched voice, he seemed to be the last person on earth who would ever make it in the movies. But he dug deep into a character, discovering unsuspected resources in conventional lines and situations. He had seen Bette not only as a pupil in plays in the John Murray Anderson Theater School, but in Blanche Yurka's *The Wild Duck* and in *Way Back Home*. He asked to see her at Warner's as a possible fellow player in *The Man Who Played God*. This was the story of a pianist stricken with deafness as a result of an explosion, whose joy comes from anonymously helping people whom he has watched in Central Park from his window and learned from reading their lips the sad and touching details of their lives. Bette was to act a girl who adored him, fascinated by his elegant hands moving over the piano keys.

Unlike many actresses and actors, Bette had a capacity for being impressed by performers. She was excited by Arliss, who told her that she had been recommended by another actor, Murray Kinnell, who had been with her in *The Menace*. He was too shy to admit he was also fascinated by and attracted to her. The interview went well. He later wrote in his memoirs that from the first moment he met

Bette Davis he clearly saw her quality, that she was the only actress he ever worked with who brought more vibrant responsiveness and interpretation to a part than was contained in the lines or was visible at first inspection. And, responding to Arliss's trust in her—his total conviction that she could play at a level equal to his own—she gave a performance alive with sincerity and intelligence. There was no bunk in her acting. She drove to the heart of an emotion. She knew *The Man Who Played God* was an important picture and, perhaps instinctively, felt Warner Brothers would be good for her.

Warners was considerably different from Universal, with its feeble guidance by Junior Laemmle. Warners, known in the business as San Quentin, was run by a no-nonsense, superefficient team headed by the tanned, blazer-wearing, wisecracking Jack Warner; the quiet persistent Hal Wallis; and the macho but hypertensive Darryl F. Zanuck. Warner pictures were made without fuss, on scratch budgets and watertight schedules. Unlike haughty MGM, Warners made pictures about the poor. They dealt with life during the Depression as it was. They showed the misery of the chain gangs, the cruelties of the Ku Klux Klan, the rough life of an office girl who had to sleep her way to the executive suite, the grueling pressures of newspaper offices, and the horror of prisons and the slums that bred their occupants.

Warner Brothers needed Bette Davis because she was an actress without pretense. She was miles above the arrogant girls who floated through high-society dramas with their noses in the air. Her gutsy, feisty, totally honest, hard-edged approach to acting melded with Warners' identical approach to picture-making. Although she didn't know it then, she had found her home.

The Man Who Played God does not wear well today. It seems heavily sanctimonious and false, and (except for the powerful moment when he realizes he has been stricken with deafness) Arliss's performance is dated. Bette's playing is on two notes: of frantic gaiety and burning intensity. Her admiration of Arliss shines through her acting; it almost makes convincing the theory that a girl of her age

79

and character would fall in love with an ancient, trembling gargoyle because of her fascination with his talent. The endless homilies and moral tags are scarcely improved by the feeble playing of the supporting cast, who seem to have just emerged from a Sunday school drama class. Only Davis seems to understand diction for the microphone; the other players are fixed in slow motion, painfully aware they are being recorded. It is unjust that *The New York Times* critic wrote only one sentence about her performance: "Bette Davis speaks too rapidly for the microphone."

Hal Wallis says: "Anyone who could hold her own with George Arliss in a scene and not look like a prop was outstanding in my book. Indeed, there were moments when you weren't looking at Arliss; you were looking at her instead. There was no question in my mind that she would go all the way to the top. She didn't just act with her eyes. She acted with her whole body, with every pore of that body. She was *alive;* she jumped out of the screen."

Bette and Ruthie, along with Bobby, who had decided to come back to California after all, were living at the time on Canyon Drive. Bette, overexcited by her new success, drove her recently acquired Auburn with such passion that she was arrested for speeding. On February 16, 1932, for a second time, she was almost burned to death. A battery short caused a sudden surge of flame to engulf her car as she was driving up to the house. She screamed and struggled with the door. Bobby rushed out of the house and dragged her from the front seat in the nick of time. The story was headlined in some of the newspapers' back pages, a sure sign that Bette Davis was on her way.

Bette also suffered at the time from a jumpy appendix that caused acute spasms, sweating, and vomiting. She was so terrified of losing work because of this problem that she postponed having an operation again and again. During the period of her sickness, Bette found another friend in the witty, acutely intelligent star, Jean Harlow. They went to parties together. Jean's husband, the producer Paul Bern, had recently committed suicide, leaving a note that intimated he was suffering from sexual impotence. Bette gave Harlow a great deal of consolation in those harrowing days.

Because of the studio's excitement over *The Man Who Played God*, Bette was kept busy under contract—rushed into no less than five pictures in 1932. Of these, *The Rich Are Always with Us* held a special place for her because during the making of it she met, and felt strongly attracted to, a handsome young Irish actor named George Brent. Dark, brown-eyed, with a football player's build, he had come from the Abbey Theatre in Dublin to success on Broadway and in Hollywood as an uninspired but reliable leading man who could be an effective foil for high-powered actresses. Unfortunately, he was mean-spirited, tough, and handicapped by a wickedly vicious tongue. His sex appeal earned him a series of conquests that made him the envy of many Hollywood men. The reasons for his appeal may have been due to his masculine self-confidence, his air of tweedy, pipe-smoking dependability and inner security. He was sturdily complacent and humorously self-satisfied. His static, stolid good looks, combined with his bland, outgoing manner, captivated Bette.

But Brent wasn't responsive to her. He was already involved with the heroine of *The Rich Are Always with Us*, Ruth Chatterton, who made up for her small stature and plump, pouter-pigeon figure with a regal manner and an imposing expression on her undistinguished oval face that convinced audiences she was a great actress. It was a confidence trick that worked. Yet today, in the absurd Hollywood version of high-society affairs that *The Rich Are Always with Us* perpetrated, Bette Davis, not Ruth Chatterton, is the one who is doing the acting. The only surviving scene of interest in this travesty of New York society is one in which Brent and Chatterton, visibly in love, are discovered in a bedroom. Brent lights two cigarettes at the same time and hands one to Chatterton.

In the latter part of the summer of 1932, Ham arrived from New York to play fanfares in turban and sash in the Olympic Games band. Only two days after he arrived, Bette had to go East on a promotional tour for *The Dark*

Horse, with the actor Warren William. Frustrated over the fact that Ham's life seemed to be at odds with hers, Bette had a depressing stay in New York in bad weather, barely tolerating Warren William's ridiculously pretentious behavior as a cut-rate John Barrymore.

Back in Los Angeles, Bette rushed through the shooting of her best picture to date: *Cabin in the Cotton.* At last, though she didn't like him, she had a real director: the brilliantly talented Michael Curtiz, a savage Hungarian who addressed everybody, including Bette, as "you bum." He screamed his instructions on the set, was disgusted by any player who chose to take lunch, liked to work well into the night, and several times got into fistfights with his crew. He strode around in riding breeches, cracking a whip and pouring out a stream of foul language. He mangled his adopted tongue and peppered his phrases with a bizarre collection of malapropisms. Skeet-shooting, polo, and pictures were his passions.

Bette has never stopped repeating the well-worn story that Curtiz called her a "no good, sexless son of a bitch," and made her play a love scene "to" the lens of a camera, almost impossible to do with any degree of conviction. What she does not acknowledge is that he forced her into her best performance of the early 1930s. As Madge, the dizzy, selfish, peroxided southern belle, she created a fully rounded character, at once ruthless, bold, and pathetic. She had little to work with in the script: a story of the conflict between labor and management on a plantation, symbolized by the internal struggles of emotion and conscience of a glum youth (Richard Barthelmess). Barthelmess, his face as fixed and expressionless as a Japanese mask, plays with morbid passivity while Bette acts up a storm as his seducer.

There is one marvelous scene, daring for its time, that succeeds in conveying a surprising degree of eroticism. Madge finally decides to corrupt her high-minded lover. Aware that he is repressed, that he has sublimated his sexuality in his devotion to the workers, she lures him into a bedroom after giving a sleepy black maid the afternoon off. Though played entirely at shoulder level, the scene conveys great power: Bette undressing in a closet, undoing the bow of her dress, and emerging, it is clearly implied, brazenly naked, as her helpless admirer slowly and frightenedly whispers her name.

It is all the more extraordinary that Bette played this scene while she was still a virgin. But Ruthie had already decided that that condition could no longer be tolerated, and Bette enthusiastically concurred. They discussed the matter as though they were talking about a business merger. It was typical of mother and daughter that every step in Bette's professional and emotional career was planned on the same level of mathematical determination. Ham was a New Englander, so the Davises and the Favors would welcome him into the family. What was more, he had managed to sign a contract with the fashionable Colony Club in Hollywood to play trumpet in its jazz band. His salary had gone up a hundred dollars a week. He could now be a husband.

Such were the narrow bourgeois considerations that Ruthie brought to bear on what should have been a spontaneous and warm coming together of a young man and a young woman. The decision for Bette and Ham to marry was based on a shaky foundation of similar tastes and backgrounds, fondness, some physical attraction, comparable earnings and prospects. Above all, it was based on a need for Bette to get rid of her troublesome virginity. It sounds, at least on paper, rather like Ruthie's acquisition of a dentist.

Ham proposed to Bette and she surprised him by accepting instantly. Ruthie probably wrote his speech. Bette said in her memoirs:

> I suppose I couldn't have expected Mother to suggest that we have an affair. Would that she had been that wise. Would that Ham and I had been. I was hopelessly puritan, helplessly passionate. . . .

The inevitable happened in August 1932, a stiflingly hot month in Los Angeles. Perhaps because she feared she might change her mind, Bette opted for an Arizona wed-

83

ding, since the California marriage laws called for a six-week waiting period. Ruthie, Bette, and Ham set off together by car to Yuma, since Bette was terrified of flying. The journey was a dusty, miserable ordeal in those days before freeways. The Auburn choked and spluttered through 115 degrees of desert heat across the California–Arizona border. Bette drove, covered in sweat; Ham wilted in the front passenger seat; and Ruthie was in a rotten state in the back. All three were soaked to the skin when they finally reached their destination. They moved into rooms in a seedy hotel and soaked in baths of cold water. Then they met in Bette's room, draped in bedspreads, while their sweat-soaked clothes dried. Finally, in late afternoon, Ham struggled into his soiled clothes and went out to buy a shirt and suit and wedding ring.

The wedding took place the next morning, conducted by the minister of an Indian mission, Rev. Mark Schalbaugh. There were no reporters, Ham temporarily lost the ring, two poodles raced around the room licking themselves vigorously, the trains tooted and shunted nearby. Bette, in her own description to the reporter Gladys Hall, said, "I wore a limp beige dress, brown gloves and shoes, and carried two limp gardenias."

That night, Bette moved into Ham's room. She described in her memoirs the joy of her wedding night, of passion excused for the Puritan by the institution of marriage. Next morning, she felt fulfilled and more madly in love with Ham than ever. Now, she felt, nothing could ever separate them.

FOUR

On the face of it, Bette and Ham seemed to have a good enough recipe for a successful marriage relationship. Bette's earnings were not all that higher than Ham's; they enjoyed the same things—music, movies, and taking weekend trips down to San Diego where Bette could relax by taking the magical ferryboat ride across the bay to the grand old Hotel Coronado. Sometimes at night Bette would watch Ham leading the Colony Club band when the regular conductor fell ill; in the tradition of the time, a voice would announce her and a thin pencil of spotlight would swing around through the darkness and settle on the table where she sat with Ruthie and Bobby, enjoying the hot jazz under the light-studded ceiling.

These happy moments were extensively described in studio handouts and fan-magazine articles. Yet often, Bette would return home at night irritable and worn-out from hours of difficult shooting under hot lights. Her dream was of a husband who could simply put his feet up and read or doze by the fire while she relaxed completely. But, in fact, Ham was off to the Colony Club every night and would not return home until the early morning hours, while she had to rise at 6:30 A.M. to drive over to Burbank from their West Hollywood house off Sunset Boulevard to go into makeup and costume fittings.

It was only on Sundays, and in the rare periods between pictures, that Bette and Ham had a chance to get to know each other. She longed for him to boss her, dominate her, take charge. She hated the fact that he complained because he had no say in family decisions. And yet at the same time she regretted in many ways the fact that he had a career of his own which made it impossible for him to share much time with her.

When she suggested that Ham should attend to tidying the house, he obeyed and she wished that he had not. It was as though she were constantly challenging both herself and Ham in order to achieve the kind of relationship which only a romantic could imagine would ever exist. She had already, unhappily, and for all her down-to-earth New England horse sense, begun to want the perfection promised by the fictitious scripts she played out in motion pictures.

Her attitude toward life was extremely cut-and-dried, far too hard and precise: She wanted life to be ordered, but it was impossible to achieve that kind of order. She gave interviewers exactly the same story over and over again; it never varied because she wanted to act out a personality that was totally organized, cool, direct, and eminently sane. She was still an easterner, and always would be. Her best friend, though she saw her seldom, was Robin Brown, a charming woman she had known from her days at Cushing Academy. New Englanders (especially her family) gave her a sense of security and firmness she never found in Hollywood people; she always tried to import into her life in Hollywood their stricter and more austere and sober virtues. The fact that Ham was New England made her forgive many of his faults, but she only wished he had a New England bedrock of firmness in his character. She, in the very bones of her being, had to win. Ham lacked her burning ambition; he could be happy just playing his trumpet in a sash and turban for the Olympic Games. Bette, on the other hand, wouldn't stop until she was Sarah Bernhardt. Ham's softness and comfortable mediocrity irritated her in spite of herself.

While Bette's name became known, Ham's, sadly, did

not. He wasn't even a radio personality; he was fixed in the dreary existence of club or hotel performances. She wanted him to be a hit in radio, and on Sundays worked with him on writing songs, hoping one would eventually be a hit. One song they composed together, "Riding on a Bus-top," was actually published, but it was a feeble effort and made no impression.

Ham's personality underwent a gradual but unnerving change. Deprived of a wife who could give him her days after his hard night's work, he had instead a wife who was constantly invited to parties to which he couldn't accompany her, and whose name was being mentioned frequently in the press as an up-and-coming star. He became bitter and jealous. He started to whine, and sometimes even cried. His gangling charm disappeared and he lashed out at Bette, even weakly hitting her when her contempt for him became too obvious. Within months, the marriage was in trouble.

Bette slowly but fatally lost her respect for Ham. As her income increased and his did not, she knew the score—she would have to foot the bills. She didn't mind that, but she very much minded that Ham complained about it. In an effort to appease him, she agreed that they would live on his salary and she would save hers, with the aid of her business managers. Instead of moving into a house justified by her rising fame, they would live on the wrong side of the tracks in a modest house, with a proper porch and clapboard front, set back from the road off Franklin Avenue: a cottage rented from Cecil B. De. Mille, who lived in splashy splendor up the road in Laughlin Park. Bette's only luxury was a maid, a black lady named Dell Pfeiffer. Bette's joy came from being able to give Ruthie and Bobby pleasant houses of their own and a succession of automobiles.

The pressures on her were constant. She was making five to six pictures a year; Ruthie's bills kept pouring in; Ham wanted new clothes; she herself had to dress well; her manager was after her constantly to try to invest more; she was forcing herself to improve daily as an actress. It is scarcely surprising that she became more fragile than ever and began to suffer from sudden and terrifying setbacks in health. She was starting to develop sinus trouble, sore throats that caused her to lose her voice, headaches, fits of weeping. The extreme severity and neuroses of her Favor strain worked against her volatile and passionate nature and made her sick with exhaustion. She flung herself into her work with a kind of desperation that gave a special edge of anxiety to her acting. Often there was a nervous, even a pathological, flavor in her performances when it wasn't called for by the script. Or, paradoxically, she would play an emotional scene in a clipped, precise, businesslike voice that destroyed the necessary feeling.

Her technique was refined, her sensitivity to the demands of a part fascinating and remarkable, but there was a certain unevenness, a lack of composure in her performances that suggested the tensions and struggles of her personal life. Her acting was affected both favorably and unfavorably by her private torment.

There were escapes from that torment in her social life. Since another man could not accompany her to premiers or parties because that would cause excessive gossip, Ruthie went with her everywhere, often walking grandiosely ahead of her (in a far more expensive costume) into lobbies crowded with photographers and fans on movie first nights. Bette made a friend of actress Marion Davies, the adorable mistress of newspaper mogul William Randolph Hearst, who invited her to a beach house at Santa Monica, where Bette mingled with the famous. She discovered the arid delights of Palm Springs and La Quinta in the California desert, where there were palm-fringed swimming pools and weekend gatherings of directors and stars.

As for work, which in the last analysis meant more to Bette Davis than anything else, it was something of an ordeal relieved only by the occasional good script. In whatever little time they had together, Bette would ask Ham to read the screenplays and give his opinion; Ham, easily pleased, would be delighted with lines that Bette would savagely denounce as stupid and banal. When he became exasperated by her wandering around the house in a trancelike condition "becoming" her character, she would suggest that he read the male lead's lines to her while she responded with the memorized lines to be spoken by the heroine. Unfortunately, Ham was a poor reader, either stumbling over the words or trying to speak them with the florid emphases of a John Barrymore. When she criticized him, Ham's voice would sink into a monotone. As a result, Bette would give up in despair and ask Ruthie or Bobby to work with her instead.

And then another problem arose: Bobby also wanted to be an actress, to be a match for her sister. Consumed with sibling rivalry, she tried again and again, but she had no talent and the industry rejected her. Always unstable and subject to severe nervous attacks bordering on schizophrenia, she had a complete collapse sometime late in 1932. Ruthie took her East for treatments. She was in isolation for periods, screaming that Bette had taken away her chances for a career. The truth was just the opposite: Bette, who put her family before everything except work, would have given anything if Bobby could have been a success in pictures.

Life in the Davis household was scarcely eased by the fact that Bette found little or no pleasure in being rushed from one trashy picture to another. Warner Brothers, in common with other studios, had its own theater chains, and pictures had to be made at express speed, even back-to-back, to satisfy the demands of the theater managers for a ceaseless flow of product. Of the pictures Bette made in 1933, during the second year of her marriage to Ham, only one, *20,000 Years in Sing Sing*, was worth seeing. In this grim story of prison life, Bette appeared with Spencer Tracy, for whom she felt a profound attraction and admiration that she still retains. Tracy had asked for her; he had seen her in *Hell's House* and had been fascinated by her odd unpredictable gaiety. Bette, Tracy later told his friends, was nervous and restless during the shooting. At one point he said to her, "You know, you could be the best actress in pictures today—I'll correct that. You *are* the most talented."

"Damn right," she snapped back characteristically. "But who are we against so many?"

Tracy's biographer, Larry Swindell, wrote:

They joked about their similarities—neither was handsome, and both had fierce tempers, and both missed the stage. They felt such rapport—it might have been that they were both Aries, and, in fact, had the same birthdate. Someday when they were rich, they planned to make more and better pictures together, but for one reason or another, they never did.

Once more, Bette found herself being directed by Michael Curtiz, who made her life miserable, but who succeeded in wringing from her a performance comparable to the one she had given in *Cabin in the Cotton*. As the convict's girl friend, at once tough and vulnerable, she created an alive, completely convincing, and rounded character, with warm touches of detail.

A sadness of those months was that Bette's terrier Boogum died. The only cure for her sorrow was to obtain another pet immediately, so she acquired an adorable Scottie; later a Sealyham, two poodles, and a large Doberman pinscher were added to the canine collection. Bette adored dogs and had great fun with her family of quadrupeds. She found an escape from the problems of her life in taking care of them.

But there were always headaches. One of them was a ridiculous journey across the country, in February 1933, aboard the *Forty-second Street Special,* a train painted gold and made of fourteen cars that traveled from Los Angeles to New York and other cities on a sixteen-day junket to promote Warner Brothers' current movie, *Forty-second Street*. Movie star Laura LaPlante, the famous swimmer Eleanor Holm, twelve singing and dancing beauties, and Tom Mix and his wonder horse set off on this grueling expedition. Frequently, the train was snowbound, and the heating and water system broke down. If anyone unwisely opened a window, a mixture of snow and soot flew in. Bette, who has always been susceptible to colds, suffered from a series of miserable ones. She often had to address crowds from the observation platform at impossible hours of the day and night. It was a thrill for Depression Era

90

crowds to see the stars; but for Bette, the only pleasure in the trip was discovering how famous she had become.

The separation scarcely helped the marriage to Ham. Yet they clung together, still romantically in love with each other in spite of everything. There was something touching and pathetic about this hanging on to the fragile raft of their relationship. Ham left the Colony Club and began to conduct dance bands in both Los Angeles and San Francisco; when he traveled north, Bette went there and holed up gallantly in a depressing motel over weekends just to be with him—but the divisions between them continued.

Much of her life was spent in longing for better scripts. Very gradually, her character was changing. Instead of the serious, subdued, but intense creature she had been, she began to become more edgy, dramatic, prone to exaggerations and to chain-smoking without inhaling: closer, in fact, to the Bette Davis we know from her screen performances. She was very different from the phony, artificial women who ruled Hollywood. She was abrasively honest and outspoken; she appreciated talent, but was quick to detect or denounce stupidity and mediocrity. If a young supporting actress was struggling, she would help her with her lines. But if she discovered incompetence in a fellow player, she would scream blue murder at everybody.

She was a great fan of her friend Jean Harlow and saw all of her pictures, calling afterward to tell her how fascinated she was by her performances. It intrigued her that Harlow could subdue a pleasant, modest nature to appear as the harsh, slangy, golddigger-type Harlow made famous. She admired Gable, and continued to worship Garbo, though she did not meet her. She was a movie buff and regretted she did not have the luxury of the MGM stars, for whom film vehicles were constructed with fanatical care.

She saw all of Katharine Hepburn's pictures and again felt acute envy from afar; Hepburn seemed to treat RKO like a country club, serving picnic lunches on the set and airily selecting all of her own scripts. Bette loved and envied Hepburn's face. She read constantly, consuming book after book and expressing extravagant enthusiasm for writers she admired. She enjoyed the works of Somerset Maugham and doted on the poems of Carl Sandburg.

She became obsessed—her life was now a series of obsessions—with the thought that she must go to RKO, Hepburn's studio, to star in the role of Mildred, the bitter, cruel waitress who mocks the crippled London intellectual in Somerset Maugham's *Of Human Bondage*. She pestered Pandro S. Berman, genial head of RKO, to take her on for the picture version; most other actresses were terrified of the part, convinced that playing a bitch would ruin their careers. She felt she had nothing to lose and, given her current misery and frustration, she was in the correct mood to act the part. She has admitted that she often taunted poor, weak Ham Nelson the way Mildred taunted Philip Carey.

Somerset Maugham knew her work and was supportive of her ambition to play Mildred. But Jack Warner, a cold and ruthless man behind his genial front, at first refused to let her go. But finally, he became so irritated by her constant phone calls that he gave in with a groan.

In the weeks it took Bette to induce everyone to let her play Mildred, she discovered she was pregnant. She would willingly have given up the supreme opportunity to make *Of Human Bondage* if she could have been the mother of a child. But to her horror, Ham, who at that moment destroyed much of her feeling for him, told her she must get rid of the child. She suddenly realized he was terrified at the thought of the expense a child would entail and ashamed to think that she might have to pay the costs. Also, she feared, he was worried that his meal ticket would be lost. A further shock came when Ruthie also opposed the idea of a baby. In a bitter passage in her memoirs, *The Lonely Life*, Bette wrote, "I saw Ruthie's point . . . I saw everyone's point . . . I understood everything intellectually. I was wretched emotionally. I did as I was told." Clearly, Ruthie was worried about her meal ticket, too.

Doing as Bette was told involved, obviously, an abortion. There is no question that this operation, followed by others in future years, affected her health and upset the emotional basis of her marriage. She struggled through a laughable example of trash called *Fashions of 1934*, through *The*

Big Shakedown, Jimmy the Gent, and the slightly superior *Fog Over Frisco* before she was able to escape at last to RKO for *Of Human Bondage* in the spring of 1934.

The director of the picture, John Cromwell, told me: "The first day I met Bette Davis I knew she *had to be Mildred.* What struck me most about her? Her courage. No other actress in Hollywood would have dared face a camera with her hair untidy and badly rinsed, her clothes cheap and tawdry, her manner vicious and ugly. She worked like a dog on her Cockney accent; she made you feel she had been on her feet all day and much of the night as well, serving food: the most exhausting of jobs for a woman, and the most humiliating. She said to me, 'A girl like Mildred must look ill: she has tuberculosis and she's poor.' I told her to do her own makeup any way she wanted, so long as she didn't overdo it. After all, Mildred couldn't seem to be literally dying; she had to have the energy of pure evil.

"I sensed a desperation in Davis. It wasn't just the desperation of an unhappy woman whose marriage was going wrong. She was frightened, really frightened that the worst thing of all would happen to her an an actress: that she would become bored with her work, that she would develop a block and would lose her career. Mildred was her chance, once and for all, to make the big time. And yet I never felt she was overdoing it. My faith in her was supported by the knowledge that her greatness would be tempered by discipline."

It is hard to believe that when she played Mildred, Bette was still, at the age of twenty-six, in many ways a sheltered and unworldly girl, whose mother's love and whose constant employment at a major studio had cut her off from the realities of the Depression. In portraying Mildred, she clearly drew from her memories of being a waitress at college, so that when she came home after working in a waitress scene, one could feel the ache in her feet, in every bone of her body. She drew on her own streak of shrewishness to show Mildred's vicious anger. Although Leslie Howard's impossibly defeated, passive Philip was hard to believe, he wasn't far removed from Ham in his character.

93

All of Bette's buried frustrations emerged in her acting. The result was a performance without compromise. And there was a problem in this. Leslie Howard, who was critical of Bette's Cockney accent, was also jealous of her, and treated her with maddening indifference. That indifference, along with the determination to convince him she was his equal, gave an almost manic edge to the hatred she conveyed in acting with him.

Somerset Maugham was the first to praise her performance. But despite good reviews from the press, audiences were disconcerted by it. The preview was a disaster; people filed out angrily, muttering that it was a dirty picture. They couldn't believe any man would accept such verbal lashings; it was perverse, ugly, against nature. The producer Pan Berman made radical cuts and changes, but *Of Human Bondage* nevertheless failed at the box office.

Back at Warners, pleased by the press reviews of *Of Human Bondage,* Bette plunged into a new series of movies of which only two, *Bordertown* and *Dangerous,* made a real impression.

In essence, *Bordertown* was just another heavy, dark melodrama of the kind in which Warners specialized. Later remade as *They Drive by Night, Bordertown* was the story of an unhappy, small-town, sex-mad girl who helps to murder her husband. It was a good part, and Bette gave it all she had, flirting with and seducing Paul Muni. And in the courtroom sequence, when she goes insane, Bette Davis ranked with the greatest stars. She could have acted the scene with hysterics, but instead she more frighteningly conveyed psychological breakdown through subtle gestures and intonations. Perhaps because her own nature was so hypersensitive, so delicately balanced, and because she knew Bobby's torment, she could provide a convincing glimpse of a psyche that had gone over the edge. Her definitive playing of the scene proved that she was not merely a broad player of melodrama. She grew in stature through this part. In doing so, she defied the director, Archie Mayo, who had a weakness for purple passages. It was a distinct case of an actress triumphing over a director and a script.

Dangerous, made several months later, was a sentimental fantasy about an actress in the Jeanne Eagels mold who feels haunted by a "jinx"—some mysterious force which drives her to destroy others and herself, and over which she has no control. She is first seen hovering on a street corner in the darkness near a theater, where she is spotted by a handsome architect (Franchot Tone). The architect picks her up, rehabilitates her, and gives her a break by financing a play for her himself. But, helpless because of her self-destructive streak, she smashes her car into a tree on opening night. It emerges that her fellow victim in the crash is her discarded husband, who remains in love with her despite her total lack of interest in him. A laughable ending has her returning to her injured husband, who smiles at her wanly through a hospital window.

This tissue of nonsense would have sunk most actresses at the start, but Bette gave the role of the actress an extraordinary realism. In scenes that were flat and mechanical, she conveyed a range of naked feeling, sometimes daringly mixing emotions, from cynical humor to despair, in the course of a single dramatic moment. For all his professional skill, and it was considerable, Franchot Tone was static and waxen alongside her amazing virtuosity. In *Dangerous*, more than in any other picture up to that time, including *Of Human Bondage*, the special quality that Bette offered could be seen most clearly. It was a courageous disclosure of feeling, a truthfulness of word and gesture, a nakedness in which the audience seemed to be seeing her thoughts without any intervention of technique. The technique fell away and exposed the nerve of suffering. It wasn't a calculated method. It was acting achieved through empathy with character and audience. Only a person with her degree of nervousness and hypersensitivity, risking her own well-being in the commitment of her playing, could have achieved this level. And always the emotion was tempered with intelligence, giving the more critical members of the audience the feeling that they were encountering somebody they would enjoy meeting. Other actresses had an equal appeal to the masses; few had an equally strong appeal to the critics.

For all its faults, *Dangerous* brought Bette great satisfaction. And the picture earned her extraordinary reviews. Although critics were severe about the manufactured nature of the production and its soap-opera lines and situations, they justly praised the firmness and honesty, the emotional depth and range, of the central performance. It was manifestly clear that Bette would be in the front running for an Academy Award when the awards were given out in February 1936.

By the late summer of 1935, Bette Davis was established as one of the big international stars. And this status resulted in countless fan-magazine articles; photographs of her posing with her Scottie, Tippy; swimming in somebody's pool (which the studio pretended was her own); being seen at "nightclubs," which in fact were corners of old nightclub sets; living the kind of life a star was supposed to live in the Depression—a life of pure fantasy spun out of celluloid. Her acting offscreen had to be as effective as her acting on.

Gradually, she learned the secret of giving press interviewers the image which she and Warner Brothers needed to sell to the public: an outgoing, cheerful, witty, nononsense kind of woman, with an answer for everything. No indication here of the pain, the nerve-wracking strain of her life with Ham, her mother, and sister; no hint of dire quarreling, of sudden threats of departure, of makings-up under stress. Nor was there an inkling of the humiliation Ham felt at being ignored at premieres or parties by people who treated him like some manager, agent, or obscure hanger-on, who shook Bette's hand or embraced her while almost literally pushing him into the background. Nor could anyone discover in these glowing, absurd articles a hint of Bette's shame at the treatment of her husband and her longing for him to be as successful as she. Even though she tried to ignore the fact, it was painful to have a husband earning a hundred dollars a week when she was earning a thousand.

Nobody seeing her smiling in photographs and at social functions would have suspected her dislike of most Hollywood people and of Hollywood talk, with its emphasis on fashion, makeup, scandal, and intrigue. It wasn't often dis-

closed that she much preferred staying at home listening to
Bing Crosby records, reading Somerset Maugham's short
stories, poring over her latest ill-written script, or adding
touches of New England to her living room in the form of
brassware, Toby mugs, and painted plates. She liked to
argue, wrangle, ride horseback, and help train guide dogs
for the blind. None of this particularly interested the magazines. There wasn't much you could make of her loving
fog, rain, arguments, and onions.

She had reached that minimal point of power at which
she could actually ask for certain parts. Whether she was
given them after *Bondage* was another matter. She had
wanted to be loaned to RKO, where Pan Berman would
have had her play Elizabeth I to Katharine Hepburn's
Mary Stuart in *Mary of Scotland*, a chance to beat her
envied rival hollow in the championship stakes. She had
wanted to play Alice in Paramount's crazy-house version of
Alice in Wonderland, with Gary Cooper as the White
Knight; but Warners had refused to let her go. Now she
became fascinated by the part of Gaby Maple in *The Petrified Forest*, which had become a big Broadway hit that
summer, with Leslie Howard in the role of a highbrow
Englishman, Alan Squier. On this occasion, she got her
wish.

The Petrified Forest was based on a typical mid-thirties
melodramatic formula about a cross section of society
trapped in an isolated milieu: in this case, a gas station in
the Arizona desert. Robert Sherwood, the author, brought
together a frail intellectual Englishman, a waitress who
dreamed of becoming a poetess, a bored society woman
whose lifelong hunger had been to play the nun in *The
Miracle*, her business-chief husband, a snarling gangster
and his henchmen, and an ancient, wiseacre grandpappy.
The plot was pure corn, the writing heavy and pretentious. Nevertheless, the play offered a basis for a good,
high-powered movie.

Bette was the perfect choice for the fragile waitress
whose yearnings for a literary career and a trip to Paris
had a touching quality of hopelessness. Again, because of

her experiences at Cushing, she knew what it was to be a waitress; her love of poetry also needed no stimulation.

She had acquired a forceful new agent, Mike Levee, along with her improved status. Levee called her one Sunday and told her, "Hal Wallis wants you for Gaby!" Memos in the studio files show she was thrilled and called Jack Warner at home in an excited state: "This is wonderful! How can I thank you enough?" Impulsive as ever, she rushed on: "It's a great honor. The finest honor I've received. My only concern is Leslie [Howard]. Will he work with me again? He hated me in *Bondage!*"

Warner assured her that Howard, who would be re-creating his stage role in the film, would give no trouble; her career had advanced tremendously and Howard would be forced to respect her. Further, while still appearing in the play, Howard had told Warner that Bette would be "quite acceptable" to him.

A problem was that Howard could spare only a few weeks to make the picture in Hollywood before having to return to New York to appear in a new play. When Bette met him on the first day of work in October 1935, she found him as cold and aloof as ever. She lied to the columnists that she "adored" him; but they seldom talked during the length of shooting. And she disliked Humphrey Bogart, who was cast as the gangster Duke Mantee, as intensely as she had when they had worked together before. He drank, was unruly and rude. He was gruff and impatient with Bette, and talked only of making enough money in Hollywood to buy a yacht and sail off into the blue for good. With her dedication to work, she was shocked by his lack of interest in picture-making and his cynical attitude toward the studio.

The unit was transferred by train in fall heat to Red Rock Canyon, a harsh location that had to double for Arizona. The white sun, the wind-blown sand, the swarms of flies that burst from the earth and the trees in small black clouds, drove the cast almost to frenzy. Bette, with her sensitive eyes and skin, suffered from severe eyestrain and freckling and burning. When she inhaled the fine gritty dust, her sinuses acted up badly.

Leslie Howard, very British, refused to work on Sundays, which incensed the director—the fat, edgy, manic Archie Mayo. Bette herself went on strike. Her throat and sinuses were so badly inflamed that she could not perform at all. When the production manager screamed at her to go to work, the other cast members rebelled along with her, and Genevieve Tobin, Leslie Howard, and Bogie all retired to the local hotel for the day.

Another problem of the shooting was that Leslie Howard disliked the director so much he would not appear on the set at the time called for each morning. He was an hour or two late on several occasions, just to annoy Mayo. This childish behavior nettled Bette. Moreover, she became increasingly sick. Back in Hollywood, she had developed a cold when the fall season suddenly changed into a chilly damp winter. Her cold now worsened, so that she had to be shifted around in the shooting schedule and some of her scenes were shot using a double.

As if this were not enough, she slipped and sprained her ankle when entering the gas-station set one morning. She limped badly and had to drop out of more scenes. She clashed with Mayo over the interpretation of her lines and in particular over the use of her voice. She pitched her voice very high; he objected to what he called its "Mickey Mouse squeakiness."

There was worse to come. To match the dust of Arizona, Mayo had a wind machine blow a poisonous substance called fuller's earth all over the set of the gas-station exterior. Bette protested that in her condition she couldn't endure this. Mayo insisted on proceeding; as a result, she often suffered from headaches and nerve rashes and became so ill she was afraid she wouldn't be able to finish the picture.

In the midst of her increasing illness, the studio offered her a new script, which the production manager, Tenny Wright, sent to the set during a break between scenes. It was a version of Dashiell Hammett's *The Maltese Falcon*, entitled *The Man with the Black Hat*. When Frank Shaw, unit manager on *The Petrified Forest*, handed it to her, she glanced through it, saw it was awful, and impatiently tossed it into her dressing room.

When Jack Warner's secretary called the next day asking for a quick response on the screenplay, Bette said that her lawyer, Martin Gang, would see Warner to discuss it, as she "most emphatically would not." But Gang failed to turn up at the meeting arranged with Warner, and Bette, who had returned to Los Angeles, cabled Warner from her home on Franklin Avenue that she needed a rest, that all the weeks on *The Petrified Forest* breathing in fuller's earth had thoroughly exhausted her, and she was sure that "anybody else" could play in *The Man with the Black Hat*.

As soon as she was well enough to return to work on *The Petrified Forest*, Roy Obringer, the studio's legal authority, went to see her on set between takes to remind her of her legal obligation to appear in anything the studio cared to send her. She became nervous and fretful, smoking constantly, and said edgily, "Valerie Purvis in *Hat* is wrong for me. There are hundreds of artists you can select for the part. I'm exhausted from this picture—*can't you see I'm exhausted*? I need a rest—my nerves are bad."

Jack Warner refused to accept this excuse and ordered her to report to the producer, Henry Blanke, on December 2 to discuss her wardrobe fittings. She did not report to Blanke, but sent another telegram to Obringer announcing that she was "physically incapable" of doing so. Obringer replied by telegram—all this across a distance of less than ten miles—saying that the studio doctor, Carl Conn, would be coming to examine her that night to see if her "incapability" was genuine. He reminded her that her contract specified that she had to submit to medical examinations at any time the studio chose to send a doctor to see her.

At six o'clock on December 2, Dr. Conn drove over to her house and found no one at home. Obringer protested by telegram. She cabled Obringer from Bobby's house, saying that she had been unable to be home when Conn called; that even if she had been home she would not have allowed him to examine her; that she was not ill and did not claim to be; and that she wanted a rest.

What annoyed her more than anything else was that,

after having just finished making a taxing, challenging, and important picture like *The Petrified Forest*, she was expected, because of the pressure to supply the exhibitors with product, to mug her way through junk like *The Man with the Black Hat*. What was more, she was genuinely exhausted, her nervous irritability more extreme than ever. Bobby was still mentally disturbed and in and out of the sanitariums. Her mother was equally upset that this kind of pressure should be applied by Warners. Ham Nelson, conducting his band every night in Hollywood, tried his best, after rising late in the morning, to calm Bette down in his ineffectual way. It was not a very happy home, that modest Cape Cod cottage, called by Bette on her stationery "The Nelson House" on Franklin Avenue. A husband who came home dead tired at all hours of the morning was not the ideal companion for an actress whose nerves were frayed.

Her temper can only be imagined when she learned that the studio had suspended her on December 3 for failing to report to wardrobe. She couldn't afford to be suspended—Mother's bills and Bobby's expenses were heavy and she had to make sure they had everything they needed in their separate homes. Moreover, so heavy had her burden of debt become, that she had already borrowed against her earnings.

On December 6, resentful, and furious with Warner, she reluctantly began work on *The Man with the Black Hat*. Wearily, she played the ludicrous scenes as best she could. And Jack Warner tossed her a bone: He yielded to her six desperately written requests to let her appear on Al Jolson's "Shell Chateau" radio program, acting out a high-powered scene from *Dangerous*. "But she mustn't," he coldly told Roy Obringer, "do anything from any material other than that film."

Bette had hoped for some rest after babbling her way through the imbecilities of *The Man with the Black Hat* (later retitled *Hard Luck Dame* and then *Satan Met a Lady*) and coping with the macho hauteur of her co-star, Warren William. But no sooner had she retired to Franklin Avenue in a state of near collapse when she was told that a crisis had developed: Kay Francis had refused to appear in

101

a nonsensical farce named *Cream Princess*, which was due to start shooting at any minute. In this emergency situation, Tenny Wright rushed the script to Bette's house, where her maid Dell Pfeiffer received it. When she returned home, Bette had to laugh. The note from Wright read: "Please prepare yourself immediately for *Cream Princess*." She couldn't believe the title, and called her friends to laugh over it some more. She had to play a former cafeteria cashier who pretends to be the madcap heiress to a cosmetic fortune and has an affair with a reporter played by George Brent.

Although she acted it out with her customary style, Bette was even more disgusted by this trash than she had been with *The Man with the Black Hat*. Many scenes were shot at the Toluca Lake Country Club golf course, in harsh sunlight that made her skin peel; she had to shoot several other scenes at Santa Monica Beach, where her sensitive easterner's complexion suffered more, and the hard glittering light beating off the Pacific Ocean gave her such a headache from eyestrain that she could scarcely proceed. On February 7, 1936, she went home early, cabling Tenny Wright from there that she was "dead after five days and nights of work . . . I cannot work tomorrow . . . I cannot do myself justice."

She hated the cameraman, Arthur Edeson, and for years refused to have him on her pictures. His harsh, realistic style of lighting made her look unattractive, always a danger, since she did not have perfectly photogenic features.

She had been in bed for several days in February when she received word to attend the Academy Awards. She struggled out of her sickbed and discovered she hadn't a single dress worthy of the occasion. She and Ruthie selected an informal checked frock for her to wear. Ruthie, of course, dressed magnificently for the event.

Bette said later that she felt completely numb when she heard her name announced as the winner of the "Best Actress" award for her role in *Dangerous*. She made her way awkwardly to the stage. She knew only too well, as she stood alongside the Irish star Victor McLaglen, who had won for *The Informer*, that she had won a sympathy vote because she had not received an award for *Of Human Bondage*. She despised *Dangerous* and wasn't overwhelmed at being awarded for her performance in it; but she also knew she had reached the summit and must now fight desperately hard to retain her position. From that moment on, she would more consciously assert her power; she *dared* not make any inferior pictures in the future.

No sooner had she received the award than Bette took the train to New York to attend the 1936 Spring Democratic Convention at Madison Square Garden. She rushed through the final scenes of *Cream Princess* in order to make the trip. Roosevelt was the idol of her existence and when Big Jim Farley asked her to appear in support of the president, it was much more exciting for her than being given the Academy Award. She arrived at Grand Central in harsh cold, to be greeted by a swarm of reporters. The Warner publicity chief Charles Einfeld was appalled when she launched into a violent attack on the Breen office, which censored motion pictures, and the problems she was having with scripts as ridiculous as that for *Cream Princess*. "*Cream Princess*!" she laughed. "What a title! Surely *that* calls for censorship!"

The press was delighted with her outspoken remarks. Most actors merely rattled off carefully memorized stock answers and gushed about their co-stars and future vehicles. The press had never met anyone quite like her before: She had a mind of her own, she was prepared to attack her bosses, she knew a good script from a bad one. She was even prepared to attack a movie in mid-production and probably imperil its commercial release! The reporters adored her and applauded spontaneously when she was through. Charles Einfeld shriveled with embarrassment.

Typically, Bette had refused the usual suite at the Plaza or the Ritz Towers and preferred the simple, quasi-British Algonquin, with its famous Round Table, its powerful intellectual associations. No other stars stayed there. The suites were cramped and the room service slow. The lobby was small and cluttered and fans could easily gather round. But Bette knew instinctively that the Algonquin crowd would pay her little attention. They were far too sophisticated to be impressed by anything as ridiculous as a Hollywood picture star.

Bette hardly had time to settle in her suite when a telegram was slipped under her door. It contained a message that drove her into rage and laughter. Jack Warner wanted her to return at once on the five-day train journey to shoot a new sequence for *Cream Princess* (retitled *The Golden Arrow*). This would show her, George Brent, and a cabbie sporting outsized shiners on their eyes.

This was the last straw. Bette cabled back that even if this meant the end of her career as an actress, she would not give up her trip to New York and the Democratic Convention to return to Hollywood to shoot this imbecilic scene. Warners could damn well wait until she was good and ready to shoot the sequence when she returned.

This was the first serious indication that Bette had assumed the will and resolution of a star. Winning the Oscar had changed her overnight from a determined church mouse into a lioness. She knew that if Warners dropped her, she could sign with any other studio in town.

She called her attorney, Martin Gang, in Hollywood and gave him lengthy instructions about what he was to convey to Jack Warner immediately. Now that she had an Oscar, she expected to be given an income and working arrangement commensurate with her importance as a star. She must have three months' vacation a year, a considerable salary increase (health and money had become obsessive concerns by 1936), the right to do an outside picture once a year (she was still fretting over being refused the chance of playing Queen Elizabeth to Hepburn's Mary Stuart), the right to do four broadcasts a year (like most stars, she loved the prestige and excitement of radio), and more consideration over scripts the studio would offer her.

Martin Gang outlined all of these requests in a letter to Jack Warner, who promptly told Ralph Lewis, the studio lawyer at the Warners attorneys, Preston and Files, that he would tolerate no further nonsense from Miss Davis. He would not agree to a new contract, since the old one was perfectly valid; and Miss Davis would come back for retakes on April 18 or she would be suspended indefinitely.

Lewis felt the letter Warner drafted was too brusque and that it should be sent only if Bette continued to refuse to do the retakes.

Receiving no reply to his letter, Gang called Lewis and was told, subtly, that little response was to be expected from Jack Warner. Fearful of his relationship with the studio being affected, Mike Levee prevailed upon Bette to return to work on the date appointed. She fumed at having her vacation cut short, but agreed when Levee pointed out she might have more chance to negotiate if she did the "black-eye scene" obediently.

Meanwhile, Hal Wallis was preparing a picture for her called *Mountain Justice*, based on the story of a girl in the backwoods who killed her parents. He rushed forty pages of script to her at Franklin Avenue and called her for wardrobe. A. A. Chang of Preston and Files, acting on behalf of Ralph Lewis, broke the news to Martin Gang that Bette's requests were rejected outright.

When she discovered she had returned to Hollywood for nothing, that she could gain nothing from her futile cutting short of a vacation she so direly needed, Bette's fury had no bounds. Here she was, an Oscar-winning, world-famous star, and the studio would do nothing to reward her at all! And she raged at Levee for having deceived her into thinking that if she came back she would be given more reasonable terms of work. She accused him of kowtowing to the studio because he was afraid of antagonizing its executives.

No sooner had Bette settled down to reading *Mountain Justice* than the studio decided temporarily to withdraw the script because of legal problems and replace it with *God's Country and the Woman*, another rural subject, about a tough girl running a lumber kingdom in the northwestern states. Bette wasn't very interested in the property; in fact, all she wanted to do was join Ruthie in Hawaii, where Ruthie was expensively vacationing on Bette's money.

Mike Levee constantly pressed her to make *God's Country and the Woman* and she gave a radio interview on KHJ on May 24 to the critic Edwin Schallert, lying that she was "looking forward" to doing it. At a meeting in Levee's office on the night of May 2, he told her that he was sure if she met Warners in an amicable frame of mind and did what they wanted, she would get a new contract. Martin Gang, however, told her to fight the studio. On May 21, Levee prevailed in a quarrel against Gang and wrote him a letter, dismissing him from any and every service on Bette's behalf. That same day Bette cabled Levee to "have nothing further to do with the negotiations; she would attend to them herself." Levee resigned, saying, "She's more grief than the commission's worth."

On June 18, A. A. Chang of Preston and Files sent Bette a continuity of *God's Country and the Woman* with a reminder that her present contract made it essential for her to do it. She was told to report for wardrobe at 10:00 A.M. on June 19. She dismissed Martin Gang, hired a new lawyer, Dudley Furse, to replace him, and summoned her business manager, Vernon Wood, to accompany her to a meeting at the studio on June 20 with Jack Warner, Hal Wallis, Roy Obringer, and Ralph Lewis. Warner had called the meeting in a last-ditch effort to persuade her to undertake the picture.

Everyone was seated when Warner said sharply to Bette: "Why will you not work in *God's Country and the Woman*? I'll make you a reasonable offer. I'll give you your favorite, Sol Polito, as cameraman. I'll increase you from sixteen hundred to two thousand dollars a week. I'll try to find better stories for you and I'll add Sally Sage* to the stock company. What more do you want? Be a trouper, Bette. Agree to do this picture!"

Bette rose and paced about the room, puffing characteristically at a cigarette. "My attitude," she said, "may be *right* or it may be *wrong*! But I'm willing to take my chances on the public rejecting me, on my *losing face* with the public, by not being in pictures in the event I don't get the terms I want! I don't want to hold up production of *God's Country and the Woman*! I am *willing*—yes, *willing*, to return and start the picture provided I am *assured* that on completion I will be given a new contract along the lines *previously requested*!"

* Her favorite double.

106

Warm and conciliatory, Vernon Wood said he hoped there would be an early settlement. "Mr. Warner," he added, "won't you consider Miss Davis's value to the company? Considering Miss Davis's potential, are we asking too much in seeking three thousand dollars a week?"

Warner snapped, "I don't want to get into money matters! I've made a fair and reasonable offer." Bette said to Hal Wallis, "You wouldn't lend me to RKO to do *Mary of Scotland*. Why?"

Wallis replied, "We didn't think the part was important enough for you. It was only one scene. It would have done you more harm than good." Jack Warner added, to no one in particular, "We build stars here. Give them every chance. Then they turn around and demand everything. I repeat my offer—two thousand dollars a week. And I'll do better. Six additional yearly options for another six years going up to four thousand eventually. I can't top that."

Bette wheeled round. "That's *a seven-year contract!*" she shouted at Warner. "*A five-year contract is long enough! And after five years I'll be too damned old to be in pictures!*"

Jack smiled. "How foolish of you, Bette, to believe you'll be too old then. You'll only be thirty-five!"

"*Thirty-three!*" she snarled back, and for a moment they laughed.

"You'll be at your best," Warner said, "with five years added to your career!" He then offered her twelve weeks vacation, without pay, divided into one six-week and two three-week consecutive periods. Up to then, all of her payless vacations had been split up in small segments over twelve months.

Bette wasn't satisfied. Now her strongest motive became clear. "*I'm entitled to more money!*" she snapped. "I don't think I'm asking for too much."

Jack said, "You're being obstinate and arbitrary."

Bette fumed. "I want more money, the chance to do outside pictures, or I'll take my chances and get out of pictures for good."

Wallis wrote on a slip of paper, "Let the first term be

107

two years only: give her $2,000 and then $2,500." Warner shook his head as he read the note.

Davis told Vernon Wood, "We're leaving." As they walked out, Jack Warner told Wood threateningly, "I want you to fix this." Wood assured Warner that Bette would make *God's Country and the Woman.**

But she would not. Denied everything she wanted, especially the money and the chance to do outside pictures, she told Wood on Sunday to call Wallis at home and tell him she was refusing all of Jack Warner's offers. She wrote a lengthy letter to Warner on June 21 saying that she was mainly objecting to the money she was being paid; she had no desire to be off the list of players; she knew he could stop her from working, a great unhappiness to her because she enjoyed working; after her vacation in New York she was so rested it hurt; and "If I'm worth anything to you at all, you can't mind letting me know in writing. If I'm not, this letter is in vain."

She went on to say that she didn't want the loan-out clause in order to be her own boss. She insisted she did not want to be autonomous. She said she'd like to have a boss give her orders, someone she could look up to, whose authority she could respect "as much as I do yours, Jack." But she knew change would do her good, that she could work better with new directors, new casts, and, she added significantly, "I also am ambitious to be known as a great actress. I *might* be one. Who can tell?"

Vacations, she continued, were important to her because they broadened her intellect and she had never been out of the country. What was more, she was essentially a high-strung person who must have rest. In mid-letter, she suddenly changed course on money, saying unpredictably that she would take even less than she was getting if she could have her rights to vacations and loan-outs. She wrote, "You ask me to be levelheaded and I believe I am. I am more than anxious to work for you again, but not as things stand. As a happy person I can work like hell—and as an unhappy one, I make everyone around me unhappy." She

* Conversation drawn from minutes in the studio files.

recognized, she continued, that in a business with a fickle public to depend on, the money should be made when it was possible, since later the public may "tell you to go to hell."

Jack Warner had heard it all before. He didn't bother to reply by either telephone or letter. Instead, Roy Obringer wrote to her: "Unless you report for *God's Country and the Woman*, you will be suspended and damages charged against you."

She left Obringer's letter unanswered. Days went by. Jack Warner ordered another rude note from Obringer, then suddenly relented and called Bette to give her one last chance. He said, "Once more, please don't break your contract, Bette. Public opinion will react against you! You are being foolish! Change your mind before it's too late!"

She hung up on him quickly and the rift seemed to be final. Jack Warner suspended her immediately. He refused to allow her to appear on any radio shows, knowing how deeply this would wound her. She sent a telegram to Warner, apparently trying to appease him by saying she was "awfully sorry" about all that had happened and "I would have enjoyed very much playing Jo Barton in *God's Country and the Woman*."

Bette was beginning to panic. She was most afraid that her dressing room, that holy of holies for a star, would be taken away from her and given to someone else, thus causing the impression at the studio that she was through as an actress. She called Jack on an impulse and begged him not to let the room go. He at last gave in and told Tenny Wright that on no condition was it to be touched in any way.

In this awkward period, a Polish producer, Ludovic Toeplitz, who operated out of London, offered Bette a chance to make two pictures in England. He had read the headlines and decided to take advantage of her rift with Warner. She accepted at once. But unfortunately no such arrangement with another producer could possibly be regarded as legal. It was a vain gesture of rebellion, and in her heart Bette knew it. She packed her bags at once.

FIVE

Leaving Hollywood was certainly a major problem. Bobby was still suffering from mental disturbances and Bette hated to leave her. She asked Vernon Wood to take care of her mother and sister, and, of course, the rent on 5346 Franklin Avenue would continue to be paid to Cecil B. De Mille. Ham, now between jobs, would go along on the trip. It was the first sustained time they would have together in a long while. It was a last-ditch effort to heal the rifts in their marriage.

Bette had never flown before, and flying in those days was uncomfortable and hazardous. For some reason, perhaps to avoid reporters, or a summons from Warners, she and Ham set out on their journey to England via Canada, instead of by the more comfortable railroad route on the *Santa Fe Chief* and *Twentieth Century Limited* to New York. They got aboard a miserable milk plane that made an all-night trip to Vancouver, touching down at all kinds of improbable places along the way, and was tossed about by the slightest turbulence. The trip was so unpleasant that years later, when Bette made an extraordinary emergency flight to her second husband, she announced she had never been in a plane before. Clearly, she had completely blotted out the earlier experience.

Bette arrived in Vancouver with her nerves in shreds. She was confronted by the very thing she had hoped to evade: a gang of trenchcoated, fedora-hatted reporters demanding to know the details of her clash with Jack Warner. She lost her cool completely, and instead of taking a comfortable middle course, once more denounced the studio and everyone connected with it for forcing her to do trashy pictures. Overlooking her radio interview with Schallert and her cable to Jack Warner, she now turned savagely on *God's Country and the Woman*, dismissing it as "some nonsense about a lady lumberjack." Far gone though she may have been, exhausted, desperate, and strained to the breaking point, she could scarcely have told the reporters her principal battle was strictly for money. But the press headlined that fact anyway.

The Warner representatives in Vancouver were faced with an impossible situation. Warners had cabled them that only one overall interview would be allowed at the airport: a general press conference. But as soon as Bette checked into the hotel with Ham, the prominent local feature writers and radio interviewers besieged the hotel, demanding to be given time with her. A local Warner chief talked to Roy Obringer by long distance and was sternly forbidden to allow anyone near Bette. Told this, she instantly went to the nearest radio station, announced herself, and appeared without warning on a show in which she said she would no longer tolerate the Warner behavior and was going to England at once to start an entirely new career.

Bette and Ham took the Canadian Pacific Railroad to Montreal, a spectacular journey through mountains, across plains, and past lakes that had her excitedly glued to the window of the compartment throughout. Without the strain of work, without the tension of the sound stage and the worry about her future career, Bette was more or less able to relax. Ham was joyful again. Together, the couple became exhilarated at the idea of Bette having a new career in England, where she was so loved. One may guess that the buried romantic side of their relationship was restored on this spectacular transcontinental journey.

They attracted enormous attention in Montreal when

112

they boarded the British ship *Duchess of Bedford* bound for Great Britain. Fellow passengers talked for years about seeing Bette, tense and popeyed in slacks, and Ham, tall and awkward-looking in a cardigan and heavy brown pants, striding the deck in the teeth of high winds. The couple didn't care who stared at them. They arrived in Britain on the fourth anniversary of their wedding—and that was entirely appropriate. They were truly married once more.

Meanwhile, Warners' lawyers in Los Angeles, Preston and Files, hired the distinguished firm of Denton, Hall and Burgin in London to act on their behalf against Bette. Denton, Hall and Burgin sent an emissary to the north of England to serve Bette with an injunction preventing her from making the film for Toeplitz. She ignored it completely. Blissfully disregarding the fact that she had no business to be proceeding with this new venture at all, she embarked on a tour of various parts of England and Wales, where she tried to find some of her distant relatives, the Davises, without success.

In London she had a pleasant meeting with Toeplitz and the former silent comedian and now-director Monty Banks, who was married to Gracie Fields and was to direct *I'll Take the Low Road* with Douglass Montgomery as Bette's co-star. She and Ham then made a lengthier journey that took in Blackpool, the Lake District, and the west of England. People would stare at her as she made her leggy compulsive entrance into various inn dining rooms, hair in a scarf, wearing a sweater and swinging skirts, briskly digging into steak-and-kidney pudding or sausage and mash. Wherever she went, she attracted people, not only because of her fame, but because of her irresistibly natural, down-to-earth talkativeness. Unlike many stars, she did not pretend that fame was a burden to her, nor did she hide ostentatiously in hotel rooms. She went everywhere and saw everything, and appeared indifferent if people were transfixed by her presence.

She loved England, and England loved her. Indeed, it is possible that the warmth of feeling for her was even greater in England than in America. It had partly to do with the fact that she had a very nearly English accent and didn't seem unbearably a Yank. She had perfect manners (rare in visitors from Hollywood), she read books, she was well informed about politics, and if she wasn't exactly an intellectual that was all to the good. She was a tweedy, tough, opinionated, humorous, and vital person with whom countless Englishwomen in the middle class could identify. What was more, at a time when emotions ran closer to the surface than they do today, women who were highly and publicly sensitive, who wrote impassioned letters and made scenes as a matter of course, also felt they were one with her. They could escape their own problems by seeing her luxurious suffering in the huge, shimmering, silver-and-black images of the screen. Their own pain seemed less significant when Bette was fighting feminist battles Up There for all Depression girls.

Bette knew in her heart that her trip to England was not much more than an expensive and controversial furlough. She made the best of it. She and Ham went to Paris, where she reveled in being dressed by well-known couturiers for Toeplitz's first film, *I'll Take the Low Road*.

In September, Warners sued her for breach of contract. She was running out of money. She had had to pay for her and Ham's trip from America, since he had little cash of his own. Because she was a star they had had to travel first class all the way, of course. Normally, during the Depression, anyone earning over a thousand dollars a week, as she was, would have been able to save sufficiently to make the trip possible. But the costs of her mother's extravagance and Bobby's hospitalization had proved to be still more crippling in the past few months. Moreover, Ruthie was talking of coming to England. Though Bette didn't mind, indeed would have loved to have seen her mother, she knew who would be paying for that trip, too.

Meantime, Bette had to find an important barrister to defend her. Unfortunately, she made a poor choice. Sir William Jowitt, later Earl Jowitt, was a distinguished member of the bar. But for reasons that remain mysterious, he did not handle her case with his usual distinction. It can be said in his defense that the case was perhaps indefensible.

114

However, having taken it on, he failed to make anything of it.

Bette was represented by the solicitors Morris, Munton and King. Warners' lawyers, Denton, Hall and Burgin, cleverly engaged Sir Patrick Hastings as their barrister. Hastings was unquestionably one of the most skilled advocates in Great Britain. His specialty was ridiculing the opposition. Judges were fond of him because he combined a remarkable grasp of the letter of the law and a perfect memory with an icy sense of humor that demolished pretense and exposed the tiniest weaknesses in an argument. He had a formidably striking appearance, heavy-browed and saturnine, and a vibrant voice that could strike terror in almost anyone. His weakness, used as a strength, was failing to take seriously anything that suggested the unusual or the foreign. This again appealed to judges, especially when they had a traditional British doubt about the virtues of "Continentals" or Americans.

Bette knew that she faced a formidable enemy in Sir Patrick. Sir William Jowitt, she discovered to her horror, required a retainer of several thousand pounds, which she did not have. In Hollywood, all her savings, and they were meager, were tied up in insurance policies to secure annuities for her in later life. Cashed in, they would have been virtually worthless. The Wood brothers advised her she could not afford to pay her attorney the equivalent of ten thousand dollars.

In this hour of extremity, not knowing how she would defend herself, Bette needed Ham's moral support more than she ever needed it before. Somehow, she felt, she would raise the money to defend herself. But it would be useless fighting the case just for herself. She was buoyed up by the thought that Ham, whose love she had so happily regained, would be at her side every minute during the agonizing experience of a trial.

But Ham was already growing restless. He was still nervous about being dependent solely on Bette for money. His masculine ego was abraded by constantly being referred to as "Mr. Davis." Much as he loved Bette, he hated having to be with her at all times and cast under her shadow. He would have to take a backseat when she was being interviewed. But *he* was an artist too—even if he was only an obscure musician and band leader.

Sadly, this fresh attempt to patch up the marriage cracked apart that September. The worst shock Bette ever received in a shock-filled life came when Ham suddenly announced, on the verge of the trial, that he was going back to America. He wanted to be his own man again, to start earning again, and he had been offered a band-leader job in Hollywood. She begged him to stay. He would not. And then, to add insult to a crushing injury, she had to pay his expensive fare home.

It is probable she reached her lowest ebb when she saw Ham off on the ship to America. She was emotionally drained and in tears when she went down to the pier and saw the vessel draw out into the gray autumn sea. Fortunately, Toeplitz put up a basic amount (refundable) to enable her to proceed with her defense. But she had to pay for a small room at the Park Lane Hotel when he discontinued payments on her suite.

It was a drizzly, bleak October day when Bette, watched with a mingling of envy and fascination by a crowd of housewives, stepped out of a cab and ran with hips characteristically swinging up the depressing stone steps and along the depressing stone halls of the Law Courts in the Strand. She walked quickly to the plain wooden bench where she was to sit for the next two days, dressed very simply in tweeds and a beret. From the moment she took her place, she settled on a theatrical actress's device; all day long she looked directly into the judge's eyes with a challenging willful stare, as though she wanted to force him to do exactly what she wanted. It was a device that backfired.

Neither the prosecution nor the defense acted admirably in the case. Despite the fact that Bette had won an Oscar and was by now famous, she was an American—and Americans were not taken seriously by high-class British legalists in that day and age. Nor indeed were movie stars of any description; pictures were simply empty-headed diversions for the masses, and Hollywood was a synonym for mindless vulgarity. Moreover, Sir William Jowitt and her

116

lawyers had absurdly allowed Bette to use as a point of defense the contention that the studio had forced her to attend a dinner for Roosevelt. This nonsense could be dismissed at once, since attending a dinner for her idol had, in fact, represented the summit of her ambitions.

Opening for Warners as plaintiffs, Hastings neatly disposed of this foolishness. He also played on the fact that Bette's salary of over a thousand dollars a week was fantastically large for any person in those years and seemed like a queen's ransom in England. Commenting on the statement that Bette was a kind of slave, he remarked to general amusement that if anyone wished to enslave him at that price he would be perfectly willing to give the offer his consideration. He called her "a very naughty young lady."

He thus unfairly skirted the issue, which was that Bette was being compelled to make pictures in which she had no interest. If Sir William Jowitt had had a better grasp of the case, he would have put it to the court that Bette's career was being ruined by the very studio that built her up. He would have cited plot details of some of her more dreadful movies and particulars of the inane characters she had to play. He made no such plea.

Sir Patrick pointed out that the case was of great importance to the film industry because the contract referred to was essentially the common form across the Atlantic. He struck home when he said that what Bette was trying to do was tear up her contract willfully and without approval for no reason at all. He made fun of Bette's complaint that she worked long hours; he emphasized that she was earning two to three thousand dollars a week when he knew perfectly well she was not; and Jowitt, though correcting the figure in his final address, failed to raise an objection on the spot. Sir Patrick reminded the judge that there were clauses in the contract making it impossible for Bette to perform for anyone other than the plaintiffs until 1942. He said he was surprised to discover that the presidential dinner to which she objected (laughter in court) included five state governors, four United States senators, and three cabinet officers, and celebrated the anniversary of the birth of

117

Thomas Jefferson. Nobody, he continued, thought that it was a breach of contract to suggest to Miss Davis that she should accept the invitation. "I cannot help thinking," he added, "that Miss Davis is letting her imagination run away with her."

Turning to the position in law, Sir Patrick pointed out that awarding damages against Miss Davis would be futile. There was no way of assessing damages over a period of seven years. All Warners wanted to do was make sure that "a competitor of theirs does not take their personal servant"—Bette sat up at the word *servant* as though she had been stung—"whom they had brought up and used her in competition with them."

Jack Warner smilingly took the stand, looking as though he were about to burst into song on the vaudeville stage. Suntanned and dapper in an elegant three-piece suit, he was a great contrast to his wan and washed-out, staring-at-the-judge star. He announced complacently that he had built Miss Davis "up almost from oblivion to what the company thinks is a very great height." Sir Patrick asked him, "How much, Mr. Warner, do you estimate the damage in money from Miss Davis walking out?"

Jack Warner replied, "That is impossible. But I can tell you this—any picture of ours in which she appears is worth six hundred thousand dollars or seven hundred thousand dollars gross in the world."

Warner went on to say, lying, that the first complaint he had had from Bette was in 1935 when she said that a part that she was playing was "not so big as previous parts that she had been given." Apart from the incorrigible pun on *So Big*, the statement, as anyone who remotely knew Bette Davis would recognize, was nonsense. She would have complained from the very first day she set foot in the studio in 1930.

He went on to add a piece of information that was entirely superfluous and already known: that she had won the Oscar for *Dangerous*.

Instead of trying to show that Warner had grossly exploited Bette, forcing her into far too many pictures a year of poor quality—a statement that would have rocked the industry's foreign image to its foundations—Sir William Jowitt feebly asked: "The prize for *Dangerous* is the highest honor the industry has to give?"

"Within the industry, yes," Jack Warner, with equal fatuity, replied.

The questions continued:

Jowitt: "Is Miss Davis ambitious to become a great actress and is she very much interested in her profession?"

Warner: "She is ambitious to become a great actress and she is very much interested in her profession."

Jowitt: "Do you agree that film-making calls for great qualities?"

Warner: "It calls for unique qualities."

After this inane exchange, Jowitt at last got down to brass tacks—more or less. He asked, "Isn't it heartbreaking for an actress to play a part that she feels to be unsuitable for her?"

It would have been better had he confronted Warner with details of inept parts, but at least this was something. Warner's reply was bizarre. He said, "Knowing how difficult it is to get film scripts, I myself, *speaking as an actor* [sic], would be willing to give and take with any producer in the matter of parts." As if this were not enough, perhaps unrivaled for sheer gall as a statement, he went on to lie that he had bought *The Petrified Forest* specifically for Bette to appear in.

Sir William Jowitt now started a red herring. Exactly where he obtained his information is not certain, but he asked the ridiculous question: "Is it true that your brother Harry Warner asked Miss Davis to sign an undertaking that she would not divorce her husband for three years?"

Jack Warner replied with the only sensible statement he had made so far: "I have not heard of that and I am sure my brother never did such a thing." But he could not resist making a hypocritical addendum: "That would not be publicity; it would be bad taste."

With Jack Warner's evidence, the proceedings, perhaps fortunately, came to a temporary close. Exactly what thoughts were swirling in Bette's brain as she returned to her room at the Park Lane Hotel can only be conjectured.

The case proceeded the following day. Gerald Gardiner, representing Toeplitz (who, disgracefully, had not even bothered to appear in court), rose and announced, irrelevantly, that allegations of criminal conduct amounting to bribery had been made against Toeplitz and there was no evidence of such charges.

Jowitt said, *inter alia*, to titters in court, "Miss Davis could not, if she wanted to, become a waitress in a Lyons tea shop or a hairdresser's assistant in the wilds of Africa, if there are any hairdressers there." This total non sequitur, eccentric and unfunny, must have caused Bette a shiver or two.

He listed a number of complicated cases including, bizarrely, *Wolverhampton and Walsall, Railway Company* v. *London and Northwest Railway* (1891), and, just as oddly, *"Rely-a-Bell" Burglar and Fire Alarm Company Limited* v. *Eisler* (1926). What a case of two railways suing each other, and a burglar alarm company accusing someone of appropriating it, had to do with Bette Davis, only Sir William Jowitt and God could possibly answer.

It is scarcely surprising that Sir Patrick Hastings omitted any mention of this Gilbert and Sullivan affair in his memoirs. The fact is, the case should never have been fought in the first place. Bette's London solicitors should have advised her to go back to Hollywood at once and forget the matter, since her contract was watertight and could not be challenged. The only advantage in the case would have been to draw attention to exploitative and sexist attitudes in Hollywood. No such purpose was achieved. Since Bette herself did not appear as a defendant in the witness box, she was deprived of the chance to give the performance of a lifetime. In every way it was a disastrous occasion and it goes without saying that she lost.

She was faced with $25,000 in legal debts and no hope for the future. But fortunately, Jack Warner's wife, Ann, a charming woman, was fond of Bette and reminded her husband of Bette's great financial potential for the studio. Warner was nothing if not money-minded. Making a grand show of mercy, he "forgave" Bette and invited his erring star back to Hollywood. He basked in public approval while Bette went to Rottingdean in Sussex to consider an appeal. She took up cycling and, chronically accident-prone, forgot to turn a corner and skinned her knees bare. Next day she caught a severe cold and spoke through her nose to the press: "I won't attend the rehearing because my hypnotism didn't work on the judge the first time. Silly of me, wasn't it? I am not a good hypnotist."

Recovering from her cold, Bette wandered the beach in a drizzle and finally made a phone call to her mother to come over and keep her company. But she abruptly canceled the invitation. She realized she couldn't afford to appeal, and a chance meeting with her old friend George Arliss made up her mind for her. Hearing she was depressed and sick, he had come to see her and to offer her tea and sympathy. He told her to go home and make her peace with Warners. She sailed for New York in November.

In Manhattan, she gave interviews to the press, saying that she was back for more years of work and that was all there was to it. She once again pretended she hadn't been fighting for money and fewer pictures. She met her mother in New York and had an uneasy reunion with Ham, who was working between jobs as an artist's manager, in his usual uncertain manner. When she arrived in Hollywood, she felt a wave of relief. It was November 18, 1936, late fall, and the sun was still shining warmly. Bobby and friends met her train. Maybe the future wouldn't be so bleak after all.

SIX

Instead of preparing an elaborate vehicle for Bette's return, Warners gave her a low-budget picture—but one that was far better written than most. At the time Bette had left for Canada, the writer Robert Rossen had made an outline for the producer Lou Edelman of a new script, *The Men Behind*, based on the trial of Lucky Luciano. Rossen worked slowly and methodically, and Hal Wallis added Paul Muni's brother-in-law Abem Finkel and Seton I. Miller to make up a trio of writers for the property. By November they had a first draft, renamed *Marked Women*, and Hal Wallis decided to assign the story to Bette. He had the title changed to *Marked Woman*, so that it would be more overtly a starring vehicle for her alone. She would play Mary Dwight, a dance hostess in a sleazy New York nightclub, who is marked by the mob. Her character was based on an actual figure in the Lucky Luciano case, and the writing was accurate and hard-hitting, in the best Warner Brothers tradition. Her co-star would be Humphrey Bogart.

As soon as Bette was settled into the Nelson house at the end of November, and Ham, their differences patched up, got a job conducting his combo at the Blossom Room of the Hollywood Roosevelt Hotel, Hal Wallis and Jack Warner called her in for a very amicable discussion. She told them she was excited by the script, feeling that at last she would be making some progress in her career, and she was impatient to get back to work at the old studio she had fought with so long. But then one of those irritating, silly, inexplicable accidents that marred her life took place.

A messenger who was supposed to take the script to her failed to do so. Tenny Wright was to follow up with a call to see whether she liked it, but, distracted by the problems of five pictures being shot at once, he forgot to phone. As a result, two and a half days before production began, Bette called Wallis when she found Warner had gone out to say she had not yet received a script. Wallis, in turn, raged at Wright and had one rushed to her immediately.

She sat up until 3:00 A.M. reading it. She couldn't sleep the rest of the night. Ham, exhausted after his stint at the Roosevelt, complained because he could not rest. Bette was wildly excited. She had seldom encountered such vivid, sure writing and character delineation. She called Wallis and rushed in for her tests. But the dark rings under her eyes, caused by nights of sleeplessness, forced Wallis to order the shots to be redone.

She plunged enthusiastically into work. The first day back was exciting; the crew applauded as she came on the sound stage. She was warm and protective with a young and nervous actress named Jane Bryan, who played her sister, a well-brought-up girl destroyed by contact with gangsterdom.

Jane Bryan told me: "Bette was absolutely spectacular. She was so patient, so considerate of me that she was almost *living* the part of being my older sister. She knew I had *terrible* nerves—still do!—and that making pictures for me was *torture*. I was lost in admiration for her. I had to tell anyone who asked that Bette was the most unselfish star I could imagine. Anyone else would have ridden roughshod over me. She did everything in her power to help me and she stood between me and the director.

"I got to know her and her mother and sister very well. I used to go to their house on Franklin Avenue with its proper front porch and I *adored* Ham. He was so gangly and sweet! But it was impossible, their marriage. And Ruthie was restless and bored. She turned to Christian Science at that time, and so did Bette. Not many people know that."

There were problems on *Marked Woman*. Bette's voice, always strained because of the constant flow of speech she addressed all day to everyone off the set on every subject under the sun, threatened to give out on her.

She used an old trick of pitching it in a higher register. Consequently, she tended to sound "singsong" and affected, and director Lloyd Bacon begged her to talk in huskier tones. She had no rapport with Bacon at all, nor he with her; he was a man's director, and here he was directing a story about women! Luckily, the script saw her through. And there was the delightful diversion of seeing Mayo Methot, a fiery, hard-drinking, small-time actress who played one of the dance-hall girls, falling headlong and ill-fatedly in love with Bogey.

Hal Wallis, as so often before, strengthened the picture by having some scenes retaken. There was a sequence in which Bette and Jane Bryan had a quarrel over Bette's profession. Bacon played it very flat; Hal Wallis asked Bette and Jane if they would redo it. Bette was to sit in a chair and Jane was to sink to her knees, fling her arms about her, and sob, "I didn't mean it! I didn't mean it!" She was to hold Bette close and drop her head on Bette's lap as Bette gazed sadly into the camera and then protectively down at her kid sister for the fade-out. Bette responded at once to the suggestion and played the scene with extraordinary tenderness. Jane had already become her "kid sister" in real life.

Before the picture was done, there was a major row; no Bette Davis movie would have been complete without one. There was a scene in which she was badly beaten. She had been to a doctor to check on the correct way she should look, and insisted on going into the makeup test with bandages on and her eyes blackened. Wallis objected to the test, writing in a memorandum, "The last makeup test of Bette with bandages on and her eyes made up is absolutely horrible . . . We are not making a comedy . . . She should have her eyes discolored and a slight swelling on one cheek . . . Let's stop trying to make her look too horrible

125

looking." But Bette won the battle and appeared in this manner in the scene.

There was some comic relief on the picture. An actor who played one of the henchmen of Eduardo Ciannelli provoked Hal Wallis's annoyance because he gave such a bad performance. "Who is that monkey?" Wallis asked Lloyd Bacon. "Why the hell didn't you get a menacing-looking character? He looks like some five-dollar extra man. Couldn't you see he wasn't right for the part of a gangster?" The reply convulsed Bette and the other players. "I'm sorry to tell you," Bacon said, "that he is one of Lucky Luciano's favorite gang members. We put him in the picture for realism!"

Jack Warner loved *Marked Woman*. For years it was one of his favorite pictures. An incorrigible punster, he ran into Bette one day in a corridor and said, "It's terrific! There's a sock in every foot!"

This response, soon to be echoed by audiences and critics alike, encouraged Bette to write to Warner on January 6, 1937 that she was in bad financial trouble. She had hoped to pay her legal expenses in England without taking an advance on her salary, but the bills arriving from London were crushing and she realized it would take her a year to pay them. She begged Warner to advance her fourteen thousand dollars on her salary so that she could meet her immediate obligations. He could make the check out to her London solicitors Morris, Munton and King direct and deduct seven hundred dollars a week for twenty weeks. She added that the whole experience had been a severe worry to her. And she added an interesting last sentence, "I am thrilled to death about Jezebel."

Jack Warner agreed to the advance, lying to the press that he had paid for everything.

Bette, in her letter to Warner, had been referring to a development that had just taken place. In February 1935, a play entitled *Jezebel*, by Owen Davis, about Julie Marsden, a ruthless southern belle in the antebellum period who steals men from their women, had been submitted through the New York office's Jake Wilk. It had been done on the stage with Miriam Hopkins. Walter McEwen of the story department in Hollywood sent it to Hal Wallis with the words, "It [the story] is not very good . . . But it could provide a good role for Bette Davis who can knock the spots off the part of a little bitch of an aristocratic southern girl . . ." Wallis agreed, but the snag was that Miriam Hopkins was determined to play the part on the screen and jointly owned the rights with the producer, Guthrie McClintic. At the time Bette mentioned being "thrilled to death" at getting a chance to play Julie Marsden, Hopkins and McClintic were locked in a violent quarrel: McClintic wanted to sell the play on any terms; Hopkins only on condition that she would play the lead. Miss Hopkins held up negotiations for several weeks, and when she heard that Bette Davis, whom she still envied savagely long after their working together at Rochester, wanted to play it, she made further violent objections. It was not until the spring of 1937 that she finally yielded for twelve thousand dollars and only after Walter McEwen lied to McClintic that Miriam would be first choice for the part when a satisfactory script was finally completed.

Meanwhile, the deadly studio pressure rushed Bette into another gangster picture: *Kid Galahad*. She quailed when she heard Curtiz would direct it but there was nothing she could do. She was consoled by a tight, fast-moving script and by the cast—not by Bogey again, but by Edward G. Robinson and her beloved Jane Bryan. It was a typical Warners programmer: a story of the boxing rackets directed with hard, slam-bang efficiency and pace.

Already, in this second picture after her return, Bette had begun to assert a formidable degree of power. Irving Rapper, who later became director of two of her most famous pictures, *Now, Voyager* and *Deception*, recalls that *Kid Galahad*, on which he was dialogue director, offered his first chance to meet her. He says, "I asked the script girl, 'What's Bette Davis like?' and the girl rolled her eyes toward heaven. 'Oh, God, don't ask me!' she replied." Now Rapper asked Michael Curtiz for his comment. "Son of a bitch, don't ask me," he also said. "You'll see her when she comes in."

Rapper's first sight of Davis was unforgettable: blue

eyes wide, long neck stretched out, body thin and angular, she ran onto the set as though onto a tennis court, formidably geared for action. In the scene Edward G. Robinson had to throw her bodily against a table. She struggled with Robinson, then fell back. Curtiz screamed at her, "That's not the way to fight him, you goddamn bum!" And Bette screamed back, "You show me what you want me to do and I'll do it!"

Curtiz, who had been a strong man in a circus, stood there while the tiny Robinson looked at him in terror. "It's okay, Eddie, throw me," Curtiz said.

"But if you struggle," Robinson wailed, "that's the end of me!"

Bette had to laugh at the sight of the runtish actor trying to throw Curtiz's 195-pound body across the room. Everyone else broke up when Curtiz did a hilarious imitation of Bette, complete with swinging hips, snapped-out delivery, and frantically puffed cigarette. Robinson pushed him. Curtiz ricocheted off the table and almost knocked Robinson over. Then he said to Bette, "Goddamnit, bum, this is what I want!" She nodded and stood in position. Robinson pushed her with all the strength he had used on Curtiz. As a result, she ricocheted so violently that she flew clean across the set and into Irving Rapper's lap as he sat watching the scene. She screamed, "My *God*! Who are you?"

He said, "I'm the dialogue director."

And she replied, "Thank *God* you caught the ball!" And they burst out laughing and became good friends.

Jezebel was still being scripted while *Kid Galahad* was being finished, and it was impossible for Bette to proceed with it. And at that moment she suffered a grievous blow. She lost what would undoubtedly have been the greatest of all her triumphs: the part of Scarlett O'Hara in *Gone With the Wind*.

It is interesting to speculate on the contradictory reasons as to why she lost the role. The most convincing one seems to be that David O. Selznick, who had bought the property, was considering Errol Flynn as Rhett Butler, and Warner had agreed to lend Flynn only on condition that Bette play Scarlett; but Bette's conviction that Flynn was wrong for

128

Butler was so intense that she preferred to surrender her chance at the picture rather than have Flynn act in it. Jack Warner characteristically rewarded her by casting Flynn opposite her in two pictures in the next two years.

In her memoirs, *The Lonely Life*, Bette says that during one of her many quarrels with Warner she saw a copy of *Gone with the Wind* on his desk and said, "I bet it's a pip!" thus encouraging him to turn it down. Another version has Selznick deciding Bette lacked the sheer physical beauty which could explain Rhett Butler's total infatuation with her over a period of years. Whatever the reason, she wasn't in the running after the first few weeks.

Would Bette have made a good Scarlett? She herself is convinced she would have been a triumph in the part. Certainly, excellent though Vivien Leigh was, she became somewhat monotonous and strident in the less satisfactory second half. Bette could have brought greater resources of thought and feeling to the picture's development. But it is possible that her lack of sheer beauty might have told against her in the long run. The essence of the book and film, the reason for their immense success, is that they are hinged on one theme: Rhett Butler's consuming sexual desire for Scarlett and her maddening refusal to commit herself totally to him. The reader and the film-goer are kept in a torment of irritated suspense during long stretches of what amounts to literary coitus interruptus. The formula worked to perfection because Margaret Mitchell convinced us that Scarlett was not only a perennial tease but a physical prize for which most men would be prepared to kill if necessary. For all her great talent and attractiveness, Bette Davis could never have answered that description.

Bette enjoyed making *Kid Galahad*—even though it was in essence a programmer. But she was annoyed that she had to follow it with a tiresome soap opera, *That Certain Woman*, in which her only consolation was working with the director-writer Edmund Goulding, an amusing and mannered English bisexual who shared Curtiz's entertaining capacity for acting out the scenes for both the actors and the actresses. In a sequence in which she had to kiss Henry Fonda, he played her part with a conviction that had everyone doubled up with laughter—and Fonda was red with embarrassment.

After *That Certain Woman*, Bette was in a state of exhaustion, weighing barely a hundred pounds. On March 15 she fled to the La Quinta Hotel near Palm Springs, refusing to come back, but Hal Wallis insisted she must—by March 28. Her attorney Dudley Furse wrote to Wallis that she had low blood pressure, a result of the flu from which she had suffered after *Marked Woman*. She also wrote Wallis saying, "Give me a week more . . . I must have a brief chance of being something more than a jittery old woman."

He did not give her the week and she had to return for *It's Love I'm After*, written by Casey Robinson and directed by Archie Mayo. It had a most amusing idea: Basil Underwood and Joyce Arden are a successful, seemingly Luntish acting team, whose romantic performances, particularly in *Romeo and Juliet*, cause a sensation on the stage. But offstage they are constantly locked in comical arguments, madly in love but at loggerheads. Olivia De Havilland played the part of a young girl who gets a crush on Basil. Bette was a feisty Joyce Arden, matched with a fierce-tempered Leslie Howard as Basil Underwood.

Oddly, the firm's situation was altered in real life: Leslie Howard, who looked so wan and delicate, was a passionate woman-chaser in private. (He could have given some points to Errol Flynn.) Howard made Olivia De Havilland's life miserable by almost literally begging her to go to bed with him; but she was staid and virginal. If she hadn't yielded to Errol Flynn, who was also persistent, she certainly wasn't about to yield to Leslie Howard.

At home, Bette still had her crosses to bear. She would come home pale and worn-out after a day of flinging herself into scenes, to find no husband to greet her; Ham, busy conducting at the Blossom Room of the Hollywood Roosevelt, didn't get home until two or three in the morning. A light, restless sleeper, she would wake on his return and sometimes could not sleep properly the rest of the night. In the morning she had to be up very early, sometimes around seven, to drive over the old Cahuenga Pass to Warners for makeup. She would wake Ham, who needed to rest until noon to recover his strength for the grueling task of standing for six hours every evening conducting his band. They scarcely saw each other; she couldn't even attend his performances because she would have attracted too much attention and might have thrown him off balance; and besides, she was too tired. Even Sundays were difficult because, under an old studio rule, she had to shoot late into the night on Saturdays, and she needed to sleep all the next day. She could only envy stars like Katharine Hepburn at RKO and Garbo at MGM who were treated like queens; Garbo would never work at night, and Hepburn would stop production for hours while she served elaborate picnic luncheons. Even Errol Flynn on her own lot was able to escape by boat to the West Indies or to Mexico the moment a picture was finished, and Humphrey Bogart also had his yacht. But her life remained severe, pinched, unglamorous. Her house was still small and in an unfashionable district; Mother (not that Bette would ever resent it) was continuing to spend money, as fast as Bette could earn it, on jewels, clothes, cars, expensive vacations; Bobby was still suffering from mental illness, and the sanitarium and psychiatric bills were crushing; there was the fourteen thousand dollars paid off to Warners for the London legal bills and the fact that the trip itself had not been entirely paid for by Ludovic Toeplitz; and Ham's job meant it was impossible for them to enjoy more than very brief trips to Palm Springs and La Quinta. Life was agonizing, and never more so than when she saw the way the studio was handing her low-budget pictures, and when she realized that her marriage was heading rapidly for the rocks.

Her early romantic life had been so warm, so innocent and fulfilling; because he was her first love, Ham had earned her undying affection. But she, even at this stage of her career, was earning $2,000 a week—she still had not attained her original goal of $2,500—and he was earning $300 a week at the Roosevelt. In those unenlightened days of the mid-1930s, a woman who was earning more than a husband could not pay the bills without feeling a deep inner resentment; in her memoirs. Bette lashes out at men who have their wives pay the household bills while spending their own money on clothes. Today, many liberated women would not resent supporting a husband, but the stigma forty years ago was almost Victorian. She claimed that Ham overcompensated by attacking her physically—uncharacteristic of so gentle a man—and that he had to assert his manhood by making her unhappy. If these physical fights did take place, it's certain it was because her temperament—challenging, infuriating, domineering—irritated him unbearably. It was because he was watching what increasing fame and success were doing to Bette: changing her from a pallid shy wren of a woman into a powerhouse full of hatred and anger and drive. The woman he had married was rapidly ceasing to exist, and it was a torment to him to see it.

He made a valiant attempt to save the marriage, gave up his band, and joined an advertising agency. But it didn't help. Obsessed with her work, Bette was, as his later divorce evidence made painfully clear, no longer attracted to him.

She enjoyed playing in *It's Love I'm After* but immediately afterward, the brief honeymoon with Warners suddenly came to an end. She moved to Santa Barbara for a rest when Hal Wallis offered her a slangy, Joan Blondell-like part in *Hollywood Hotel*. She flatly refused to play it. She felt, she told Wallis on July 17, 1937, that his offer to her was a great mistake; that she had had only four weeks vacation after *It's Love I'm After* and that she wasn't fit enough to tackle another picture; that she had hoped for a complete rest at the beach for the twelve weeks she was allowed, after making three movies in five months; and that she was still feeling the effects of these pictures and the harrowing ordeal of the court battle in England. She was underweight; surely Joan Blondell could play this nonsense instead? In a confirming note, she said, "I'm sure you must believe me when I tell you I've been through a little bit of hell." The letter, dashed off in her bold, rounded hand in garish green ink on thin paper, still breathes anxiety and mental and physical exhaustion forty years later.

Wallis ordered her to appear for wardrobe on July 28—or she would be suspended. It seemed as though her whole fight had been for nothing. She had obtained three superior programmers, that was all, and *Jezebel* seemed as far away as ever. She failed to turn up for wardrobe, and when the studio demanded to know why, her secretary, Bridget Price, called to say that Miss Davis had been so severely burned while sunbathing at Carpinteria that she had a case of sunstroke. Her mother and Dr. C. Horace Goshow confirmed the statement; according to a friend, Bette was simply putting on a performance worthy of those she gave on the screen, in order to avoid acting in the dreaded *Hollywood Hotel*. She was also extremely upset because in revenge for her behavior, the studio was forbidding her to do one radio show after another—a familiar way of punishing rebellious stars.

The row grew louder. When Roy Obringer insisted she do a Warner Brothers radio show on KFWB, she declined on the grounds that she had not been allowed to do the Chase and Sanborn Show or the Lux shows. Finally, she did all the shows in "fair trade."

There is another side to the story. Bridget Price wrote to Jack Warner and Hal Wallis on July 29 that Bette had second-degree burns and that she was feverish and fretful—particularly since she was getting second billing to Leslie Howard in *It's Love I'm After*. Price wrote, "Bette asked me to express her deep regret to you regarding her present illness: I do feel that this enforced rest, although painful at the moment, will make her really strong and well for the first time in a year!" She went on. "If you can wait for Bette's recovery, she will give her very best to her work, even to *Hollywood Hotel*, as she always does, even though she thinks she isn't right for a picture."

The sunstroke won the battle, and she didn't work again until, at long suffering last, *Jezebel* was scripted in the fall. The rest at Carpinteria did her some good. She gained weight and she began to feel that in *Jezebel* she would have a chance to become a very great star.

Miriam Hopkins had given up wanting the role, and Robert Buckner, a dignified and elegant gentleman-writer,

133

produced a smooth first-draft screenplay of *Jezebel*. But it did not solve the problem of a rambling, diffuse structure, or overcome the fact that it was impossible to sympathize with Julie Marsden, the spoiled little southern vixen. Buckner finally hit on the idea that at the end of the picture she is regenerated by suffering. Edmund Goulding was supposed to direct the picture, but he disliked the script and dropped out. Hal Wallis had a writer named Clements Ripley work on it, with writer Abem Finkel supplying additional pages. Finally, there came the problem of obtaining a leading man. Hal Wallis wanted Jeffrey Lind, later known at Jeffrey Lynn, who was appearing in a play in Chicago, but negotiations broke down and instead—fortunately—he cast Henry Fonda in the part. Bette, who had liked Fonda during the shooting of *That Certain Woman*, was very pleased indeed.

Wallis hit on the bold idea of hiring William Wyler, then under contract to Sam Goldwyn, to make the picture. Wyler was at that time one of the two or three most important directors in Hollywood. In his early thirties, he was compelled by great energy, ruthless in his attack, a perfectionist who would take scenes over and over in order to achieve perfection. Small, impish, with a wickedly smart sense of humor, he was extremely attractive to women. From the moment she met him, Bette fell in love with him, and there is no question that he upset the balance of her life at the same moment as he drastically enhanced it.

Hal Wallis and Bette's double Sally Sage recall that during the shooting Bette impulsively entered into a romance with Wyler. There is no doubt that his genius, blunt Jewish looks, fierce drive under a seemingly quiet exterior, and, most important, his grasp of her potential as an actress, overcame her fear of him and enslaved her as only she could be enslaved. She became convinced (she always had the power to convince herself of anything) that this would be the most complete and permanent relationship she would ever know. Wyler had recently been divorced from Margaret Sullavan, whose willful, mercurial, unreliable, and perverse nature was the exact opposite of Davis's. Wyler had more in common with Bette; both were disciplined, severe spirits, dedicated to achieving extraordinary levels in their working careers. Yet in some ways Wyler was as incompatible with Bette as he had been with Sullavan. He was born in Alsace-Lorraine, which made him almost as German as if he had been born in Germany. There was a strictness and severity in Wyler behind the genial, driving personality that resisted most readily the endless fire and fever of Davis's nature. Neurosis in a woman irritated him; he was infuriated by Bette's tortured spirit, even when he most admired her. He was at once drawn to her and exasperated by her. Bette was partly excited by the idea of being dominated by a man at last—the woman in her was excited. But her mind and her ego found it impossible to accept that domination. She was afraid of being consumed by Wyler. She wanted to be in charge of everything herself; even a visit to the hairdresser or dentist irritated her because someone else was in charge. She was torn as always by conflicts of desire and what was best for her. The tension exhausted her. She was running too fast on her shaky engine.

Fear of exposure and fear of being consumed ate away at Bette's fragile health. She lost weight and played many scenes with a darting, stabbing intensity that no doubt resulted from her state of terror.

And then there were the intolerable logistics of having the affair at all. On no account must the gossip columnists get wind of it: Hedda and Louella did not—or else they were sports about it and kept silent. If it were found out that she was having a relationship with her director, the vultures of the women's club would have swept down on her like so much carrion. Bette was a person without surreptitiousness. Yet at night, after long hours of tearing, rending work, she had to dodge off with Wyler and somehow avoid having Ham make a public spectacle of her.

Her marriage to Ham was steadily disintegrating, and she must have thought wistfully of the days when they were just an ambitious young couple starting out—before her career as a star had placed her so far ahead of him. Wyler was everything Ham was not: rich, famous, domineering, unafraid, secure, and prepared to confront her head-on in any argument. His judgment, she recognized, was better than hers. For the first time in her career, since John Cromwell directed her, she had found an artistic guide who could bring out the best in her.

And Wyler, right at the outset of their working together, hit on a brilliant notion. He brought in Walter Huston's tall loping son John as co-author, rewriting the last half of the picture in its entirety to deepen the character of Julie Marsden and to make her regeneration believable. Wyler talked to Bette both at the studio and in the evenings they were able to spend together, teaching her how to control her energy and enthusiasm, how to tame her too-desperate anxiety to do every sequence as perfectly as possible. His memoranda to Hal Wallis and the producer Henry Blanke at the time indicate this. One (October 15, 1937) reads: "She comes in during the morning eager to do it right, maybe to overdo it . . . and I tell her to take it easy. I tell her a scene is important, but not every scene . . . so she learns not to act everything at the same pressure, as though her life depends on it . . ."

He taught her to modulate her style, to allow herself soft as well as overweening passages, and to adapt herself to Henry Fonda's quieter, subtler approach. Wyler's love of endless takes, always so infuriating to the studio front office, proved effective in her case, because he simply drained her energy by having her rush in and out of rooms dozens of times until she acted like a normal person. Her anguished state of mind might have ruined her performance, but he taught her, with great patience and skill, to use the stresses she was suffering from to enhance her interpretation.

This patience and cunning meant that the production moved very slowly indeed. And when Henry Fonda arrived, ten days after production began, the actor soon made it clear that he would have to be released as quickly as possible, because his wife was expecting their first child, who turned out to be Jane Fonda. Bette's nervous strain resulted in a small red swelling, a kind of pimple on her face; and no closeups could be shot of her for several days.

Worse, her makeup, which was highly toxic, inflamed the spot still further and she became ill, returning home for several days until the production, with Fonda becoming increasingly fretful, slipped twelve days behind schedule.

As a result, and in order to release Fonda, much of the movie could not be shot according to schedule. Bette developed a "charley horse" that made it impossible for her to film, on the days appointed, the important ballroom scene in which Julie shocks New Orleans society by wearing a revealing red dress. The sequence had to be postponed again and again. On the night of December 20, after eleven consecutive hours of very slowly shooting disconnected pieces of sequences, Bette became hysterical, collapsing in floods of tears in her dressing room. Her depression at the constant rearrangements for the birth of Fonda's child, Wyler's driving of her, and her devotion to making Julie her greatest role had shattered her precariously balanced nature.

A month behind schedule, the production dragged on through the cold damp winter of 1937 into the later hours of Christmas Eve and into the New Year. Bette was frayed, exhausted, ill, and then she was stunned by a jolt of bad news. While she was still shooting on New Year's Day 1938, her father died suddenly in Boston and she could not be spared for the week or more it would have taken to attend the funeral because the cumbersome picture was by now twenty-four and a half days behind.

Tormented by the fact that she could not go to Boston, she had to shoot exteriors on rainy days on the back lot, and she came down with bronchitis and a miserable cold. She had to shoot a strange scene in which she sang along with the plantation blacks (cut from most released versions), and her voice, always troublesome, gave out, so that she had to rehearse for days on end and then struggle, with days of sickness in between, to match up shots. By January 17 the picture still wasn't finished and Hal Wallis decided to let William Dieterle finish it. Bette protested violently, saying that after "all she had been through" she would not "tolerate anybody else taking the picture on." Much as she hated the work, she was by now not only in love with Wyler, but engulfed by admiration of his talent.

By the end of January 1938, Bette was so sick that her physician, Dr. Noys, told the studio in a memorandum dated January 30 that she would be in no shape to begin any picture in the near future. Indeed, he added, he was amazed she had managed to struggle through to the last day's shooting of *Jezebel*. Her condition did not allow for the kind of nervous strain she had undergone. She should have two months off now, whether her contract allowed for it or not, "because she is going on grit alone." He added: "She is not actually medically ill, but her general physical and emotional makeup is such that if we rush her into another picture she will be in danger of collapse."

She had her two months off, in February and March, when her affair with Wyler ran into trouble. She evidently was terrified by the idea of being comsumed by an ego even larger than her own. She had no desire to work. When the studio's Benjamin Glazer brought a trashy story called *Comet Over Broadway* to her front door in March, she had her maid tell Glazer she was in bed and could not get up. Glazer returned later in the morning and she had gone out; her maid Dell said she had gone to Bobby's house. But when Glazer arrived at Bobby's, Bette was not there. Not surprisingly, he reported to Jack Warner, "I believe we are getting the old run-around."

She gave an elaborate dinner party at the Beverly Hills Hotel to raise money for the Tailwaggers Club—a dog-lovers' organization. The guest of honor was Howard Hughes. She says in her memoirs, discreetly, "I became involved in a catastrophic relationship . . . he was extremely attractive and one of the wealthiest men in the West—or East, for that matter." She says that she met him for the first time at the club. But she does not name Hughes.

At the time, Hughes was in his thirties, handsome, overwhelmingly wealthy, a great flier whose picture *Hell's Angels* had been the ultimate in aviation movies. But Hughes was nervous, awkward, shy, and self-conscious. He hid in corners at parties and was clumsy and ill-at-ease with women. He was like a great gangling country bumpkin. Women wanted to mother him.

His physical self-consciousness was so extreme that he suffered from recurrent ejaculatory impotence with women. It came as a considerable shock to Bette when she discovered this. He had been through an enormously publicized romance with Katharine Hepburn.

Hughes had romanced Hepburn in a very old-fashioned manner. He had dipped his wings when he flew over her house; he had even taught her to fly. As fanatically private as she, he was always dodging in and out of cars, trains, and planes with her in an attempt to avoid publicity which, like Garbo's, inevitably resulted in an excess of it. When Hepburn went off on a tour of *Jane Eyre* in severe winter weather, Hughes followed her by plane at considerable danger to himself, and put a fresh emerald on her dressing table every night she performed.

There is no evidence that he treated Bette with equal attentiveness and indeed he soon returned to Hepburn with whom, it seems, he had more personal empathy. But in one respect Bette Davis was closer to him than Hepburn. Bette, who was not beautiful and thus was not threatening, told her friends she managed to help him overcome his impotence. She was sweet and kind and good to Hughes—she set his mind free of anxiety.

Yet curing an impotent male, after the bitter disappointment of the relationship with Ham, was very far from being what Bette wanted. Wyler drew her back quickly from the complicated, struggling personality of Hughes.

And then came a severe shock. Ham Nelson, threatened, maddened by Bette's attraction to Wyler, and still more exasperated by her fascination with Hughes, suddenly went off the rails. He decided to bug the house he now shared with her in Coldwater Canyon (they had moved from Franklin Avenue the year before) and with the aid of a well-known private detective fixed up a recording system (discs in those days) in the walls of the bedroom and living room to be able to prove the physical details of the affair.

139

He obtained a sound truck to which the wires leading from the recording devices were attached and late at night he parked the truck in a secluded side street in the canyon just above the house. In an agony of mind that can scarcely be guessed at, he heard Bette and Hughes together. As he listened on that dark street at night, he suddenly could endure no more. He raced down to the back door, let himself in with a key, and burst into the bedroom. Hughes tried to punch Ham in the face. He flubbed it. Ham said that the instant his recordings were released, Bette's reputation as a star would be ruined, because in those days adultery was a sin so serious that the Legion of Decency could wreck a career if they discovered it. Bette became hysterical as Ham ran out. This scene, at once grotesque, comic, and nightmarish, was followed by one even more extreme. Ham blackmailed Hughes for seventy thousand dollars in return for agreeing to destroy the recording.

Hughes was deathly afraid of his potency problem being made known to his macho friends. He hired a professional gangster to kill Ham, but then learned that Ham had advised the police that if he were murdered, Hughes would be responsible for the killing.

The ghastly episode destroyed Bette's relationship with Hughes, as Ham hoped it would. Bette was scarcely able to sleep and retreated to Bobby's house. Hughes rushed a check to Ham for the demanded figure. The records were smashed in front of Bette. Then she took a loan on future earnings and, with great decency, as a matter of honor, paid Hughes back the full seventy thousand dollars. Hughes never forgot her gesture but, fabulously wealthy though he was, he wasn't good enough to refuse it. Instead, he indulged in the theatrical gesture of sending her a single flower every year for the rest of his life on the anniversary of the repayment.

SEVEN

Jezebel established Bette as a top star; Wyler's fanatical direction paid off. Bette's interpretation was startlingly vivid, making Julie Marsden's petulance and drive understandable and sympathetic. She was justly praised for her performance and won her second Oscar for it the following year.

In June 1938, Bette began work for the fair-haired, elegant director Anatole Litvak in *The Sisters*, a contrived romantic melodrama about the fortunes of three young women in the early years of the twentieth century. Third choice after Irene Dunne and Ginger Rogers, she was cast as a girl who falls in love with an impoverished newspaperman and moves to San Francisco at the time of the earthquake. She played opposite Errol Flynn, who was fourth choice after Fredric March, Franchot Tone, and George Brent—all of whom refused the picture. Flynn was earning $4,500 a week to Bette's $2,250; there was no question of who was the bigger star or who was more admired by Jack Warner. Although she wasn't his type, Errol made a conventional pass at Bette which she peremptorily rebuffed.

Her absenteeism on the picture was more remarkable than ever. Even though she was playing in high summer, she took sick with influenza and lost her voice again on June 27. Jack Sullivan, the assistant director, wrote an acid memorandum to his superior Tenny Wright, saying, "I

141

don't know whether she's sick or getting too much social life." This was a sly reference to the persistent studio rumors that she had been dating Howard Hughes.

And once again the extraordinary rivalry between herself and Miriam Hopkins flared up. Miriam was fuming that Bette had played in *her* drama, *Jezebel*, and now she began accusing Litvak, her recently acquired husband, of having an affair with her envied and hated enemy at the same time he was directing her. Actually, her charges were groundless; Bette was by no means over Wyler, and it was not until some months later that her fascination with Litvak developed into a brief, ill-fated, much gossiped-about romance.

Miriam Hopkins was still a remarkable personage. With her crinkly hair, snapping eyes, contemptuous mouth, and southern drawl, she was prettier and more cruel than ever. She was jealous—consumingly so of Bette. Her drive and ambition had ensured her success in such movies as *Dr. Jekyll and Mr. Hyde*, *Becky Sharp*, *The Story of Temple Drake*, *Trouble in Paradise*, and *These Three*. She acted even her most trivial scenes with an intensity belied by her cool dismissal of her film performances in private; of all stage—and literature—snobs, she was among the snootiest. She never quite reached actual stardom; the failure of *Becky Sharp*, an adroit bowdlerization of *Vanity Fair*, suggested to everyone in Hollywood that she shouldn't warrant a picture on her own. Maybe audiences picked up that she was too "intellectual" and high-hat, that she was a southern belle slumming vigorously in pictures. And she also lacked that ice-cold sex that Bette projected to perfection.

Litvak was a Russian who had made his name quickly with his polished direction of *Mayerling*, a romanticizing of the famous historical episode, with Danielle Darrieux and Charles Boyer. Litvak was everything Miriam was not: gregarious, charming, tactful, with a passion for the glamour and luxury that still existed in Hollywood in 1937. He loved nightclubs and parties; she hated them. Inevitably, too, he would fail to have a rapport with Bette because her life was so cramped, so dark, so meager, with Bette's penny-pinching and her troubled sister. Litvak wanted to enjoy Ciro's, the Trocadero, the Clover Club, cocktails and laughter; Bette was interested in rushing home from work to kick off her shoes and devour a script more hungrily than she ever devoured any meal or kissed any lover.

Her affair with Litvak lay in the future. In the late summer Bette was busy pushing for the role of Judith Traherne in *Dark Victory*, a play in which Tallulah Bankhead had flopped. It was currently owned by David O. Selznick, who planned to co-star Katharine Hepburn and Fredric March in it, or possibly Garbo and March, with a screen play by Philip Barry. In January 1938, Walter McEwen, head of Warners story department, bought the play from Selznick for Kay Francis at a price of twenty thousand dollars; but Miss Francis turned it down because she was superstitious—she was afraid of playing a dying woman. The story dealt with an heiress to a fortune, a typical 1930s Park Avenue brat, who is stricken with a fatal disease: a cross between *My Man Godfrey* and *One-Way Passage*. Casey Robinson, perhaps the most gifted writer of "women's" scripts in the business, had been hoping to do the picture for three years, and had mentioned the possibilities of it to Bette. He longed for Spencer Tracy to play the doctor who diagnoses the heiress's ailment and falls in love with her; and she, who still admired Tracy more than almost any other actor, was hugely excited by the idea.

Instead, Jack Warner decided to avoid the difficult negotiations with MGM that hiring Tracy, who was under contract to Metro, would involve; he was also afraid of Tracy's alcoholism. He chose George Brent, his favorite stopgap for virtually every picture then being made that lacked a leading man.

The choice was more intelligent than it may have seemed. Brent exuded integrity, warmth, and a quiet, composed good humor. Although by no means a fine actor, he had a gift for playing foil to major actresses, and he could certainly be a convincing doctor—nobody in pictures had a more polished bedside manner. Despite her disappointment over Tracy, Bette was pleased by the choice. Warners advanced her salary to three thousand dollars a week, due to rise in annual increments to four thousand by 1942. And Jack Warner personally wrote to her, at long last, sweeping away the remainder of her fourteen-thousand-dollar loan.

There was no question that Bette was in anguish after Ham walked out following the Hughes episode. It is easy to imagine her state of mind. Her rage and contempt for him, particularly over the blackmailing of Hughes, had been followed by remorse, because both David Lewis and Hal Wallis recall that she was fearfully distressed by the collapse of her marriage as she began preparing for *Dark Victory* three weeks later.

No sooner had she begun the picture in October than she experienced another trauma. She had been quarreling with Wyler, who wanted her to marry him most desperately, but who was also seeing a beautiful young girl named Margaret Tallichet. One evening, when Bette returned home after a day of shooting, she found a letter from Wyler, which had been hand-delivered, on her entrance-hall table. She was too angry with him after their latest collision to open it.

A week later she finally decided to read the letter. She put it down and burst into tears. It said that unless she agreed to marry him then and there, he would wed Margaret the following Wednesday. The day she read the letter was a Wednesday. And the moment she finished it, a radio announcer stated that William Wyler and Margaret Tallichet had been married that same morning.

Bette did not return to the set for several days. She refused to see anyone. She realized that not opening the letter was the most serious mistake of her life. It is extraordinary to reflect that her next picture with Wyler was entitled . . . *The Letter*.

For those who made *Dark Victory*, Bette's absence was most infuriating. Edmund Goulding wrote to Hal Wallis on October 26, 1938:

> We were advised [from her home] that she would not appear when we were on the set in the morning, ready to shoot lineups that had been rehearsed and arranged the night before. On each occasion it has been neces-

sary to rush actors from their homes and dig into the script out of continuity . . . wait while the actors come from their homes, wait while the actors learn their parts, and on the last occasion complete a new set and install new plumbing . . .

After receiving this note, Hal Wallis sent for Bette, but she failed to appear at the meeting. He was annoyed but there was nothing he could do; and her absence remained unexplained until she called him and told him she was leaving the picture for good. He was horrified, especially since she had been interested in playing it as soon as he told her that Kay Francis had declined it—she even told people she had begged for the part for years. She explained that she was headed for a nervous breakdown and empathized with the stricken Judith Traherne so completely that she couldn't bear any more talk of disease and death. Wallis talked her back into the picture, explaining to her how to use her anguish creatively in her work. She went back on the set—very courageously indeed—and played with a nervous vulnerability and sensitivity, a sense of open, daringly expressed pain and despair that she never equaled before or since.

She and Brent and Goulding worked together very well, hampered only slightly by the cameraman, Ernest Haller, who took inordinate amounts of time arranging lights. Only occasionally, as in a quarrel scene in which she wheeled around in a doorway and threw down a muff, shouting at Brent in anger, was there evidence of overacting, and this was quickly corrected; for the rest of the movie she played with restraint and subdued realism.

In the wake of Wyler's marriage, she needed someone desperately. George Brent was the stopgap in life as he had been in the picture. He was indispensable male company and knew that Bette, still recovering from Hughes and smarting over the loss of William Wyler, needed strength, calm, and emotional security. They had an affair which lasted the length of the shooting of *Dark Victory* and a year beyond. By now she was firmly separated from Ham

145

Nelson and about to face Ham's divorcing her. She and Brent spent many evenings together at her house in Coldwater Canyon or at his home after the day's work. It was commonplace, and often privately smiled on by the studios, for stars to have brief romances with their fellow leading performers to help give conviction to the love scenes. Only the columnists had to be cautioned to silence, because Bette and Ham were still married, and in an age when blue-noses still ruled America, any hint of adultery might upset Bette's career.

However, the affair with Brent was a problem. Temperamentally, once again, they were ill-matched. She was more than ever all fire and fury and sudden unnerving switches of mood, and since this was "real" life or what passed for it in Hollywood, he did not have the saintly, static, waxen calm called for by a Casey Robinson script. He was human too: Acid and sharp, he was unable to cope with the behavior of a temperamental and nervous woman. Her tightness with money annoyed him as well. He couldn't understand how she could live so modestly. Brent did not know that Bette's mother and sister were such heavy burdens and that even though she was earning three-thousand dollars a week, it was difficult to pay out fifteen hundred dollars a month rent. And then she had to dress according to her new status, drive an expensive car, and be seen now and again in expensive restaurants and nightclubs.

If *Jezebel* propelled Bette into major stardom, then *Dark Victory* undoubtedly confirmed it. Her exquisitely modulated acting raised the picture from soap to tragedy. The number of articles devoted to Bette in fan magazines and women's slicks notably increased. Her fan mail grew so massive that her ever-loyal and devoted secretary, Bridget Price, had her time cut out answering it; Bette was frequently interviewed in the press and on the radio, expertly fielding questions about her impending divorce. In England her number of fans grew enormously and she was voted most popular actress by many magazines across the world. She had had cause to be gratified by her role of Duse of the Depression, Queen of the Warner Lot, and Rival to

Garbo; but she was still displeased by her salary, which was dwarfed by Loretta Young's and Charles Boyer's and Marlene Dietrich's and even by Ginger Rogers's. It is amazing to realize that when she played opposite Charles Boyer two years later in *All This and Heaven Too*, he was earning $12,500 a week—$9,500 more than she was.

Even while she was meeting the taxing histrionic problems of *Dark Victory*, problems that required every ounce of skill and concentration she possessed, she was under pressure to climb into hooped skirts and tight bodices for *Juarez*, her next picture, in which she played Carlota, the ill-fated empress of Mexico. Al Alleborn, assistant director to Dieterle, constantly bugged her on the set of *Dark Victory*, asking her over and over to come to wardrobe; and even when Orry-Kelly approached her personally, she declined. Clearly, she realized that her performance as Judith Traherne would be affected by any sudden assumption of an entirely different woman's wardrobe and wigs, and she wisely postponed the tests until the principal photography of *Dark Victory* was completely over.

And that end of shooting was greatly delayed because despite George Brent's supportiveness, she was ill again. Hal Wallis recalls that she was brooding about Wyler. She had walked out on the love of her life and it gnawed at her. *Juarez* had to be postponed again and again—all the way into December 1938.

A year earlier Hal Wallis and Jack Warner had concluded arrangements for buying *The Phantom Crown*, a biography of Maximilian and Carlota of Austria, and a play on the same theme by Franz Werfel. As early as 1935, Wallis had talked about the idea of making a movie about Maximilian, Carlota, and Juarez with Max Reinhardt in Salzburg. After some discussion with Luther Adler for the part of Juarez, Wallis decided to give the part to Paul Muni, who had been greatly successful in two other biographies, *The Story of Louis Pasteur* and *The Life of Emile Zola*. On October 12, 1938, when Bette was working on *Dark Victory*, Wallis offered her the part of Carlota. The part was small, but she had always begged for a chance to play character roles, and there was a bang-up Davis sequence in which she could go mad after berating Louis Napoleon for his neglect of her husband. Europe was on the brink of war, so Warners had begun to turn from subjects that would be of interest there and had begun to look for material in neighboring countries.

Paul Muni was the imperial head of the star list at Warners. Withdrawn, haughty, never a mixer, he was looked on with a mixture of awe and dislike by the crews. Very few dared address him as anything but "Mr. Muni." A note from Hal Wallis to Muni dated October 22 indicates that even the head of production did not approach this monarch with impunity: "Mike Levee has informed us of your willingness to permit us to co-star Bette Davis with you in *Juarez*. I want you to know that we appreciate very much your graciousness in acceding to this request."

Even on the first day of work, Bette's behavior was erratic. She had had several days in La Quinta to accustom herself to the script, but when she actually came onto the set of the Emperor Maximilian's study on December 13, two weeks into the production, she suddenly froze and ran out, telling Al Alleborn that she could not continue, that she did not know the scene well enough to do it sufficient justice. He begged her to work; Brian Aherne, who played Maximilian, pleaded with her, but she was adamant. For the first time in her life she told the director she would not proceed with the sequence in hand; she turned around, changed out of her starched dress, and drove home in tears.

The picture had to close down at great expense for several days. Tuesday, Wednesday, went by; she refused to work. No sooner was she back on the set than the weather turned rainy and threatening and she became more fretful and nervous than ever. By Christmas, she was yet again close to a nervous breakdown. Shooting a sequence on Christmas Eve, she slumped to the floor, announcing that her costume called for "a stunt woman, not an actress." The company looked at her dumbfounded and at last she pulled herself together.

Just after Christmas, she had sharp stabbing pains in the side of her chest, pains that were acutely aggravated by violent attacks of coughing. She thought she must be dying.

148

She rushed to the doctor, who told her she had a severe case of pleurisy. Almost everyone else on the picture had colds. She stayed in bed until 3:00 P.M. for several days and came in to play major dramatic scenes with a temperature raging over 100 degrees. When she had to do a complicated wardrobe change on the same day to play two scenes, in a Paris hotel and in a coach in Mexico, she once more collapsed—in her dressing room—and had to be taken home.

When it was time for the very big scene in which Carlota confronted Napoleon III, played by Claude Rains, in the council room of the Tuileries, she simply announced she could not come in to work. The scene was held for her for two days until at last she struggled out of bed in mid-afternoon and drove through violent rain and wind over Coldwater Canyon, in those days a perilous drive at best, all the way to Burbank, wrapped heavily in furs. It says much for her courage that she gave one of her finest dramatic performances in that particular sequence, with the rain beating savagely on the studio walls and thunder bursting overhead.

The shooting, which continued throughout the winter of 1938, proved to be heavy and boring. She had never particularly warmed to Dieterle, finding him pompous and pedantic, and devoid of the electric drive of Wyler or the subtle intelligence of Goulding.

In her memoirs Bette accused Paul Muni of adding fifty pages to enhance his own part of Juarez, but the studio records show that no such enlargement took place. In fact this is an actress's rationalization of the fact that her part from the beginning was comparatively minor. No actor, even one as powerful as Muni, could possibly order fifty extra pages of any script.

The truth is that as early as August 1937, even before The Phantom Crown had been bought, Aeneas MacKenzie, a favorite writer of Hal Wallis, had been hired to build up the part of Juarez for Muni. It is also true that Muni's performance, glowering and obsessed, dominates the film. Aside from her own and Muni's acting, it is not a very good movie; the preview was a disaster. The picture had to be recut in its entirety, whole sequences cut and trans-posed, and even after it was rendered less cumbersome, the public was understandably indifferent.

It was during the shooting of *Juarez*—not *Jezebel* or *Dark Victory*, as has so often been stated—that Bette and Ham were divorced—on December 6, 1938.

During the last year, Ham claimed in court, Bette had been "so engrossed in her profession that she had neglected and failed to perform her duties as a wife; that she had been inattentive, casual, and distant to him to the point of rudeness and embarrassment; that during their times together she had insisted on occupying herself with reading to an unnecessary degree"; and that when Ham asked her for "conjugal friendliness and affection" she had become enraged and rude and indulged in "a blatant array of epithets and derision." He went on to say that she would upset the entire household and unnerve and humiliate him.

He charged that she wouldn't go out with his friends; that, to his extreme embarrassment and humiliation, when he did bring friends to the house she would read intently in their presence, ignore them, and make them feel uncomfortable and unwelcome, and that this in effect upset those friendships and, he implied, affected his possible gain from them.

He added that she was often not present at mealtimes, vanishing without explanation, that she would not enjoy her vacation with him but rather with her mother and sister, and that after he had chosen one location for a vacation and she had agreed to go there, she suddenly departed with her sister to another. He said that she spoke embarrassingly in front of friends and business associates about the instability of her marriage, that she had said she did not want to go on living with him and asked him to leave her alone with her work and her family. Finally she had spoken to him so bitingly and caustically, her comments were so cruel, that he had left Coldwater Canyon and her life for good.

The divorce was finalized quickly, and Bette did not contest it. As she grew as a star, Bette could no longer cope with a man inferior to her professionally and intellectually. She had changed utterly; he had not.

Financially, Ham was the victor. Their property was divided down the middle. There was no real estate, stocks, or bonds. They had accounts in various banks, insurance policies, and three cars between them; not much else. Ham had only one thought: to get out of California as fast as he could. He resigned his job with a local advertising agency and obtained a position with Young and Rubicam in New York.

Bette failed to respond to the two summonses to appear to settle the matter and Ham begged the court to rush the divorce through or he would lose the New York job. The divorce was finalized on December 6, and he left at once for the eastern states.

Bette finished *Juarez* after two long drawn-out months of hard work in February 1939; the film was as solemn and turgid as she had feared. Still weak from pleurisy, she had to lie down in her dressing room between shots, and because the sound stage was so cold and damp, she feared a recurrence of the sickness and arranged for a private bathroom with tub and furnace and toilet to be installed in her dressing room. Jack Warner, ungenerous to his great star, failed to pick up the tab of $702.05, and she had to pay it out of her own purse. It was worth it to her to have this convenience, not to have to make her way to a seedy, drafty ladies' room when she felt ill.

She went to her beloved La Quinta Hotel to rest and try to repair her increasingly poor health. Hal Wallis decided to add a final scene in which she returned to visit her husband's grave and knelt before a shrine erected in his memory, a scene that disappeared from many release prints of the picture. She was slow in returning from La Quinta, begging for some grace so that she could look reasonably presentable at the Academy Awards dinner on February 15, at which she was given the Oscar for *Jezebel*. She looked fine.

Most of February was spent recovering from her influenza in La Quinta and fussing over the installation of the tub and furnace in her dressing room; when she was too exhausted to come to Hollywood for the installation arrangements Ruthie took over.

In early March, she began reading her part in her next movie, *The Old Maid*, and confronting everyone at the studio with a series of complaints about her billing in *Juarez;* she was adamant about not receiving first billing, as the picture had the title of a man's name; she claimed that the fans would think her vain for assuming such billing. Actually she was fuming over the fact that the picture really belonged to Muni.

The Old Maid was certainly a dangerous undertaking. In this soap opera of the antebellum period, based on a novel by Edith Wharton, two women spent their lives locked in a struggle over a child. Hal Wallis cast Miriam Hopkins as Bette's rival—amusing, considering that Hopkins was still convinced Bette was in love with Anatole Litvak, and hated her most intensely. The director, Edmund Goulding, wanted fireworks on the screen; and certainly he got fireworks on the set. Every day both actresses argued over their scenes with Goulding, and there was a further problem: Humphrey Bogart was cast as the romantic hero, and after two days of work he was so hopeless in a scene at a railroad station in which he left for the Civil War, looking so thin and pathetic in his uniform and so unromantic in his last wave good-bye, that Jack Warner demanded he be fired. Goulding and Wallis were forced to tell him he was dismissed. Bogart shrugged and walked off the set. At Bette's urgent recommendation, George Brent took over, despite the fact that the part was small.

All through March, Bette and Miriam indulged in a battle of champions. But Miriam did something deadly; instead of fighting Bette in the actual performance of the picture, she played her part on a note of sweetness and consideration that went entirely against the grain of her character. Bette, who wanted her to be unsympathetic, as the part called for, soon realized that Miriam was lusting for the audience to care for her. She would be vindictive and sharp in rehearsal, and then once the scenes began, she would be all marshmallow softness and easy southern charm. She also used her authentic Georgia drawl to show up Bette's less convincing, too-clipped accent. In desperation, Bette said to the writer, Casey Robinson, one day, "Throwing a cue at this woman is like throwing a tennis ball in a blanket." Whenever Bette would make such complaints, Miriam underplayed so drastically that Bette was forced to do all the work. Miriam upstaged her at every opportunity. She was being supersweet, but without the strength of sweetness; just retiring and mincing around meaninglessly.

As if this behavior were not enough, she argued over her dialogue constantly, and Robinson had to come back from a desert vacation to rewrite it. Miriam vanished off the set for days because she claimed her eyes were swollen "from a period" and she felt very low. She refused to do closeups. Bette took ill, also, and both ladies were away from the set so often the picture fell eleven days behind and ran well over schedule.

Bette was drastically concerned, that late winter and early spring, with the title of a film about Queen Elizabeth. She wrote to Jack Warner on April 28 that she was angry and frustrated because every effort to reach him through her lawyer, Oscar Cummins, had failed. She rejected *Essex and Elizabeth* and *The Knight and the Lady*, as these would place her second in the billing, and, as on *Juarez*, she would not claim first billing against the order of the title for fear her fans would think her vain. She wrote demanding, not asking, for first billing; the present title favored Errol Flynn, whom Hal Wallis had cast as Essex. She went on, "You force me to refuse the picture unless the billing is mine. If you'd be willing to discuss it with me, I'd be more than willing."

Warner was not willing. Nevertheless, at the end of April, in order to placate her, he changed the title to *The Private Lives of Elizabeth and Essex*. Robert Lord, the associate producer on the picture, was agonizing over her state of anxiety. He sent a memo to Warner (April 30, 1939) reading: "How about health insurance on Davis?

Once she starts shooting we have no work without her. If she folds up, we stop shooting. I have been studying the lady and in my opinion she is in a rather serious condition of nerves. At most she is frail and she is going into a very tough picture when she is a long way from her best."

Warner refused to pay for any such insurance, convinced that Bette was "playacting" sickness to get more money and more power. Yet the same days that he was dismissing her as a "hungry climber," he also granted her permission to have first billing and first place in the title.

During the row over *Elizabeth and Essex*—her mere week of rest after *The Old Maid*, her anger over the title, and over Flynn's casting (she wanted Laurence Olivier)— Warner secretly tested Geraldine Fitzgerald for the part of Elizabeth, and even tried to get Hal Wallis to approve the casting. Wallis utterly refused to hear of it. Only Bette could play the part, and he was right.

Bette spent many hours working out a correct makeup with Perc Westmore. She went over the clothes with Orry-Kelly, comparing them stitch by stitch, paste jewel by paste jewel, with the various royal portraits dug out of the files by the research chief, Herman Lissauer. Much of her incredibly brief "vacation" was absorbed in the work and she had to arrive even earlier than usual, about 5:30 A.M. every day, to spend two or three hours being made up and dressed and stitched into the cumbersome clothes. She blew up again when Hal Wallis rejected a costume to be used in a courtroom scene because he thought it was too elaborate. She memoed Wallis that the costume was startlingly authentic and she must have it no matter what. Wallis agreed.

Bette attacked the problems of the part with her customary vigor and enterprise. Studying the Holbein portraits, she realized that historical references to Queen Elizabeth's baldness were not exaggerated. She had her close friend Perc Westmore, the able makeup chief at Warners, shave back her hairline to the crown of her head, and she had him fashion a red wig for her, made of real hair, laced through with jewels. She even had her eyebrows shaved so that she began to look, as Westmore said, "like a terrific baby."

154

She read book after book on the queen, determining that Elizabeth's character was flinty, overbearing, and harsh. Yet she also determined that Elizabeth had tender feelings too, that she was capable of affection, even love. The script's writers took the line that Elizabeth's one abiding hunger in life was to keep England great, that this patriotism and sense of duty to the throne was the passion that devoured all others. Bette found this interpretation to her liking. And she welcomed the chance to play someone far removed from the fragile nervous women she had acted hitherto.

The chief problem with the picture was Errol Flynn as the Earl of Essex. She was not pleased with his casting, and futilely demanded his removal from the picture. He was then at the peak of his career, but he had never learned to take movies seriously; he secretly yearned to be a stage actor, playing Shakespeare in London and New York. Yet— so contradictory was his nature—he refused to provide the time and energy that would improve his acting; he thought more of his dog, his sailing, his amorous adventures, how he could force the studio to pay him more money, than he did of working on his scenes. He relied on his glamorous face and figure to get him through the picture, and Bette longed to pit her strength against a "real" actor. Someone like Olivier.

She became fretful and irritable, her scripted arguments with Essex acquiring a disturbingly realistic edge that suggested she was going beyond the point of merely acting them. Flynn's behavior—forgetting lines, yawning off camera at her when she played hers, tweaking her bottom whenever the opportunity arose, making rude gestures at her—drove her into paroxysms of fury. He laughed uproariously at her discomfort. The summer heat in those days before air conditioning proved more insufferable than ever, especially in the heavy, stifling period clothes; she paid a heavy price for her sense of accuracy—wearing layer over layer of stiff brocade; high, starched lace collars, masses of jewelry.

One trouble followed another. The first weeks were consumed in quarrels with Orry-Kelly, Curtiz, and the studio executives over flaws in her costumes. On June 20, Flynn and his wife Lili Damita were driving down a street off Sunset Boulevard when they slammed into a truck. Flynn was away from work for several days, nursing cuts and abrasions to his head, fending off reporters who were convinced the injury was caused by Mrs. Flynn's powerful blows with a champagne bottle.

Next day, Bette also took to her bed, announcing to the world at large that she had ruptured several blood vessels in her throat. She was told to rest and not to talk—a very tall order in her case. She sent a note to Hal Wallis: "I feel bad about leaving the set . . . this was one picture I wanted to do . . . I will do nothing to interfere with it." Oscar Cummins went to see her and found her coughing badly, wheezing disappointment that she had to cancel a "Lux Radio Theater" broadcast. Asked by Roy Obringer of the studio legal department whether Warners' Dr. Conn could check her over to see if she was all right, her lawyer said, "No dice. She'll know you're wanting to see if she's lying. It will annoy her terribly."

She began to lose weight—and realized as the picture went on that yet again her health was starting to fail. When Flynn bounced back on the set without a trace of his injury, bursting with vigor and vitality, she was more upset with him than ever. At one stage she threatened to box his ears. She was amazed to see him turn pale and walk quickly from her dressing room. She never found out the truth: that he had had double mastoid operations and a severe blow of her beringed hand could have deafened him or even killed him. Nor did she know that this famous male beauty was a victim of tuberculosis, who spent much of his life flat on his back in a sickbed.

Probably because of her discomfort and anger, which gave her playing too strident and coarse an edge, and because of Flynn's indifference, which made his Essex weak, soft, and self-indulgent, *The Private Lives of Elizabeth and Essex* emerged as a stiff and awkward pageant, dead under its lavish trappings and dull despite the rousing musical score of Max Steiner. Once it was over, Bette called a halt to work. She packed her bags and fled East for a long and much-needed rambling vacation in New England.

The studio begged her to start preparations for yet another picture, but she was determined that she would do nothing. She wrote to Jack Warner from New York on August 31: "After making five pictures in twelve months, with one week in between three of them, I am ordered to be on the lot. I am sure if I were in my coffin you would be finally convinced I am really exhausted and that I cannot turn them out like a machine anymore . . ." She added that she knew it would be better for Warners if she could do just that, and she said she was "truly sorry" there was such a lack in her; that some agreement would have to be reached about the future, "for your sake and mine."

She gave countless interviews in that difficult time, supplying a stream of opinions on marriage, men, and women. Her observations to a writer for *Photoplay* ran as follows:

> Men continually work and fret themselves into bad tempers over their sex resentment of Women's newfound independence in their careers. And what they don't know is the Great Fuss is in vain. Women never have, never will, never can be independent of the men they love—and be happy! All women know this. Only men are blind to it. And because it has made them so unhappy in general, this, to my mind, is the most important thing men do not know about themselves.

She added:

> *Men should boss women more!* This is particularly true of American men. Women adore feeling they are possessed, that they belong to a dominant male. As I see it, the great danger in Woman's new place in the scheme of things is not nearly so menacing to women in that they will upset the apple cart by wearing the pants—as it is that men are going to let them get

157

away with it! All men need to do is quit pouting over their lack of dominance, and begin to assert it more. The women won't mind. They'll love it.

While she welcomed women's independence, she insisted women be dominated at home, scarcely a point of view most women today would readily accept. Yet it was a point of view she retained against her own nature for years. She overlooked the fact that any man who tried to dominate and overpower her in or out of her own home would certainly not last long. One probable cause of her constant irritation and edginess was that her theories utterly failed to connect with her personal behavior.

EIGHT

At thirty-one, Bette was at the height of her career. Yet her life was still scaled-down, simple, devoid of glamour, dogged by sickness, exhaustion, and depression. With two Oscars behind her, an extraordinary number of flattering reviews that called her the greatest actress on the screen, countless fan magazine articles, the adulation of millions of people, she was, in this period just before the outbreak of World War II, obsessed with the problems of the future. How, her letters to Jack Warner repeat over and over again, could she maintain her standards? How could she continue to work at a frantic pace and still give good performances? How—in brief—could she live? Her career had affected her personal happiness: Her intelligence, her stabbing speech, her streams of opinions upon everything, her sharp temper, her electric bursts of humor, her chain-smoking, her feverish movements around rooms, her compulsion to dig into the heart of a character to expose herself nakedly in her playing, her exhilaration followed by depression and exhaustion, all wore out her men, who were conditioned to dealing with subservient sexpots. Hers was the tragedy of a woman whose vivid intelligence and aggression prevented her from achieving fulfillment in a relationship.

Her life, even in a period of convalescence, was not devoid of pleasure. Back in her beloved New England after *Elizabeth and Essex*, she was able to throw herself into leisure almost as wholeheartedly as she threw herself into her work. She strode briskly down country roads with her dogs, she dug into clam and lobster dishes, she sat by night fires and told Hollywood anecdotes to friends with loud bursts of raucous laughter, she picked flowers and thrust them expertly into vases, she drove about in unpretentious automobiles, took in neighborhood movies and plays, and roamed the countryside taking up or dropping off acquaintances. It was good to be back in the real world after the airless sound stages and klieg-glare sunlight of Hollywood.

While she wandered about on a free and pleasurable ramble through several New England states, Jack Warner was doggedly determined to have her back. He flew to New York, checked into the Waldorf Towers, and wrote or called her at various addresses trying to locate her. His visit was a secret; the public mustn't find out that this all-powerful studio chief had so humiliated himself he would chase after a reluctant star. But that, in fact, is what he did.

He was anxious to have Bette appear in 'Til We Meet Again, a remake of the famous old weepie One-Way Passage, in which Kay Francis and William Powell had previously starred. It was the story of a woman stricken with a terminal illness who takes a last pleasure cruise and falls in love with a condemned criminal, not knowing that his life is also doomed. Bette was not drawn to the subject; the experience of making Dark Victory remained a harrowing memory; the script was dumb and sentimental; and she was discouraging to Jack Warner when he called her from the Waldorf about it.

Oscar Cummins was in New York and Jack Warner at first considered going with Cummins to see Bette. But he finally decided it would be more flattering and appropriate to make the journey alone.

Warner cabled Hal Wallis in Hollywood that he was making arrangements to see "our young lady" and that Vivien Leigh was not to be offered 'Til We Meet Again until the Davis matter was resolved. Then somebody at Warners made the mistake of announcing that George Brent and Vivien Leigh would co-star in 'Til We Meet Again. Bette saw the item in the paper. She sent a telegram to Warner saying that it was clear he had no problem replacing her in *'Til We Meet Again;* she was shocked to learn that her business managers, Vernon and C. J. Wood, had been barred from the Warner lot; that all this proved that Warner had no interest in coming to terms with her; that if this was the case she would like to know, as she wanted to make plans for the winter.

Jack Warner took this latest storm with weathered assurance. He simply proceeded to make arrangements to drive out to see Bette on Sunday, October 22, 1939. She decided not to have him up to Peckett's Inn, Franconia, New Hampshire, where she was then staying, probably because their meeting would be widely commented on locally and picked up by the press. He and she were still determined to keep their discussion a secret, and in one telegram to Hollywood, Jack Warner opened with a warning that sounded like an instruction to a plumber: THERE MUST BE NO LEAK.

Instead, the summit meeting was to be at the Ogden Farm, a magnificently luxurious place in New Hampshire owned by a metal-parts manufacturer. It was a reconstructed Dutch farmhouse, with elaborate guest quarters where the barn had been, pegged floors, and an office in a converted stable. The farm was a difficult place to find, and Bette called Warner with instructions which still, in Jack Warner's scrawling penciled hand, are to be found in the studio files. Warner drove down dirt roads with elms forming canopies overhead, in exquisite fall weather, unobserved by the press, to talk for hours with his hip-swinging, uptight, cigarette-puffing, far-from-happy star.

This was unheard of: the head of a studio making a lengthy and difficult journey to persuade a major actress to appear in a soap opera remake. Unheard of and a failure —because for all his charm, Warner failed to persuade Bette to make *'Til We Meet Again*. However, he did succeed in calming her to the point where she agreed to come back to work at Christmas, after what amounted to a five-month leave. They discussed several properties. She expressed a preference for Maugham's *Up at a Villa* or an obscure property called *That Woman Brown*. She agreed also to do *Anna Christie* with James Cagney if the right

161

script would be written; it was thrilling for her to think she might challenge Garbo, who had made such a hit in the same part at the outset of the talkie period. If none of these projects worked out, she agreed to consider Rachel Field's currently successful *All This and Heaven Too*, about a governess caught up in a French murder case. Oddly enough, the film's producer, David Lewis, had been trying unsuccessfully to persuade Garbo to play the part of the governess for over a year.

In those weeks of rest and recuperation, Bette became strongly attracted to the young, tweed-jacketed airman and aircraft engineer who worked part-time as a night manager at Peckett's Inn. His name was Arthur Farnsworth. He came from a good, bedrock New England family, with a mother as stern and formidable as Gladys Cooper in *Now, Voyager*. He had very broad shoulders, a powerful chest, a short neck, with an old-fashioned all-American style of good looks. He wore sturdy leather, denims, brogues; he was like a figure in a Norman Rockwell illustration. He had a clipped, well-educated voice, perfect manners, and he would inherit money one day. He was a flier, who had had a crackup he never talked about, and had developed a condition similar to epilepsy, caused by a slight injury to the brain. Bette, attracted to beefy, broad, outdoorsy men's men, found him virtually irresistible. Like Ham, he was musical. Also, he was deeply and genuinely fond of Bette; there wasn't the feeling that he was desperately struggling to make it in show business. He *had* to be New England to qualify as a husband; this decent, not too overbearing, kindly man was a buffer against life as well. But the problem was that he was essentially a nothing; he couldn't match Bette in career, money, or temperament.

Once again, she was faced with the poignance of her problem: a longing to have a man as an equal—a mate, a chum; and the painful knowledge that only a man whose achievements matched hers in some other field—a banker, a business chief, a politician—could team up with her, take her on as combatant and lover. And again, there was the feeling that any prominent and powerful figure of commerce or politics wouldn't want a Bette Davis for a wife. He would want someone bland, supportive, careerless: a hostess for his friends, an ornament of the country club, a face in a family photograph. She plunged into the affair with Farney with all of the recklessness and optimism that marked her affairs on screen. She was as desperate for personal happiness as any of her characters.

Stocky as Tracy, smooth as Henreid, soothing as Brent, Farney was for a time the hero of her dreams. And to her delight, her closest friends, Geraldine ("Fitzie") Fitzgerald and Jane Bryan (who was soon to fall in love herself, with the attractive and wealthy Justin Dart), her sister and mother, all gave Farney the stamp of approval, overlooking his streak of valetlike parasitism. There was rejoicing in the Davis camp that summer. She and Farney could enjoy the life of New Hampshire together: they reveled in harness races, country walks, cookouts, picnics, riding on bridle trails. Passionately addicted though she was to her career, Bette was happier in this rural life than in any other.

Under Farney's slavish care, she at last grew stronger and put on a few much-needed pounds. She began to laugh again: that deep, contagious, loud laugh that seemed to start at her feet and rise like a gush of water through her being until it exploded into the room. She read endless books and magazines, chain-smoking defiantly. She was starting to live again.

It was in those weeks that Bette found Butternut—a broken-down house at Littleton, near Franconia, at Sugar Hill. The roof was almost off, the walls falling apart; but she saw at once it could be an enchanted place. Knowing how slow the local workers were, and how costly, how could she possibly afford the time and money to rebuild Butternut, to make it the house of her dreams?

She took a bold step; she contacted a chief carpenter at Warners, who bootlegged work between jobs on a nonunion basis, and flew him with a team of five studio men to New Hampshire. Thus, Butternut became a kind of movie set for her to live in, in real life; it was put together with amazing skill, economy, and expertise by the very people

163

who created the dream world of her movies. The results were entirely charming, and Farney helped her furnish the house and take care of it. Butternut bound them closely together.

Bette enjoyed the pleasure Butternut brought her: the rich smell of a barn full of hay; joining in the local choir for hymn-singing; finding antiques in out-of-the-way places, and cutting the pages of finely bound books on winter mornings; seeing snow swirl around Butternut while she was safe and snug inside with friends or Farney; going for sleigh rides; listening to the New York Philharmonic broadcasts on a Sunday; and receiving *The New York Times* on her doorstep every morning (the *Los Angeles Times* could never be a substitute for that). Life at Butternut was informal, but she made the house beautiful with her perfect New England housekeeping. She pressed and laid out her linen; she always bought dozens of handkerchiefs at a time, especially lace ones; and the beds were aired, the sheets and blankets shaken, the pillows plumped, with joyful expertise. She loved the ease, the relaxation of Butternut, far from the pressures of the sound stages. Photographs show her, sporty in riding breeches or slacks, striding down the long path that led to Butternut, attacking the problems of gardening or making preserves, smoking and laughing and running to greet the mailman with all of the electricity she brought to her major roles on the screen.

One of the few problems in that time occurred when Oscar Cummins, whom she had fired as her lawyer, arrived one night at Peckett's Inn without warning, insisting on being paid the $69,500 he said she owed him. Alerted by Farney, she ducked out the back door—and Cummins went home and sued her. The case was settled out of court. She had no lawyer now, but at least she was investing in property. Aside from the many rolling acres of New Hampshire, her business managers bought a house in Glendale near Los Angeles to come back to: the romantically beautiful, Grimm's fairy-tale house known as Riverbottom, on Rancho Drive. Perfect to this day, with trees growing wildly in the garden, Riverbottom stands very close to the still unspoiled greenery and bridle trails and oak trees of Griffith Park. It was peaceful there then, the quiet disturbed only by the gentle clop-clop of hooves, the murmuring voices of riders, wings of birds brushing through leaves, the gentle movement of a stream.

Riverbottom had been built by hand by its original owner Earl Callam; he had bought scorched tile for the roof and tiled it himself; he had fashioned bold timber beams for the open-beamed ceilings of the living room; he had a great fireplace and a wonderful sense of space. Bette returned happily to preoccupy herself with furnishing the house, using many of her beloved New England things. And soon she finished Butternut on her New Hampshire property. It was very similar to the Ogden House, reconstituted Dutch in mood, with pegged floors and lofty ceilings and a hurricane cellar because it was in the hurricane district. Like Ogden, it had richly planted paths, elms that met overhead, a feeling of comfort and ease rather than ostentatious luxury. Bobby and Bette's mother fell in love with both houses at once, and for years Riverbottom and Butternut became Bette's havens against the world.

At the beginning of 1940, Bette arrived at Warners ready for work. But she had a kind of relapse as soon as she moved into Riverbottom and completed the task of furnishing it in a New England mode; she had the next picture postponed until February, wresting a promise that she would be able to travel to Honolulu right afterward.

The movie ideas for *That Woman Brown* and *Anna Christie* had failed to gel. So *All This and Heaven Too* was chosen for Bette's "comeback," despite her misgivings about another period drama. The novel was overdone but had an interesting plot, based on an episode that had actually taken place in Paris. Henriette Déluzy-Desportes was a governess (related to an ancestor of the novel's author) attached to the family of the Duc de Praslin in Paris in the 1840s. When the duke murdered his wife, this innocent, mousy little woman became caught up in a major political and social scandal.

David Lewis, the producer, recalls that Bette was totally uninterested in the part of Henriette Déluzy-Desportes; she wanted instead to play the part of the vicious and sullen Duchesse de Praslin. She had a theory that the Duchess should be slatternly and unpleasant, whereas in historical fact the Duchess was immensely rich and distinguished and of a refined if somewhat neurotic character. She asked Lewis confidentially, "If I didn't play Henriette, whom would you have do the part?" and he replied, "Garbo." "That would be divine!" she exclaimed happily. But there was a problem: Lewis had recently asked Garbo to appear in a version of Evelyn Eaton's trashy novel *Quietly, My Captain Waits*, and Garbo's friend, Salka Viertel, had conveyed the news. Garbo had rejected the part because it involved acting with a child, and now the same difficulty arose over *All This and Heaven Too:* The part called for her to be the governess to four children and she hated them. "That horrible monster Freddie Bartholomew!" Garbo said to Lewis. "How boring he was in *Anna Karenina*! How I hated acting with him! No! No! I will never work with children again!" And Garbo was superstitious; she would never work away from MGM and from her star's dressing room. So the idea was abandoned, and Bette agreed to act as Henriette, with Barbara O'Neil as the Duchess (she played Scarlett O'Hara's mother in *Gone With the Wind*) and Charles Boyer as the Duke.

Boyer fascinated everyone. He was secretive, withdrawn, private, monastically dedicated to his art. He was small, pot-bellied, and balding; but by heroic acts of artifice he changed himself, with toupée, corset, makeup, and lifts, into a glamorous heroic figure. Bette told her stand-in, Sally Sage, she would never forget the moment when she saw him, prematurely aged, wigless, fat, for the first time; she didn't recognize him at first; she was about to order him off the set; she almost cried out with shock and astonishment when she realized who he was. He was excellent as the Duke: his pale, oval face, his heavylidded, dreamily reflective, deeply melancholy eyes, his aristocratic manner, his incredible skill in wearing clothes, especially a superb, long, black-and-silver striped robe he wore toward the end of the picture—all were ideal for the part. Barbara O'Neil, moody and sulky, made a perfect foil. She disliked Hollywood, the part, the picture, working in pictures; she was just over a relationship with Joshua Logan that had resulted in an unhappy marriage; her look of ponderous despondency was perfect, and Anatole Litvak used it well.

Bette's situation with Litvak was extremely uncomfortable. She was over her impossible relationship with him and was apparently embarrassed by it. She did not like his directorial approach, which she found solemn, heavy, and obvious.

The biggest problem arose in the trial scene, when Henriette fell to her knees and pleaded to the judge that she was innocent. Litvak told her the scene was horrible. He told her to stand up straight and face her accusers. She stormed into David Lewis's office. "That son of a bitch!" she screamed. "He won't let me play that scene the way I want!" Lewis came to the set and watched her play it both ways. There was no comparison in the warmth and passion with which she played it as she knelt, and Litvak had to give in.

Today the movie seems excessively overlong and overstuffed—too turgid and too faithful to the book; mired in the novel's stolid construction. But there are very good things in it: the children's Halloween party, not in the novel and drawn by Casey Robinson from Dumas *fils;* the schoolroom scenes in America, when Henriette cows a cruel schoolgirl who has come to bait her; the murder of the Duchess; and the big death scene, played to perfection by Boyer. Bette's performance is among her most controlled and subdued.

Her health still not fully recovered after the experiences of the previous year, fretting over the countless ways in which Litvak had frustrated her, disappointed (according to David Lewis) about not having played the Duchesse de Praslin, Bette had to wrangle to obtain a promised one month's vacation.

As part of her deal she had to rush through costume

tests for her next picture, *The Letter*, to be directed by her beloved William Wyler, in order to be free to make the voyage to Hawaii. Farney was back East, their romantic interest in each other thwarted temporarily by distance.

She had a pleasant stay in the islands and on the voyage back became friendly with a nice Warners publicity man, Bob Taphinger, whose name was linked to hers romantically in gossip columns for several months thereafter. But she was very preoccupied with Farney—and soon she would be engaged to him.

Refreshed by the sun and surf of Hawaii and the leisurely, week-long sea voyage each way, Bette was healthier and stronger than she had been in years when she attacked the part of Leslie Crosbie in Somerset Maugham's *The Letter* that spring of 1940. It was a marvelous crocodile's feast of a role about a planter's adulterous wife in Malaya who shoots her lover, stands trial, and forces her lawyer to deceive the jury in order to escape the hangman. Jeanne Eagels had made a great success in the part in an early talkie, and Katharine Cornell in New York and Gladys Cooper in London had also made vivid impressions. Bette had been fascinated by Jeanne Eagels since girlhood; it was flattering and exciting to be creating a new interpretation of a murderess.

It was a daring theme for the time—a killer as a protagonist who does not even try to elicit the audience's sympathy—and few actresses would have dared to play such a part. They feared identification more than anything else, but Bette, bold, fierce, and at the height of her career, was enthralled by the chance.

Together with Howard Koch, the writer, Wyler worked out an ingenious idea based on an idea of Maugham's, to illustrate the character of the killer, Leslie Crosbie. He would have Mrs. Crosbie work away grimly at a lace shawl, stitching it piece by tiny piece as a symbol of her complex pattern of deceit. She would apply the needle to the small, white, oval parts of the whole with a fanatical concentration not altered even by the tension of waiting for the verdict. Everyone applauded the idea: Bette herself liked to do needlework in real life to keep her hands controlled, her nerves steady; Wyler, as her former lover, knew this better than anyone, and here gave it a brilliant melodramatic application.

Koch worked out another device for her, enhanced by Tony Gaudio's lacquered photography. She would be obsessed by the moon; it would seem to control her fate. She would look up at it after she shot her lover on the bungalow steps; she would look up at it again when after her acquittal she walked to her death in the tropical garden. When a knife was left by her intending killers on the rattan floor of her room, she would again glance up, the white intense light shining in her eyes.

The two devices, the lace and the moon, give the movie a poetic intensity that raises it above the level of melodrama, and the picture contains perhaps Davis's finest performance on the screen. Her interpretation most intriguingly differs from Jeanne Eagels's; whereas Eagels had been brilliantly fluttery, nervous, insecure, Bette is cold and implacable. Eagels played the scene in which she learns she may be hanged with a hand clutching her throat, as though she were already anticpating the hangman's noose. Bette becomes more and more taut, until at last her will suddenly gives out and she falls fainting to the floor.

After the hard but rewarding experience of making *The Letter* was over, Bette gratefully returned to Butternut for a brief vacation. Often she was alone there, or accompanied only by her beloved maid, Dell Pfeiffer. Farney was there whenever he could be. Now that war had broken out in Europe he was, because of his considerable experience in aeronautics, being asked to take part in some very secret investigations into aircraft construction, and soon he would go to Minneapolis, to the important Honeywell plant.

Their relationship developed easily and comfortably. Because Farney had a good family and a little money of his own, there were few of the miserable imbalances of Bette's relationship with Ham. The couple planned to be married at the New Year. They were happy working on the house together, the house that would be their home for a time.

Back to the grindstone at Burbank, Bette found herself saddled with a wretched picture she had accepted in a weak moment—*The Great Lie*. It was the story of two women: Sandra, a famous pianist, and Maggie, an ordinary middle-class housewife. The hero, with whom both women are in love, is a flier of the Farney mold, and even more oddly, he is involved in important work in aeronautics. Amusingly, too, he was played by Bette's previous flame, George Brent. The story is an absurdity: Sandra marries the flier in a hurry, becomes pregnant, and no longer wants the baby. But she is too selfish to part with it to Maggie, who wants to have her flier's child. Finally, Maggie gives Sandra a life income so that she can have the baby in return. Soap opera had seldom been sudsier, or situations more improbable.

Casting Sandra, the pianist, proved to be a major headache. Miriam Hopkins, who might have been used, was not even considered; nobody could face her tantrums anymore. Anna Sten, a fine actress in European films who had been ruined by Goldwyn, was offered the part, but the executives were unhappy with her test. Sylvia Sidney was also tested, then Mary Astor, then Muriel Angelus and Katherine Locke.

Bette never liked to look at her own rushes, hating virtually everything about herself except her hair, but she did enjoy seeing these tests and giving her opinions loudly and clearly to anyone who would listen. She was shocked that Mary Astor, who was by far the most striking of the contestants, had simply been passed over, and demanded that Hal Wallis and Jack Warner arrange another test, this time with Mary banging away at a piano. Mary, with her dark hair, mysterious dark eyes, delicate features, and look of infinite melancholy, would undoubtedly bring glamour and allure to an intolerably ill-written role. She would be a worthy contestant: Bette loved playing against powerful actresses who worked hard at trying to outmatch her in scenes.

The executives hung fire, and Bette was furious. She had to start the picture without the part of Sandra firmly cast. Edmund Goulding was to direct, which was nice; but he was edgy, and there were many quarrels. Bette got a sore throat from shouting at him and grumbling loudly over the lines. Because of her laryngitis the picture was closed down—on November 6 and 7, 1940. When Bette returned, she insisted that Goulding, the producer Henry Blanke, and the writer Lenore Coffee come in and produce words she could speak and situations she could play.

Mary Astor walked into the midst of this highly charged situation. She was cast on November 8—on Bette's further and angrier insistence. Bette was so irritable at the delays and problems she sat in her chair on the sidelines smoking furiously, with one leg tucked under her and the other swinging dangerously, when Astor walked onto the set for the first time. But they were friends at once.

Bette's unselfishness toward other actors was always one of her most attractive features. She had befriended Geraldine Fitzgerald on *Dark Victory*, when Geraldine wrongly feared that Bette would upstage her, force her into corners; and now she eased Mary Astor's insecurity, lulling her, telling her they must work together to improve the story. Lenore Coffee was on the set day after day reworking scenes with Bette to enhance the conflict between the two women in the story, to shear away the laughable triangle stuff that threatened to sink it at the outset.

Bette was responsible for the simple, close-cut, short bob—almost masculine and very daring for the time—that Mary wore in the picture. The style instantly became a fashion. Despite differences between them, Bette again found Goulding a delight. His bisexuality was a constant cause of ribbing, as he first played out Bette's part—all swinging hips and clipped nervous speeches and sudden highfalutin "Hepburn" imitations—and then Mary's—all somber stares and glares and murky exhausted side glances and a look of having been at several successive funerals. Bette and Mary broke up at these witty mimicries.

In a scene in which Mary had a baby in a remote desert cabin, Astor recalls, "Bette insisted on striding up and down outside the room in riding breeches in an imitation of 'waiting for the baby' that had us all in stitches." There is a scene in which Mary asks for a brandy (Goulding summed up her part as "a piano, brandy, and men"). Bette tells her, "The doctor says you can have *an ounce*." After a hasty conference, Bette, Mary, and Lenore Coffee came up with the line, "Whoever heard of an *ounce* of brandy!" Everyone laughed and Edmund Goulding said, "Why don't you two gals take over the studio. And Coffee, how about another brandy?"

There were uncomfortable problems on the picture. Because Mary had come onto the set so late, the entire schedule had to be redrawn from top to bottom. The baby that was supposed to be Mary's was ill for much of the shooting, and then a nurse dropped the child and injured him so badly he had to be replaced. There was a major lawsuit over this. Mary was having trouble with her husband and insisted he accompany her on location to Victorville in the desert where the childbirth scene was to be shot. No sooner had she secured permission than he refused to go. Bette again suffered from a charley horse and had to cut down work. George Brent and Mary were ill for so many days that the picture had to be shut down. The desert dust and glare again played havoc with Bette's eyes and throat. Sometimes scenes were so bad that, when the front office refused to tolerate rewrites, Bette, Mary, and Goulding would make two versions: the original scene and the revised one, and show both to Hal Wallis, who acted as judge.

As Christmas approached, everyone was heartily sick of *The Great Lie*. Even in its rewritten form it was 100 percent soap: just a series of quarrels and financial arrangements, partings and reunions, without a grain of realism. Bette virtually played herself: her healthier, more vibrant, outgoing self, not the nervous, vulnerable, breakdown-prone self hidden from the public. Mary didn't steal the picture; Bette gave it to her on a silver platter. It wasn't worth having, but Mary won an Oscar for it.

Bette was determined to finish by Christmas Eve. Goulding was slow, but, in the words of the assistant director, Al Alleborn, "Miss Davis insisted we must finish before the holidays. She was determined the crew would enjoy the season with their families, and that she and Brent and Astor would too. She literally pulled the whole troupe with her so we could have a great Christmas. She was the trouper of all time."

In a break following a particularly overwrought dramatic scene in the picture, Bette received a comedy script from Hal Wallis entitled *The Bride Came C.O.D.* She laughed at the title; she and Farney, who was visiting from the East, would surely be married right after the holidays. She said she would love to make the picture, without seriously considering its essential stupidity.

She had managed, with remarkable skill, to keep her marriage a secret from the press. She announced it only on December 30, when most newspapers were operating on minimum staffs for the holidays and when photographers were at a premium. She even failed to advise the studio publicity department, which infuriated several flacks who had hoped to capitalize on the wedding to publicize *The Bride Came C.O.D.*

She decided to hold the ceremony on New Year's Eve at the home of her beloved Jane Bryan and Justin Dart in Arizona. A Methodist minister was chosen because of Farney's faith: the Reverend Price, of Clarksburg. Bette chose white for her wedding gown: a jersey evening dress with long sleeves, decorated with lilies of the valley. Bobby's husband Robert Pelgram was best man and Jane Dart was matron of honor. Among those present were Ruthie and Bobby, Bette's cousin John Favor, and makeup man Perc Westmore and his girl friend and later wife, Bette's favorite hairdresser Margaret Donovan. The marriage took place in the magnificent living room of the Spanish-style ranch house in the fifteen-thousand-acre tract. It was Farney's second marriage; he had formerly been married to a woman flier who had joined him in several flights.

It was an extremely joyous occasion. The Darts were certainly Bette's closest friends, and she would not have tolerated the absence of Westmore, to whom she felt she owed everything for making her "beautiful" on the world's screens. She was delighted to see Farney's parents and sisters once more. The honeymoon, however, was extremely brief. Bette had to report for work at the studio almost immediately.

Perhaps because of the excitement of her second and

more promising marriage, Bette almost immediately lost enthusiasm for *The Bride Came C.O.D.* On January 7, 1941, Al Alleborn, assistant director on the picture, called her and asked her when she would be coming in for her wardrobe tests. This was a mistake; because of the rushed schedule, Hal Wallis had ordered Bette not to have a special wardrobe made for the picture, but instead, and astonishingly, to buy all her clothes for the picture at I. Magnin's store. Therefore, Alleborn's call was distinctly misjudged. She snapped testily: "I've already gotten my wardrobe from some store or other. I won't have to test, thank God."

Alleborn stammered, "There seems to be some question about your wardrobe."

"There is no question!" she shouted and hung up.

Alleborn took a deep breath, counted up to ten, and called her back. He said, "We're leaving for Death Valley on Sunday."

"Oh, my *God*!" she replied and hung up again.

Leave for Death Valley she did. After the long and complicated journey back from Arizona, it was not pleasing to have to leave her husband and set off again. Even in January, the heat in Death Valley was well over 100 degrees in the daytime and dropped alarmingly to chilly conditions at night. A consolation was that the cocky, high-strung, aggressively humorous James Cagney was her co-star. They both despised the script and laughed nightly over the crazy lines and situations.

One afternoon, the script included a sequence in which an airplane piloted by Cagney made a forced landing, with its tail in the air. Bette was supposed to open a door and jump into a sandhill. She obeyed, when the director William Keighley shouted a command, only to plunge into a cactus patch. According to the Warner's publicity department, she screamed and was carried off in agony, bristling with forty-five spines in her rear, to a local hotel where a doctor painfully removed the spines one by one. Recovering bravely, she picked up a new page for the script for the following day. It announced that she was to receive a sling-

174

shot in her behind, aimed by Cagney. The scene was post-poned—and her fall in the cactus patch included in the picture. A photograph was run in the press, leading many to suspect that the entire episode was invented for publicity purposes. The caption read: "Forty-five point landing; fundamentally speaking, a patch of cactus is no bed of roses."

The picture was as nonsensical as Bette had feared. Yet it contained some sequences in which her little-known flair for comedy was agreeably exploited.

After *The Bride Came C.O.D.* ground tiresomely to its conclusion, Bette was confronted with a very different project. William Wyler had been pestering her to make a screen version of Lillian Hellman's savage play about greed and cruelty in the Deep South, *The Little Foxes*. Wyler was convinced she would be ideal in the part of Regina Giddens, a former southern belle warped by frustration and repression into becoming a monster obsessed by money.

Tallulah Bankhead had been very successful as Regina on the stage. She had played the part with great boldness, warmth, and authority, forcing the audience to sympathize with her as a woman in a world of men, making them understand why she had been turned into a demoniacal force by the contempt with which her corrupt macho brothers had treated her. Bette, very much against her own judgment, yielded to Wyler when he insisted she see Miss Bankhead in the play. It was a mistake. She was so over-awed by Tallulah's performance that she overcompensated by working out a completely different interpretation of the part. Once Wyler talked her into playing Regina, she decided to emphasize the coldness, the calculation of the character. Instead of Tallulah's sexuality, her full-blown thwarted voluptuousness, Bette decided to portray a woman whose sexuality had been destroyed by competition with men. She had grown frigid, so that when she made up her face to greet her husband and try to seduce him into following the purpose of her will, she simply produced a death mask of white powder. With the aid of Perc Westmore, Bette worked out her own makeup, an icy resistant appearance that suggested the sterility of Regina's spirit but at the same time greatly reduced the range of the actress's expression.

No sooner had Bette reluctantly yielded to pressure to play the part than Jack Warner refused to loan her to Sam Goldwyn, who owned the rights. It seemed that Tallulah might be hired after all when suddenly Goldwyn decided to use Miriam Hopkins. Miss Hopkins was gleeful that she would replace her hated rival in so important a vehicle, and indeed she would probably have been brilliant in a part that was very close to her own character. Wyler refused to proceed with her and Goldwyn was forced to try to make a deal with Warners.

He had a stroke of luck. Jack Warner and Hal Wallis ran into casting problems on the picture *Sergeant York,* a story of the World War I hero, and they needed an actor immediately for the title role. Gary Cooper was the perfect choice. They had to have him. Goldwyn was eager for the money that a loan-out of Cooper would bring. He traded: Cooper for Davis. Bette was freed at a price of $150,000 to Jack Warner while still paid her usual $3,000 a week for twelve weeks. Thus, Warner made a profit of $114,000 on the deal.

Bette was annoyed about this, but soon other problems consumed her. Farney, so soon after their marriage, had to return to Minneapolis for secret work on planes, and the separation was extremely painful to her. She was lonely and desperately needed affection from Wyler at the time. Sally Sage, her stand-in, says she even sought a resumption of her earlier romance with Wyler; this is unlikely, since she was friendly with Wyler and his wife Margaret, and she was, at the least, fond of Farney. She did need warmth, consideration, and support at this time. But from the beginning Wyler was furious with her because she would not play the part with the warmth and womanliness he wanted.

She insisted that the house occupied by her clan, the Hubbards, was too opulent; that it should have a frayed, run-down look to indicate the family's desperate need for cash which consumed their lives. She also felt that if she exuded sexual charm, it would be incomprehensible to the viewer that there was no man in her life. In this she was entirely

176

logical but Wyler obstinately refused to see the point. Worse, Goldwyn changed his mind from day to day over her costumes. He also kept shifting her hairstyles and makeup from one day to another. This indecision very nearly drove her mad. The cold rage with which she played the part extended into her behavior off the set.

Much as she had criticized Warners, she hated being away from "home," from her own studio. Both Wyler and Goldwyn criticized her appearance: they hated the almost "Japanese" quality of her white makeup. A big explosion came just before the big scene in which Regina, seated in the foreground, lets her husband suffer a heart attack on a staircase by failing to bring him a medicine bottle. Bette pointed out that if the audience was sympathetic to Regina at this stage, then surely they would not tolerate what amounted to a form of murder. Surely this, more than anything else, proved her to be correct in her interpretation. Wyler said that he wanted a shock to the audience: by making her monstrous from the beginning Bette had provided no illuminating change in character at a moment of crisis.

The arguments went on and on, screaming match after screaming match with no resolution. Wyler, despite his dislike of the interpretation, gave Bette the full star treatment, placing her at the exact center of almost every shot, forming the cast around her in geometric patterns. He allowed her to reflect her character in her clothing, her hair tightly and forbiddingly wound up *à la concierge*, her dresses tight-fitting and corseted and made of intricate handmade lace. Nevertheless, she was not consoled. One evening, following a particularly bad argument, she literally ran from Wyler's office. She had scarcely slept for the past week, and, her nerves tight, drove to a pharmacist who had prepared a sedative for her on a doctor's prescription. By accident, she was given household ammonia in the bottle. She swallowed the poisonous substance and was seized by wracking convulsions. She collapsed and her maid rushed her to the hospital where the application of a stomach pump just saved her life.

This horrifying episode unsettled her drastically. Wyler

continued to announce as she came on the set that a particular costume was lousy and the designer would say the opposite. She would stand there fuming while the argument raged around her, and finally joined in enthusiastically herself. The real crisis came during a big dinner party scene at the Hubbard house. She played it with a neurotic edge, whereas Wyler wanted a glow of hospitality barely concealing an inner bitterness. She could not come to grips with the part as Wyler wanted it; she could not, in the parlance of the industry, get "into" it. Wyler let the sequence play out and then said to everyone on the set, "That's the lousiest goddamn dinner scene I ever saw." He added the cruelest cut of all, "Maybe we'd better get Bankhead."

Something snapped. Bette had again reached the end of her tether. She burst into hysterical tears, and ran to her dressing room, slamming the door. For only the second time in her life, she went off a picture. To be insulted like this by the man she most admired and perhaps still loved was unbearable. She drove off to the beach for a week and the picture was shot around her while she was given sick leave.*

The studio files show that Wyler and Goldwyn seriously considered scrapping the footage and bringing in Hopkins, who was waiting gleefully in the wings, but they realized this was insanity; they had to complete the picture with Bette. They rudely tried to prove she was faking when her doctor reported she was having a nervous breakdown but failed to make the case stick. Unsmilingly, very far from feeling like a happy newlywed and desperately needing Farney, she fought her way back to work on June 7, 1941.

No sooner had she started than Hal Wallis sent her a script entitled *The Gay Sisters*. It was the story of three heiresses to a fortune whose father goes down on the *Lusitania;* most of the action was taken up with quarrels in boardrooms. She found the script dull and laden with too much talk. She wrote Wallis that she was tired of playing women older than she was; the part of the older sister seemed to be poorly written; it called for someone who had

---

* Conversation from studio minutes.

a hard and bitter quality in her acting which did not have to be assumed; she was tired of pretending to be hard and bitter in her late thirties as she was in *Foxes;* there was "plenty of time for that later on." (She was now thirty-three.) She said, "I would be so grateful if you could give *The Gay Sisters* to someone else." Wallis did—to Barbara Stanwyck.

She proceeded miserably with *The Little Foxes.* Wyler soon began to carp yet again about her sternness and grimness in playing the scenes. She yielded to his entreaties by playing some of the sequences with a bitter laugh, an antic savage humor.

The picture turned out to be, surprisingly, a major work. Seen today, Bette's performance is quote "modern." By removing all sentiment and softness from her character, by playing it on an even note of steely effrontery, she is entirely ahead of her time and undoubtedly made the right choices in almost every scene. The warmth and charm Wyler wanted would have been wrong in the context: Hellman had written a symbolic story of American bourgeois greed, and Bette showed by inference how a desire for money in many Americans overcame a desire for sex and destroyed marital love. The reviews were mixed but she undoubtedly added to her stature by undertaking the picture. It has improved with time; its coldness and hardness now seem more acceptable than they may have seemed in a romantic and sentimental age.

NINE

After *The Little Foxes,* Bette had another breakdown; she was so depressed that she lay crying all day long; when Hal Wallis and Jack Warner tried to reach her to discuss her playing in her next picture, *The Man Who Came to Dinner,* she refused to accept their calls and simply lay on her bed, sobbing and sobbing. She longed for Farney, but he was tied up in Minneapolis. She finally did write to Wallis, thanking him for the flowers he sent, and saying, "When I cry all day long there really is something wrong," and asking him to help a friend of hers, Dwight Fiske, obtain work as a writer. She was needed for the part of Maggie, secretary to the extravagantly boorish Sheridan Whiteside, a parody of Alexander Woollcott on whom the play was based. It was the one sentimental and ill-written role in the play, yet it offered chances to act somebody brisk, nononsense, efficient, and tough—in other words, the image the public had of Bette in private, an image fostered by her own extraordinary command of her own publicity.

For the public knew nothing of the "other" Bette: of her hysteria, her shattered nerves, her outbursts of tears and fury, her sheer temperament; they knew only her alter ego from the fan magazine articles she vetted or wrote to be only a cheerful, outgoing, extroverted, warm, composed, and assured human being—like Maggie. It is therefore ironical that, just as she was considering the script for *The*

Man Who Came to Dinner, she was virtually bedridden, and crying miserably from morning to night.

And when at last she did pull herself together, when at last she began turning herself into the film's brisk cool character the public thought she was, when she forced herself to accept Monty Woolley instead of John Barrymore whom she wanted for the part of Sheridan Whiteside—one of those weird inexplicable accidents occurred that marred her life and upset everything.

She was playing with a Scottie when the dog bit her: this devoted, dog-loving president of the Tailwaggers. Bit her on the most prominent public feature: her nose. She screamed at the pain; but, adoring dogs, she did not punish the animal. She was terrified of blood poisoning, and summoned her doctor; she learned she had been saved from poisoning but might be disfigured; and that the deep and dangerous wound would take weeks to heal.

She was already involved in costume fittings for *Dinner* when this bizarre accident, as bizarre as that with the ammonia bottle, took place. Much to the distress of Jack Warner, Hal Wallis, and everyone else at the studio, she announced the picture would have to be postponed while her nose healed up. She was doubly embarrassed by the fact that she had asked for the part of Maggie, which certainly wasn't a starring role. Now she acted with characteristic bad judgment. Instead of staying in town, when at least she would have been handy for discussions, she suddenly and impetuously left for New Hampshire. She spent the entire journey on the train confined to her drawing room, petrified that somebody would see her and leak the story that she was disfigured.

She rested and recuperated at the Farnsworth farm in Vermont, and Farney got leave to visit with her from Minneapolis. Her telegrams to the studio became increasingly more bizarre, making as many references to her nose as Cyrano de Bergerac did to his in the famous play. Her nose seemed to loom larger in her life than the Statue of Liberty: now it was not as red as the day before; now the scab was about to fall off; now the swelling was down; now it would not be gross and disfiguring; now it was its small, unassuming self again; now it would be ready for church on Sunday; now she could even sniff flowers and, presumably, poke it into other people's business . . . the telegrams and letters have a surrealist black humor, an antic, frantic oddity, that make them irresistibly outlandish and comic today. And at last her world-famous proboscis did mend, and she came back to Hollywood with a large piece of adhesive tape attached to its now modest dimensions, to confront a helplessly giggling cast on her first day of work, playing her scenes with her back to the camera and snapping out her lines too acidly—beyond the demands of the script.

She was in a temper when she started *The Man Who Came to Dinner,* and the fact shows in her expert but too hard-edged and bitter playing of Maggie Cutler. Her dislike of Monty Woolley seems to go beyond the demands of the part, which calls for Maggie to show a wry, skeptical attitude toward the great man she is working for. She is skillful enough to pretend affection for the newspaperman in the story, but her "love" scenes are notably brittle and artificial. Nevertheless, she brings great style—almost too much style—to a part that could easily have proved a liability: her long swooping rushes of greeting to Reginald Gardiner (as a parody of Noel Coward) and Jimmy Durante (improbable as a version of Harpo Marx) are in themselves marvels of simulated enthusiasm.

Most of all, it is fascinating to see how she triumphs over breakdown and dog bite to give a cheerful naturalistic performance. She worked barely two weeks. She began reading the script for *In This Our Life* almost at once: she had been denied, like a naughty schoolgirl, the right to her usual vacation between pictures because she had taken leave to go to New Hampshire over her dog bite. *In This Our Life,* based on a gloomy, repetitious, and poorly written novel by Ellen Glasgow, about two sisters in conflict, was for some reason admired by her; she did not feel equally happy with the screenplay.

On October 20, she was in costume and wig fittings for *In This Our Life* when she received a telegram saying that Farney had been stricken with a severe case of pneumonia and had been rushed to a hospital in Minneapolis. She completely lost control. Refusing to wait for a scheduled flight, which would involve changing planes several times, she called Farney's best friend, the famous stunt flier Paul Mantz, and asked him if he would fly her to Minneapolis. The conversation, word for word, is in the studio files.

"Bette, I'd love to help," that tough aviator replied. Referring to the great distance to Minnesota, which was already in the grip of foul autumn weather, he added: "And my plane is only a single-motor job."

"Is that bad?" Bette screamed down the line. "What difference does it make? Doesn't it fly with one motor? What does it matter so long as it gets there?"

"It's one hell of a flight. We'd have to stop every hundred miles," Mantz replied.

She told him she would go anyway and he promised to help. But Hal Wallis and Jack Warner were adamant she must take no such risk. She immediately called Howard Hughes and asked him to give her a private TWA plane. They had scarcely spoken since that horrible night in Coldwater Canyon.

"The weather's pretty thick," he said. "I wouldn't advise the trip, Bette."

"Does that mean bad?" she asked.

"It does, Bette," he told her. "But if you want to chance it, I'll arrange a transport for you."

While she waited, chain-smoking, for Hughes to phone her back, Farney managed to get to a telephone from his sickbed and call her. His voice sounded creaky and weak, and she was unable to sleep all night. She had to laugh when he told her his doctor's name was Jay Davis. "Poor darling!" she told a friend. "He just *had* to have a doctor whose name was Davis!"

When Dr. Davis called her, she called everyone, saying "Dr. Davis says there's no fat on Farney. Is that good or bad? His white corpuscle count is up. Is that good or bad?"

Bette and her mother. At five-and-a-half months Bette was still Ruth Elizabeth Davis. (Culver Pictures)

Bette, at about age eight, with her younger sister, Bobby. (Culver Pictures)

Showing off her newly bobbed hair. (Culver Pictures)

With Donald Meek in *Broken Dishes* at the Ritz Theatre in New York City, 1929. (Culver Pictures)

Hostessing a party at the Beverly Hills Hotel, Bette greets Howard Hughes.

Bette with her first husband, Harmon "Ham" Oscar Nelson. (Culver Pictures)

Between dips on Pebble Beach, California, 1932. (Culver Pictures)

Henry Fonda was Bette's co-star in *Jezebel*, 1938. (Courtesy United Artists)

With Ronald Reagan in *Dark Victory* (Warner Bros.), 1939.

In 1939 with Errol Flynn in *The Private Lives of Elizabeth and Essex*. (Culver Pictures)

Bette as the empress Carlota in *Juarez* (Warner Bros.), 1939. Donald Crisp (left) stands next to Brian Aherne, who played Maximilian; Gilbert Roland is at Bette's left. (Courtesy United Artists)

Bette and Bobby at the Cocoanut Grove, 1940. (Culver Pictures)

At the premiere of *All This and Heaven Too* with Ruthie. (Culver Pictures)

As Henriette Déluzy-Desportes on the witness stand in *All This and Heaven Too*, 1940. (Courtesy United Artists)

The Letter (Warner Bros.), 1940.

Wedding party, December 31, 1940, of Bette and her second husband, Arthur "Farney" Farnsworth. (Culver Pictures)

With Mary Astor in *The Great Lie* (Warner Bros.), 1941.

With Harry Davenport and James Cagney in *The Bride Came C.O.D.* (Warner Bros.), 1941.

As Regina Giddens in *The Little Foxes*, 1941. (Culver Pictures)

Dennis Morgan visits the set of *In This Our Life* (Warner Bros.), 1942, to congratulate Bette on the day she was elected president of the Motion Picture Academy.

With Paul Henreid in the famous two-cigarettes scene from *Now, Voyager* (Warner Bros.), 1942.

Young Fanny with her admirers in *Mr. Skeffington,* 1944. Walter Abel on stairs; Jerome Cowan, right. (Courtesy United Artists)

November 29, 1945, at reception for Bette's wedding to third husband, William Grant Sherry. Shown here (left to right): Woodbury Palmer; Seymour Fox, the best man; "Skip," the groom's brother; Sherry; Bette; sister Bobby; Rev. Francis C. Ellis; and Sherry's mother, Marion. (Culver Pictures)

Playing identical twins in *A Stolen Life* (Warner Bros.), 1946.

A scene with Claude Rains from *Deception* (Warner Bros.), 1946.

Sherry and Bette at
daughter B.D.'s christening.
(Culver Pictures)

As Rosa Moline in *Beyond
the Forest* (Warner Bros.),
1949.

Bette, as Margo Channing, with Gary Merrill and Anne Baxter in *All About Eve* (20th Century-Fox), 1950.

Merrlll and Bette enjoy a laugh on the set of *The Virgin Queen,* 1955. (Culver Pictures)

Bette and Joan Crawford (back to camera) in *What Ever Happened to Baby Jane?* (Warner Bros.), 1962.

With B.D. and Michael in
1963. (Hedda Hopper
Collection)

With Mike Douglas on his TV show in March 1976. (Hedda
Hopper Collection)

At last Hughes fixed her up with a TWA plane just for herself. All other aircraft were grounded. She and her traveling companion, her new manager, Lester Linsk, and a friend, Elaine Byers, were half an hour late for the flight. They flew through fog and stormy weather. She was terrified the plane would crash, feeling such violent rocking that she feared she would have to sit in the middle in order to balance the plane. She constantly bugged the pilot for word on whether conditions would improve.

She and her companions landed in Kansas City and were transferred to a special Hughes-chartered clipper in which they were again the only passengers. Paul Richter, vice-president of TWA, and a close personal friend of Hughes's, piloted the plane himself. Fog was so bad that he had to make an unscheduled landing in Des Moines, Iowa. Bette paced up and down the airport lounge, her nerves in shreds after a sleepless night. At last there was a clearance. A Warners representative in Chicago called Bette and told her on orders: "Farney is well, his temperature is normal." She decided to go ahead; her instinct told her Farney was still desperately ill and she was right. She knew the studio hated her undertaking the flight with all the planes grounded and bad weather conditions all along the route.

She was barely able to endure the constant bumping, trembling, and rocking of the plane. She wondered if she would ever make it to Farney. Lester Linsk and Mrs. Byers tried to calm her. It says much for her courage and determination that despite her terror she pressed on, driven by her intense love, in an adventure that surpassed any she experienced in pictures.

The travelers arrived in Minneapolis after a two-thousand-mile flight on October 22. Bette was so exhausted and helpless with long hours of crying and nights without rest that at first Farney's Dr. Jay Davis felt she would have to go into the hospital herself. She checked into the Curtis Hotel, dodging a mob of fans in the airport and hotel lobby, and against Lester Linsk's advice insisted on going to Farney at once. He was in intensive care, still on the critical list, and she sat with him all afternoon; he was too ill to recognize her.

She feared she might lose him; and she still could not stop crying. Her fans among the nurses and personnel constantly peeked through the door to catch a glimpse of her. Dr. Davis begged them to go away. She was so pale and weak by sundown that the doctor demanded she return to the hotel and go to bed. She did—but again lay awake through much of the night.

She had been married for only ten months. Surely Farney couldn't die now: that robust, vigorous former flier? That outdoorsman and athlete, trim and strong, who loved her so tenderly?

She told Dr. Davis the next morning, "If Farney isn't better by tomorrow, I want you to find a room near him and check me into it." The doctor explained this was against hospital policy, but she insisted the policy be overridden, and indeed she did move into the room.

Meanwhile, Jack Warner bombarded her with cables callously demanding that she return at once for costume fittings on *In This Our Life*. The sheer ruthlessness of the messages in the Warner files is shocking, Bette's resolution to stick by her husband beautiful and moving.

Bette was not too pleased by the merciless pressure. The same day, she cabled Warner that she had already received three wires from him and from Taplinger; that she was sorry to be such a nuisance but still had no intention of leaving until Farney was in no danger of a relapse; that this was no vacation she was taking; that she would try to return by air, weather permitting; and why would she stay longer than necessary? She was usually, she added in conclusion, fairly honest about such things.

She sent the telegram in a state so drained of energy, so utterly exhausted, she thought she might die. Dr. Davis forbade her outright to make the entire journey to Los Angeles by plane. He demanded she have a few days' rest before flying to Chicago to join the *Santa Fe Chief* train to Los Angeles. He was worried that Farney would be upset, and would get worse, if he learned that Bette was going to

186

fly in bad weather. He cabled Jack Warner that she was still worn-out from her trip north and that the strain was so severe she might break down completely at any moment.

With her usual energy, she suddenly bounced back on October 24 and greeted Farney's mother and brother, Dan, a musician who played with the Renaissance Quintet of Ancient Instruments. She made a tour of the Honeywell plant in Minneapolis and even managed to play hostess to the press at a conference on October 26. She won them over completely with her charm. Seemingly untouched by her experience, chipper and full of fun, she gave scarcely an inkling of her condition the day before. The Minneapolis papers described her curled up with her feet beneath her in a chair, wrinkling her forehead, cupping her chin in her hands, chortling or roaring with laughter, and talking a blue streak.

It was a big performance, as good as any she had given on screen, and marred only by the fact that her hunger for a good dinner afterward was repressed because the doctor refused to allow her to eat a solid meal along with her in-laws at the Curtis Hotel dining room.

On October 27, she was pleased to find Farney sitting up in bed with some color in his cheeks. Propped up on pillows, he urged her weakly to go back to Hollywood and her new picture. He promised he would follow her soon. She insisted he come to California to recuperate. He must not risk catching pneumonia again. The work he was doing was tiring, with endless pressure and very long hours. There was much to do in California in aircraft plants, because of Roosevelt's defense plans now that war was so far advanced in Europe.

So fierce was Jack Warner's determination to have Bette get to work that she had to go straight from the *Santa Fe Chief* to the studio for makeup and clothing tests without a break. She was very thin, her eyes seemingly the only living features in a chalk-white face, her nerves more seriously stretched out than ever before. She quarreled with the producers over her hairstyle, insisting on unbecoming bangs that made her look ridiculous and caused laughs at

187

the previews, and she made Orry-Kelly redesign her clothes, defying Hal Wallis as she supervised a drastically unbecoming wardrobe.

She was unhappy about everything. She had wanted to play the good sister in the story of a corrosive clan, with Olivia De Havilland cast against type as the bad sister, but Olivia had refused to risk her public image. Hal Wallis thought it ridiculous that Bette's character should be given a man's name, Stanley; but she thought the name interesting. ("Besides," she told Wallis, "it's in the novel.") Olivia was exceptionally nervous herself; overweight, she had been ordered to lose a pound a day and was losing only half a pound—by starving herself so much she felt weak, ill, and uncomfortable. John Huston, who was directing, fell in love with Olivia, and Bette was upset with him, feeling he was taking advantage. She interfered to the annoyance of all concerned. She meant well, but the associate producer David Lewis recalls that this protectiveness caused severe friction between her and the director, which upset the whole picture from the start. Night after night Bette would visit Olivia and talk things over while Olivia soaked in a hot tub to relax her nerves.

As if she did not have enough to contend with in this difficult period, Bette rashly took on the prestigious position of president of the Academy of Motion Picture Arts and Sciences. It was a mistake. She had responded to the invitation before the crisis over Farney. Instead of canceling and backing out, she resolutely pushed ahead. But she had no time to attend to Academy business. The fret over Farney, the worry over *In This Our Life*, and her poor state of health conspired against her success in this important position. She clashed over policy with members of the board and was surprised to find a grimly conservative and rearguard atmosphere in the upper echelons. She was shocked to learn that the Academy intended canceling the annual dinners for the duration of the war and insisted that it was essential for the industry's prestige and morale that the Oscar presentations be retained. In this one point she was victorious and indeed her point was a good one. She resigned only a few weeks after she took up her position—with great relief.

On December 1, Farney arrived in Hollywood, pale and weak but over the pneumonia, and Bette insisted on going to meet his train, thereby holding up production for the day. She was ill with worry during much of the time she was waiting for him; and Olivia, torn between Bette's sisterly advice and Huston's manful pursuit, was ill, too—on some days announcing she would not begin work until after lunch. Bette constantly imitated Hepburn, leaning against a doorway and saying, exhaustedly, in a flat Hepburn voice, "All I want to do is drive, drive, drive." Then, to make matters worse, Olivia began to imitate Bette imitating Hepburn.

Once Farney was back, Bette had little sleep. She had her maid Dell Pfeiffer call twice to say she was so exhausted from insomnia she would not go to work. Six days later, news of Pearl Harbor came over the radio and again she was sleepless. Matters came to a head on December 10. Huston had to leave town on a War Department assignment. Raoul Walsh was brought in to direct a scene in which Stanley, played by Bette, goes to the house of her Uncle William, played by Charles Coburn, sees him, then gets into her car and drives off into the night. Police pick her up for speeding. The scene was supposed to be played stealthily, so that Stanley would not be seen entering her uncle's house. But Bette, disliking Walsh and in a rage with the whole picture, got out of her car, slammed the door, slammed into the house, slammed out again, got back in her car, slammed the door again—and Walsh screamed, "*Cut!*" He told her to do the scene as he wanted and she refused. She rushed home and wrote to Jack Warner that it was ridiculous to do the scene again. She also refused to do retakes of a scene in a shanty and a Baltimore apartment, citing, amusingly, the economy wave as a reason. Surely, she said, it would be a waste of money in a national emergency to do the scenes again, as she didn't know how she could possibly play them any differently. Wallis canceled the retakes but demanded she redo the scene at Uncle William's house as he wanted it. She said—reluctantly—she would. A day later she lost her voice and took to her bed, fuming inwardly, making it impossible for her to do the promised scene. The studio kept calling her house and getting Farney. She returned on Christmas Eve—when it was too late to set up the sequence.

She finally submitted to order on January 1, 1942. She was supposed not only to play the "exit and entrance" scene at Uncle William's house but a further scene in which she argued with police. She refused to play any of the lines in the manner Walsh wanted. He told his assistant he was going to walk off the picture. Wallis called up and demanded to know what was going on. There was a major row on the telephone. Finally, Bette played the scene in a compromise between her interpretation and Walsh's. Wallis suddenly decided to reshoot the Baltimore apartment sequence after all. Bette refused to do it. Wallis insisted. She just managed to stop herself from walking off. She played the scene, but in a manner Wallis found unacceptable. And when he ran the "exit and entrance" scene, she was still slamming doors as before.

Between January 8 and 10 the sequences had to be re-done yet again. Bette was at the end of her tether. So were Walsh and Wallis. Inevitably, Bette reached a new series of compromises. But she wrote the picture off in her mind and indeed gave her worst performance in what was perhaps her worst major picture and Huston's as well. Scene after scene verged on the amateurish. The preview was a disaster. Comment cards attacked Bette's hairdo and make-up and clothing. She would have been mortified—if she had cared at that stage. She thanked God there was a better picture ahead: *Now, Voyager*, from the novel by Olive Higgins Prouty.

Hal Wallis had discovered Mrs. Prouty's novel in the late summer of 1941: a soap opera in the tradition of the author's earlier *Stella Dallas,* it was a wish-fulfillment fantasy about a repressed, unhappy Bostonian girl who escapes her dragon mother through the aid of a psychiatrist, breaks her glasses, and emerges from two days of a pleasure cruise with a new face and figure and the chance of a romance with a Continental charmer. Originally the story was set partly in Europe, but because of the outbreak of war, it had to be transferred to prewar Boston, the Caribbean, and South America. The story achieved a kind of abstract quality, belonging to no particular era and dealing in a group of impossibly noble or ignoble characters who had little or no resemblance to living people. The author of the book wanted the picture to be made in rich colors, with the flashbacks shot silent, subtitled; apparently unaware that war was taking place, she wanted locations shot in Italy.

Hal Wallis felt Irene Dunne was right for the central role: the Dunne-Boyer *Love Affair* had been a hit, and the reason the picture was bought was to cash in on the current public interest in romantic fantasies set aboard luxury liners. Originally, Edmund Goulding was to have directed it; he was asked to supply his own script. But he became involved with another picture. Meanwhile, Norma Shearer expressed a warm interest; Wallis sent her a copy of the book. Charles Feldman represented her as well as Irene Dunne. He refused to convey a firm offer to Miss Dunne because he was afraid Norma would be upset, and would accuse him of playing one client against another. When Norma finally decided not to go ahead, Irene Dunne was already committed elsewhere. Wallis sent the book to Ginger Rogers, who had won an Oscar for another soap opera, *Kitty Foyle.*

Bette heard about these negotiations while vacationing in New Hampshire and flew into a rage, demanding to know why she, a Bostonian herself, had not been considered for the part. Nobody was rude enough to point out that Jack Warner did not think she could achieve a transition to great beauty from sheer ugliness; that audiences would find it impossible to accept the change. She made it clear that for Charlotte Vale, the ugly duckling in the story, to become Irene Dunne or Ginger Rogers would be laughable: Bette with her attractive plainness would be a far more likely figure. She argued the point in letters. She sent telegrams. Ginger turned the part down. Bette, busy with Roosevelt's cause, attending a mass Democratic Convention at Madison Square Garden to support her idol, and joined by Farney, who was distantly related to the Roosevelts, pressed her cause still more firmly. And finally Jack Warner, influenced by Hal Wallis, agreed.

Why was Jack Warner so adamant at first that Bette should not play in *Now, Voyager*? Because he was drastically upset by her performance in *In This Our Life* and by the audience comment cards. Bette returned, refreshed after six weeks' leave and the exhilaration of the convention, thrilled that she would play Charlotte Vale starting March 16. She was annoyed to hear that Michael Curtiz was supposed to direct after he finished the patriotic musical *Yankee Doodle Dandy*, but much to her relief he was replaced by Irving Rapper. She remembered the witty, intelligent Rapper with great pleasure from his job as dialogue director of *Kid Galahad* and *Jezebel*—and he had allowed her as a gag to play a bit part as a nurse in his movie *Shining Victory*.

Bette left New York for Chicago on March 12. She was on the train, looking forward to seeing Ethel Barrymore in *The Corn Is Green*, which she planned to make as a film. Suddenly she was stricken with agonizing stomach pains and an attack of vomiting. There was no doctor on the train and she had to suffer miserably through the night until she arrived in Chicago, where she was carried off on a stretcher to the hospital. It seemed she had eaten something in New York which had given her ptomaine poisoning.

She finally rallied, and managed to sit up in her bed and check her luggage. She was dismayed to discover that one of the pieces was missing. It was a train trunk containing a fur coat, suits, dresses, lingerie, and silk stockings, valued at a total of $3,150. She was very upset, realizing that some member of the train's staff had taken advantage of her serious condition to rob her of her possessions. She called the police, who came to see her at the hotel. In a bad mood, she attended Miss Barrymore's performance. She was electrified by it. Typically, she bounced back from sickness and gloom to high-powered enthusiasm and admiration. She rushed backstage and congratulated Miss Barrymore on her acting.

Bette was determined now that she must play in *The Corn Is Green* in pictures, but meantime there was the business of making *Now, Voyager*. Given the fact that it was nonsense, she knew she would have to play the part of Charlotte Vale as realistically as possible. She consulted with Orry-Kelly on the matter of her wardrobe, which was to show the transition from a miserable girl to an assured and attractive woman. She suggested an ugly Foulard dress with a heavy pattern for the early scenes and stylish costumes for the cruise. Orry-Kelly made the clothes timeless, with an emphasis on hats which at first shadowed Bette's face, suggesting the character's extreme shyness and only gradual change.

Another matter which concerned Bette from the outset was the casting of the part of her mother, the formidable Mrs. Vale. Irving Rapper came up with the idea of Gladys Cooper, who had played in *The Letter* in London. Bette, who had admired Cooper on Broadway, was delighted with the idea; and indeed, as the angry and pathetic matriarch, Cooper's performance provided powerful competition for Bette's own.

Shooting the picture was a slow and laborious business; it dragged on weeks over schedule. Rapper was an accomplished craftsman, but every time he wanted Davis to interpret a scene in a particular manner, he had to wheedle and cajole her like a courtier. She and Perc Westmore together worked out a makeup for the ugly duckling Boston girl that was overemphatic: the great beetling eyebrows and overstuffed figure made her laughable instead of tragic. And even though Rapper forced this preposterous disguise to be played down, it still seemed impossible, crude, in the final movie; just as the transition to good looks and a slim figure—and even the cure of an eyesight problem—seemed improbably swift; it was too much from the pages of a fairy tale.

Both Jack Warner and Hal Wallis, whose "independent" production this was, grumbled constantly over the slowness of the shooting, the excessive costs; but the results, seen in the screening room each night, were surprisingly effective. *Now, Voyager* was a camp classic, undoubtedly: well-made, polished, expert.

A tiny but potent controversy has swirled about the origin of the famous sequence in which Paul Henreid places two cigarettes in his mouth, lights them simultaneously, and passes one to Bette. Irving Rapper unhesitatingly states that he invented this particular bit of business, inspired by a similiar passage in the novel. On several public occasions, Henreid and Davis have denied Rapper's claim, stating that they cooked up the sequence together on the set while he, presumably, was out to lunch. Casey Robinson, who wrote the script, recalled including it long before the star was cast. The screenplay prepared before shooting clearly indicates that he was right, but it is possible Bette may have influenced the precise direction of the scene. It had occurred much earlier, as we know, between Ruth Chatterton and George Brent in *The Rich Are Always with Us*, when the actors performed the same gesture in a bedroom scene.

Scripts in those days were explicitly tailored for stars and Robinson included many touches that suggested Bette's New England background. Out of his long friendship with her, he drew the moment when the heroine takes from her handbag a photograph of aunts and uncles ranged before the camera in a somber Boston living room as though before a firing squad. We might as well be back in Lowell, with Bette's family similarly arranged for a wedding or a funeral. There is a waxen quality about the group, a sense of moral purpose and rectitude, that ideally reflects Bette's background. There is a good scene later on in which the heroine has to confront her relatives after she has been transformed from an ugly duckling into a swan. The same formidable figures that appeared in the group portrait now appear in person, challenging her, threatening her with ancient shibboleths and customs.

Now, Voyager provided a fantasy for millions of women during the war years: No matter how plain or badly done by a woman might be, she could, through the attention of a psychiatrist and a Continental lover in a white suit, achieve a sublime existence. But so strict were the moral codes of the era, she must not go unpunished. Because she had an affair with a married man, she must be condemned to occupy a Back Street role, forever suffering in a remote compartment of her architect lover's life while he continued to devote most of the year to a humorless and unattractive spouse. "Why ask for the moon? We have the stars!" uttered by Bette in a final transcendent moment, is supposed to keep the audience pleasantly uncomfortable as it goes home. After all, the public settled for second best in everything, so why shouldn't the figures in movie dramas?

As a dream, a shimmering fantasy, the movie still works. All the formidable resources of a major studio were brought to bear on an insubstantial plot, including the throbbing music of Max Steiner, with rich, sweet melodies that lull the audience into submission before the most rampant absurdities. But above all it is Davis's performance which sustains the work. Her atmosphere of brisk New England common sense, her uncanny ability to hold the eye, overcome many weak or soggy passages. She has a logic, energy, drive, and charm that no dialogue can defeat. By seemingly believing in the plot, the star almost makes one accept it.

Now, Voyager was perhaps Bette's most successful picture to date. A pleased Jack Warner grudgingly increased her salary to four thousand dollars a week. Girls, many of them unhappy, plain, or crippled, all of them burning with identification, wrote to her in droves.

In 1942, during the shooting of *Now, Voyager*, Bette became involved in a project designed to give entertainment to servicemen on leave or stationed in and around Los Angeles. This was the Hollywood Canteen. The inspiration for it came from John Garfield, who was determined to do something for the war effort when he was rejected for military service. He asked to have lunch with her one day in the Warner's commissary and outlined his concept: a canteen to be run by the stars. She was fascinated and delighted with the idea. When Garfield asked her to be chairwoman, she exploded with an uproarious cry of "*Yes!*" Electrified into action as only she could be, Bette began scouring Hollywood for the location. She soon discovered it and flung herself into weekends of eighteen-hour workdays to raise money and decorate the place.

She went to her agent, the tight-fisted Jules Stein, and pushed him into taking charge of the financial committee and even pouring money into it himself. Stein's wife, Doris, charming and energetic, took charge of assigning the hostesses from the ranks of leading actresses. The most prominent among these, Marlene Dietrich, gave herself vigorously to scrubbing floors, washing dishes, and cooking food. Dietrich's admiration of Davis was so intense that for years she sent her a fresh rose at regular intervals.

During the shooting of *Now, Voyager*, Hal Wallis had closed a deal with Lillian Hellman to film *Watch on the Rhine*, from her famous stage play about an expatriate German family that arrives in a typical American home. The play, a telling exposure of American isolationism, would make an ideal propaganda picture in time of war.

There was no question of Bette being offered the part of Sara Muller, the tormented wife of an underground leader and patriot. She was tied up in *Now, Voyager*, which, in view of its countless delays, would not be finished until the summer of 1942. While Miss Hellman's lover, Dashiell Hammett, began work on the screenplay at their farm in Pleasantville, New York, Wallis began casting around for a suitable actress. He offered it to Irene Dunne, who liked the material but didn't think the part important enough for her. Her agent, Charles Feldman, agreed. Wallis thought of Margaret Sullavan but she proved so uninterested she didn't even bother to return his telephone calls. Willful and mercurial, Miss Sullavan now suddenly announced she was interested, but when Wallis sent a New York representative to see her at her apartment, she wasn't at home. Wallis began to think about the British actress Edna Best, or possibly Rosemary de Camp. Meanwhile, the potential director, a friend of Lillian Hellman and Dashiell Hammett named Herman Shumlin, who had directed the play on the stage, suggested Helen Hayes. Wallis rejected the idea.

Paul Lukas was not at first considered as the patriotic Franz Muller. Charles Boyer was the first choice, but he became nervous about not having a German accent and backed out.

Finally, Hammett injured his back and work on the script was delayed to the point at which *Now, Voyager* was finished. In the last days of shooting, Wallis sent Bette Dashiell Hammett's first few pages. She accepted at once; as ardent a supporter of Roosevelt as she had ever been, fiercely patriotic and a leader of anti-Nazism, she found a deep personal attraction in the play. Lillian Hellman was delighted with the choice and came to Hollywood in May to do a final polish of the script and to confer with Hal Wallis. On Wallis's advice, she created additional scenes to build the character for the basis of a star performance; in the opening scene Bette would make a headlong run from the street into her family home and lovingly rediscover it room by room. Other scenes in which Bette was shown in Washington had to be cut because of wartime restrictions on the filming of government buildings.

As so often before, Bette was upset over her billing. She insisted she should be in second place to Paul Lukas, finally cast as her husband. She said people would think her ridiculous in assuming first position when her part was secondary. She quarreled incessantly with Wallis over this. But the publicity department was adamant that the picture could not be sold on Lukas, only on her. The flacks won the battle.

Bette had never worked with Herman Shumlin before. She was extremely superstitious. No one must whistle in her dressing room or wear green socks. If anyone spilled salt, it had to be thrown over a shoulder immediately. She was constantly touching wood. She would never walk under a ladder or open an umbrella in the house. When Shumlin walked into her dressing room for the first time, he removed his hat. She watched, paralyzed with dismay, as he placed it on the sofa she sometimes used as a bed. He never forgot her shock.

It was a forewarning. She had waived her vacation to do *Watch on the Rhine*, which started on June 15, only seven days after *Now, Voyager* finished. As a result, she was on edge, and Shumlin was lacking in the experience that would win her respect. She began arguing with him almost from the beginning. She overacted several scenes, drawing attention to herself when she was supposed to be one of an ensemble. Wallis had to send a stream of notes to Shumlin warning him to "hold Bette down" whenever the dialogue became strongly emotional in tone. Bette did not have a rapport with Lucile Watson, who played the dominating matriarch of the clan and shows a gradually eroded isolationism in the action. Miss Watson was an extreme Republican whose haughty manner and high-powered right-winged politics contrasted ironically with the part she played. Bette, a Democrat to the core, found her tiresome and made no bones about showing it.

Although stagy and heavy-handed, its political message too crudely spelled out, *Watch on the Rhine* was a valuable contribution to the war effort. Unfortunately, Bette's performance, though sincere and deeply felt, was altogether too strong for the film. Her crisp theatrical delivery and great command of action made her too dominant in scenes that called for subdued underplaying. Paul Lukas, a stolid actor who exuded little sympathy or warmth, was so clearly outacted by her that the focus of the story became blurred.

A pleasant experience of the picture was meeting Geraldine Fitzgerald again; Miss Fitzgerald played the part of the unhappy wife of a Nazi agent. She had kept in touch with Bette in the years since *Dark Victory;* they had many evenings together after the day's work.

Arthur Farnsworth was in Hollywood now, on secret war work connected with Honeywell. The marriage bumped along fairly comfortably, only occasionally interrupted by strenuous arguments. There was much to do on weekends improving Riverbottom, their lovely house in Glendale. They continued to have an intense personal affection for each other, based on shared backgrounds, interests, and friends. Justin and Jane Bryan Dart and Perc Westmore and Margaret Donovan remained their closest and dearest

198

friends. Bobby was much recovered from her years of mental disturbances and had married. Ruthie was enjoying the relaxation of relishing her daughter's enormous success. The family was closer than ever, Bette's circle deliberately restricted, her work on the Hollywood Canteen occupying her pleasurably in every moment she could spare.

This, undoubtedly, was the best period of Bette's life, perhaps the only time in which she achieved complete fulfillment and happiness on a personal and professional level. The summer of 1942 was her apex: She was thirty-four years old, she was happily married to a man she respected, she had made a huge box-office hit followed by a valuable patriotic film, she was personally involved in the war effort through the Canteen, her health was markedly improved from previous years, and her difficult contentious nature was almost serene. But it was a summer that was quickly doomed.

TEN

As early as 1940, Hal Wallis had planned to make a film of John Van Druten's stage play *Old Acquaintance*, which starred Peggy Wood and Jane Cowl on Broadway. It was the story of two girlhood friends, one ruthless and selfish, the other cheerfully down-to-earth and outgoing who, rivals from the outset, become novelists in competition. It was a thin mechanical contrivance enlivened by witty dialogue and skillful touches of characterization.

In the period just before and during the first months of America's entry to World War II, the play provided the ideal escapist entertainment. Edmund Goulding, fascinated as always by the bitchy quarrels of neurotic women, very much wanted to direct it on the screen, but right away the project seemed an impossibility. When Wallis sent it to one of his favorite producers, the German expatriate Henry Blanke, Blanke saw major problems in its thinness and poor construction. When he sent it to Joseph Breen of the Hays office, Breen rejected it outright, saying that since it showed a middle-aged woman with a young lover it would be totally unacceptable; that it displayed gross illicit sex; that it showed the heroine as having had numerous sexual affairs; that the characters were frequently drinking alcohol; and that the entire work was damaging to the image of the industry.

201

Wallis decided to go ahead, but work was very slow. He put screenwriter Lenore Coffee onto it but she was distracted by other work on *In This Our Life* and on the Errol Flynn vehicle *They Died with Their Boots On*. She had to fill out the plot with particulars of the early lives of the two women. Finally, she gave up in despair; she was unable to lick the material. Wallis brought Howard Koch, who had written the adaptation of *The Letter,* into the production, and he struggled with the script for several months, followed by a writer named Ann Frolick.

By March 1942, there was still no satisfactory screenplay. Rosalind Russell was determined to play the part of Kit, the more decent of the two female characters, and she would have been ideal for it. But she was delayed by a commitment to *My Sister Eileen,* and Hal Wallis was greatly disappointed to find that even for $150,000 for the picture she could not be released in time to begin work. Wallis then offered the part to Irene Dunne, but she couldn't make up her mind and negotiations dragged on for months.

In June, John Van Druten began working with Edmund Goulding on the script at the Hotel Pierre in New York. Basing their work on Lenore Coffee's original draft, they filled the action with many entertaining New York "in" jokes and references, and more clearly defined the contrast between the two women. Finally, Irene Dunne decided not to go ahead.

It was not until late June that Bette, last choice as usual, was added to the cast. And even then it wasn't sure whether she would play the nice, no-nonsense Kit or the ferocious self-pitying Millie. She told everyone she would be perfectly happy in either part.

In New York, the witty Goulding sent a stream of letters on Hotel Pierre stationery to the associate producer Henry Blanke beginning, "Darling Heinz." At first, the letters were filled with enthusiasm, but soon Goulding, who was British, became weighed down with the triviality of what he was doing in the face of his country's peril in time of war. He wrote to Blanke on July 23: "Alas, when you come down to it, it is a very light cream puff with no cream. And in the light of the furious things that are going on in the world, the petty quarrels of a couple of bitches seem fragile and inconsequential."

Jack Warner read the letter and said to Blanke, "The only cream puff in this matter is Eddie Goulding. Tell him to get back to the pastry kitchen and produce something that will keep the public's mind off this goddamn war."

Warner wanted Mary Astor to play Mildred, the villainess of the piece. He said to Blanke, "The Astor dame was mixed up in a scandal. If she plays the good girl we're finished at the box office." Goulding suggested Miriam Hopkins in a telegram to Warner, who responded: "Yes, a bitch she is!" Miriam was cast. Bette groaned, but agreed Hopkins would be ideal—as the bitch. While these discussions went on, she quickly appeared in a war-effort extravaganza, *Thank Your Lucky Stars,* singing "They're Either Too Young or Too Old" with great bravura and allowing herself to be thrown about in jitterbug routine—a perennial joy to her fans.

She enjoyed this brief respite but, fuming that she had been last choice for Kit, dreading Hopkins, Bette was in a very poor state of mind that summer. Suddenly, Miss Hopkins again proved difficult: She wanted an enormous amount of money to play the part, twice as much as Bette, and insisted she be allowed to supervise her own wardrobe, makeup, and hairstyles without the slightest interference from anyone. As a result, she was put on hold while everyone began looking for an alternative. Goulding and Van Druten, who had been concocting numerous vicious lines which they knew Hopkins would spit out in her inimitable way, suddenly had to pause, wondering if the entire screenplay would have to be rewritten.

Wallis offered the part of Millie to Margaret Sullavan, who declined once more even to see the studio representatives and announced that she found it insulting that she would be asked to play a bitch. Instead of saying this in private, she said it in a radio interview, which annoyed everyone intensely. Henry Blanke came up with the crazy idea of casting Janet Gaynor, the saccharine heroine of numerous romantic novelettes, and of having the authors re-write the part to resemble a kind of Billie Burke character. John Van Druten and Goulding were adamant that Gaynor's sweetness would be impossible: "I do not feel" [Van Druten wrote to Wallis] "Gaynor can play it. . . . The actress needs great physical force and strength for her out-bursts and attacks of hysterics. . . . This would be swell for Hopkins . . . This is *pure* Hopkins stuff . . ."

Jack Warner suggested Constance Bennett but at last everyone groaned, shrugged, and decided to put up with Miriam's predictable tantrums on and off the set.

A tremendous row blew up over the cameraman. In August 1942, Bette refused to tolerate any photographer except Sol Polito. She flatly refused to work with Tony Gaudio, who had shot *The Letter*. Edmund Goulding was furious. He sent a cable to Wallis from New York:

> I AM EITHER WORKING FOR WARNER BROTHERS OR MISS DAVIS AND THERE IS A DIFFERENCE. URGE YOU NOT TO COMMIT YOURSELF TO ANY PROMISE ON CAMERAMAN UNTIL AFTER TALK WITH ME. THAT WOULD PUT ME IN A POSITION OF DAVIS, HOPKINS, MOODS, FADS, AND NONSENSE.

Needless to say, Bette won: Polito, not Gaudio, photographed the picture.

The arguments dragged on. Miriam Hopkins came to Hollywood in October only to find nobody to meet her at the depot or at the hotel. No one was interested in speaking to her until it became essential. She received no invitations to dinner and sat alone in her suite in the Beverly Wilshire Hotel in a state of seemingly permanent fury, threatening to return at once to New York.

Goulding received several phone calls from her filled with violent complaints. He became so exhausted from the endless hours of work with Van Druten, often extending through the night, and from Miss Hopkins's stream of hour-long calls, that he had a heart attack the day after he arrived in Hollywood and was carried off to the Good Samaritan Hospital. The director Julien Duvivier was offered the picture but declined it, and finally Vincent Sherman was signed. Nobody, in those ruthless days of Hollywood, considered waiting until Goulding recovered. All of his long months of work were wasted, months that resulted in his almost losing his life.

Sherman was very worried about the script, even in its final draft. Work began in the rainy November of 1942. Bette was in Palm Springs with a severe throat condition when shooting began. She was uneasy, sick, about working with a new director; she was unfamiliar with Sherman's work and wasn't sure if she would get along with him. After five days she walked into the studio with her agent Jules Stein's partner, Lew Wasserman. She asked Sherman in her dressing room, "How are things going?"

"Very well," he replied.

"How is Miriam behaving?"

"Fine," he told her.

She looked amazed. Sherman asked her, "Why don't you look at the rushes?" She was delighted because she knew from looking at Sherman's work she would be able to tell how he was handling the picture. She went to the projection room and sat enthralled. Merciless with incompetence, she instantly recognized quality. Sherman had done wonders with Miriam: He had effectively used her harshness, her vicious edge, to illustrate the self-destructive nastiness of the character. Sherman came in a little uneasily to determine her reaction. Snapping her cigarette lighter open and lighting up a cigarette she said, "It's fantastic. All I want to know is, when do I report for work?"

Smiling, Sherman replied, "Nine o'clock tomorrow morning."

Bette thrust the lighter into her handbag with a brisk touch of finality. "I'll be there," she said. "You're doing wonderful things with Miriam!"

Everyone expected trouble on the set, but nobody could have foreseen the extent of it. Even though Miriam was better paid than Bette, she regarded herself as a visitor on the picture, forced to overcompensate for the fact that Bette was the reigning queen of the lot. Every time there was an over-the-shoulder shot from Miriam to Bette, Miriam would bring up a cigarette lighter across Bette's face and light a cigarette with it, blowing the smoke slowly and deliberately into Bette's eyes. Whenever Bette went into a speech that demanded Miriam's unswerving attention, Miriam would discover that one flower in a vase was set unevenly with the others and painstakingly fix it into position. On one occasion, when the scene called for Miriam to hang on every word Bette uttered, she went to a clock and reset the hands. She would drop a handkerchief and go to extensive business to retrieve it or straighten a painting on a wall or even tinkle the keys of a piano. Bette exploded again and again, and Miriam would smile sweetly saying, "But nobody was looking at me."

On January 11, 1943, Vincent Sherman blew up. Bette had been giving him extended advice on handling Miriam for several days, and in desperation he had turned to her worst enemy for consolation. "I'm going to have a showdown," he said to Miriam. "Either she directs the picture or I do. I'm not going on in this way."

Miriam's reaction was typical. She said, "Vince, don't talk it over with me. She's been riding roughshod over me from the beginning. I'm better out of it. I'm an innocent in this matter. I never did any harm to her. I don't know what she's talking about."

Miriam complained constantly that she was having fewer closeups than Bette. Sherman sent a note to her reading:

> Miriam, if I had my own mother in the film I wouldn't favor her over any other actress because I do what I think is best for the film and not what I think is best for any individual . . . There's no such thing as giving a person a closeup more often than another in a position of equal strength in the cast . . .

About halfway through the shooting, Miriam developed a habit of pretending to be suffering from an attack of temporary deafness whenever Bette spoke to her off the

206

set. She would take an elaborate hearing aid from her purse and fix it in her ear while Bette was going into a tirade and then discover to her pretended distress that it was failing to function. When Bette came at her as though about to strike one cheek, she turned the other. Every time Bette would order a "blue page" or revised passage in the script, Miriam would bring in a pink one. On one occasion, when Bette said that Miriam had played a scene like a dead person, Miriam appeared on the set in black. When Miriam played a lengthy crying scene, Bette stood on the sidelines commenting on it as though it were a horse race at Santa Anita. In revenge, Miriam gave the crew small radios, encouraging them to listen to the races the following day when Bette was playing a love scene with a younger man. She was delighted when the announcer rapidly described the neck-and-neck finish, just as Bette passionately kissed the actor.

Miriam became so nervous as she was leaving the shower one morning, she skidded on a piece of soap and fell on a steel fixture which split her ear and cracked her head. She swore absurdly that Bette had put the soap there. She lay in bed for a week, grumbling incessantly, and Bette, perhaps in competition, was also absent because of illness for a time. During the shooting, both women were absent, often on alternate days; Bette's old problem of laryngitis was flaring up.

Bette's biggest scene was one in which she learned that her lover had abandoned her and was going to marry her own daughter. She insisted Miriam be kept off the set and played the scene with great skill. But it proved impossible to get the closeup Vincent Sherman wanted of her face crumpling when she receives the news. Sherman deliberately waited until 2:00 A.M. on a Sunday morning after many hours of difficult shooting to retake the closeup. Bette was exhausted and her face was drawn and pale when he made the shot. At the preview, the producer Jesse Lasky said to Sherman, "That woman is the most remarkable actress I've ever seen in my life. She aged in one shot."

"That's not surprising," Sherman replied. "I took that last closeup three months after the rest of the scene!"

Perhaps the most famous sequence in *Old Acquaintance* was that in which Bette shook Miriam and threw her onto a couch. Everyone was waiting eagerly for this to take place. The crew knew Bette would play the scene with more commitment than she had played anything else in her career. On the big day, not only the rest of the cast and crew called for work, but also everybody possible from every office in the studio and every other picture in production jammed the sound stage to see the event of the season.

Bette had to advance across a living room, take Miriam by each shoulder, and force her down into a sitting position. Bette strode vigorously to the attack. She took Miriam's shoulders in a powerful grip. Suddenly, Miriam went completely loose, like a rag doll, so that when Bette shook her she seemed to have no bones in her body. Bette stepped back. "This is impossible," she said. "She isn't fighting me."

Sherman said, "Miriam, for God's sake struggle with her."

"But I *am* struggling!" Miriam said.

The scene began again. Bette walked, took Miriam's shoulders, and Miriam again went slack. Bette gave up. She said, "It's impossible. I can't do anything with her." Vincent told her to try again. The scene dragged on all afternoon. Finally, by clever camera-faking, something approaching an adequate sequence was shot. Bette, knowing everyone was watching, infuriated Miriam by not screaming at her directly. But when she returned home, she screamed to anyone who would listen for over an hour.

Through the entire production there was trouble over Bette's and Sherman's rewrites of the script. In one memorandum from Chuck Hansen, unit manager, to the studio manager T. C. Wright, Hansen wrote: "Considerable time is spent in rehearsing, but in my opinion there is still a lot of rewriting being done. Of course, a lot of this is Miss Davis's idea, as she is not satisfied with the dialogue. Nothing can be done about it, as they are trying to make a good picture—only it is being done the hard way."

Jack Warner cabled Sherman from New York:

SEE YOU ARE UP TO YOUR OLD TRICKS AGAIN. RECEIVED THIS MORNING 14 PAGES REWRITE ON OLD ACQUAINTANCE. WHY DON'T YOU STOP REWRITING THE SCRIPT. IT WAS DAMN GOOD WHEN YOU STARTED. YOU'RE 16 DAYS BEHIND SCHEDULE. NOW MAKE SOME OF THIS TIME UP AND GET THROUGH WITH THIS PRODUCTION.

There was further trouble in October 1943 when Bette walked past a record store and saw a copy of the song entitled "Old Acquaintance" showing her and Miriam toasting each other on the cover. She had never given permission for this and became hysterical, saying that the lyrics printed under the image suggested lesbianism.

Bette didn't stop complaining about the implication of a love relationship between her and Miriam for weeks. She was almost as annoyed when a columnist ran the following comment on the picture being thirty-six days behind schedule due to absenteeism:

Now listen, folks. This was the schedule in January:

1/5/43	Miriam ill.	1/22/43	Bette ill.
1/6/43	Miriam ill.	1/23/43	Miriam ill.
1/7/43	Miriam ill.	1/24/43	Bette ill.
1/20/43	Bette ill.	1/25/43	Miriam ill.
1/21/43	Bette ill.	1/26/43	Bette ill.

Is it any wonder, folks, that the picture didn't finish until St. Valentine's Day?

Old Acquaintance turned out to be a great popular success. Bette was ideally matched in the conflict of personalties that gave the picture the appeal of a championship boxing match. Everyone in the industry made sure they saw it. They knew so much about its making that it became one of the most talked-about movies of the year.

Bette traveled to Mexico in the early summer of 1943 with her friend, Dorothy, Contessa di Frasso; it was a combined personal appearance tour and vacation. As far as she was concerned, Dorothy, the former lover of Gary Cooper, was simply a fascinating and much-traveled sophis-

209

ticate who gave marvelous parties in Beverly Hills and Palm Springs. Bette could not possibly have known that Dorothy had traveled to Italy in 1940 with her close friend Bugsy Siegel, the gangster, to sell an explosive device to Mussolini, or that Dorothy was a paid agent of the Italian government, involved in criminal and Fascist activities.

Throughout the Mexican trip, FBI agents followed the two women; Bette, of course, was known to be a completely loyal and dedicated super-American who had worked more for the war effort than any other woman star. In the end, nothing could be proven against di Frasso and the hunt was called off. Bette remained unaware of the whole matter.

From Mexico, Bette traveled to Butternut in New Hampshire and spent the rest of the season with Farney, who was on vacation from Honeywell. One afternoon, Farney was standing at the head of the stairs when the telephone rang. Some weeks before, Farney had had a fall from a horse, caused by his earlier injury in the plane. Now, at the sound of the phone, he spun around on his heel, tripped, and fell the full length of the staircase. He cracked his head on the hard parquet floor of the entrance hall. Bette heard the fall and rushed to his side.

He began to suffer from blackouts, drowsy or dizzy spells; and at times he limped quite painfully. He swam zigzag in the pool.

Farnsworth was a silent uncomplaining man's man who thought discussion of physical problems was a sign of weakness. Bette and Farney decided he should come back to Riverbottom in Glendale, where he could rest. But no sooner had he returned with her by train than he began working very hard once more.

He continued his secret war work as liaison between local airplane production plants and Honeywell, and he also supervised the drawings of airplanes executed by Walt Disney's team of animators for the full-length cartoon *Victory Through Air Power*. He also became involved in an affair with a married woman, conducted in great secrecy because her husband was intensely jealous and suspicious.

Bette did not find out about the affair until much later.

She coexisted with Farney in a relationship that was more like that of brother and sister than husband and wife. She fed herself with the fantasy that she had at last obtained a perfect relationship.

It is an irony of Bette's life that, scarcely able to achieve more than passing contentment in her private life, she suddenly assumed the role of Miss Lonelyhearts by running an advice to the lovelorn column in *Photoplay,* the reigning fan magazine at the time. Letters poured in from young girls having trouble with their boyfriends, suffering from separations caused by the draft, struggling with hostility from parents, or trying to be actresses.

In 1939, the English novelist Mary Annette Beauchamp Russell, known professionally as "Elizabeth," published in British *Good Housekeeping* and later with Heinemann and Doubleday a book entitled *Mr. Skeffington,* suggested by the character of the American actress Fanny Ward, a selfish beauty who had settled in London just before the war. The central figure of the novel was Fanny Skeffington, a dizzy and self-centered society beauty, and the setting was the world of high society in Mayfair and Kensington and of country weekends in mansions in the south of England. Paramount had bought the property but was unable to make use of it; the fashion for British high-flown romances and melodramas had decreased. Warners obtained the rights and assigned the picture to David Lewis. Lenore Coffee wrote a first draft and it was forwarded to Jack Warner's assistant Richard Gully, a cousin of Anthony Eden and an authority on British manners. Gully pointed out that London postmen never use a whistle but knock on doors; no barrel-organ-player could afford a cigar; a maid would address Mrs. Skeffington as "M'lady," not "Your Ladyship"; a particular kind of knight of the realm would not wear a flower in his buttonhole; and "Who else would you like to have to dinner?" should be "Whom else would you like to have to dinner?" Jack Warner became impatient with these trivialities; he didn't trust anyone on his staff to deal with this pretentious material. He also felt that American audiences would become bored by all the affected social situations, and that, if it had to be done, this kind of property was best left to MGM.

As a result, in July 1941, Minna Wallis and Andy Lawlor of the Sam Jaffe Agency were authorized by Warners to find a buyer for the property. Not a single person in Hollywood was interested and in desperation Jack Warner and Hal Wallis hired the witty twins Julius J. and Philip G. Epstein to produce and write it. They settled at once on transferring the story to New York in the first part of the century leading up to the present day. Bette had rejected the part when it had originally been offered to her, feeling that whereas she had managed a special accent for *Elizabeth and Essex,* she was not able to speak in an upper-class British accent for this production. When the director, Vincent Sherman, told Bette he had a new draft script for *Mr. Skeffington,* she said, "Oh, brother! I read that turkey years ago. It was a dreary story! I hated that silly affected woman so much!"

Sherman explained that the Epsteins had given the trifling material depth and had succeeded in bringing the characters to life. Bette took the material home to Glendale, read it in an evening, and called Sherman the following morning. She said. "It's magnificent. I'm dying to do it. I'll call Jack and tell him." She telephoned Jack Warner, who was delighted she would go ahead. Production was due to begin in September 1943. Bette, for once offered a part before anyone else, flung herself into hairdress and makeup tests with enthusiasm. Her excitement was shared by Farney, Ruthie, Bobby, Margaret Donovan, and her faithful secretary of many years, Bridget Price.

On August 23, 1943, a hot and sultry Los Angeles day, Farney picked up a stole for Bette at Magnin, then drove to Hollywood to discuss the purchase of some real estate with Bette's attorney Dudley Furse. He was walking along Hollywood Boulevard past a cigar store only a few blocks from the home Bette had shared with Ham. Dave Freedman, proprietor of the store, his assistant Rosalie Day, and a customer Gilbert Wright were standing just inside the entrance discussing the war news when they heard a terrifying scream.

212

They ran out and saw Farney, who was carrying a briefcase. He fell straight backward in an odd, awkward movement, screaming again as he did so. His head struck the concrete sidewalk; he began to hemorrhage from his nose and ears. His convulsions were so violent that people came running to the scene. Somehow, in the confusion, the briefcase disappeared; Farney was also carrying a dispatch case, which was not taken. Freedman called the Hollywood Receiving Hospital, which sent an ambulance. From papers in Farney's wallet, attendants found the address and phone number of his physician, Dr. Paul Moore. Moore raced to Hollywood Receiving. He called Bette, who was at Riverbottom. She was shocked to tears. But he insisted that she remain at home, while Farney was transferred to Hollywood Presbyterian. It was the beginning of an ordeal even more severe than Farney's bout with pneumonia in Minneapolis. Farney's injury was diagnosed as a skull fracture. When Bette finally came to visit him at the hospital, he barely recognized her.

Reporters constantly besieged her for comment, and police from the Hollywood Homicide Bureau questioned her. Because Farney was on secret war work, there were implications that someone may have tried to kill him for whatever was in the briefcase. But the reports remained maddeningly inexact in the press. Every day the newspapers contradicted what they said the day before. Nobody mentioned epilepsy, a taboo subject.

Mrs. Farnsworth flew in from New York, and Bette's conversations with her were awkward and strained. Mrs. Farnsworth was harsh, unfriendly. Farney continued to hover between life and death. At last he gave up the unequal struggle. He passed away in his sleep.

The authorities were far from satisfied that the death was accidental. The autopsy report, which has since been destroyed, was disturbing. Assistant County Surgeon Homer R. Keyes told the inquest court: "A basal skull injury probably caused this man's death. It didn't result from the fall, but instigated it. Consider the blood in the fracture. It is black and coagulated, not merely purple and partially congealed as it would have been if the injury had been received as a result of the fall. The fracture must have been inflicted about fourteen days ago. Farnsworth must have been walking around with the condition fructifying until it eventually caused his death."

Dr. Keyes went on to say, and his statement was confirmed by other doctors, that the blow must have been caused by the butt of a gun or some other blunt instrument. The witnesses dismissed any suggestion that a black and coagulated mass of blood would have remained as a result of the fall at Butternut, which had long since healed; nor could Farnsworth have simply fallen some two weeks earlier in another place.

Pale and without makeup after nights without sleep, Bette remained in an anteroom while the other witnesses gave their testimony. She took the stand in an acute state of distress. She told of the accident at Butternut, but was unable to cast any light on the blow which caused the death. Then, in contradiction of the evidence, the inquest verdict was that the earlier fall had caused the seizure and subsequent death of the subject.

The funeral was as quiet as the Farnsworth family and Bette could manage. They had begged the public not to swamp them, and their request was surprisingly honored. Only a handful of people showed up for the services at the Church of the Recessional in Forest Lawn. Among those present were Jack Warner, John Garfield, Perc Westmore, Ruthie, Mrs. Farnsworth, Farney's brother Dan, and stunt-man Paul Mantz.

Bette's uncle, the Rev. Paul Favor, now living at Laguna Beach, performed the service. Bette chose the 121st and 123rd Psalms (Farney's favorites). The casket was banked with floral pieces of gladioli, dahlias, and other flowers, as it lay beneath the three stained glass windows of the church.

Bette had to travel East by train to attend the second funeral at Butternut. The occasion was a horrible experience. Mrs. Farnsworth insisted on having a wake. She forced Bette to sit all night by the open coffin, flanked by candles, in vigil with the rest of the clan. One of Farns-

214

worth's aunts became hysterical and began dragging the body out of the coffin.

Next night a team of workmen arrived to blast away solid rock and saw down trees to make room for Farney's grave on the hill. Bette tossed and turned all night at the noise. Then, when at last it seemed Farney was to be laid to his final rest, Mrs. Farnsworth decided her beloved son shouldn't be at Butternut at all but in the family vault in Vermont. She told Bette that Farney would have to be dug up again and shipped there. Once more, Bette had to listen to the drills and the blasting. But she couldn't face the third funeral. Ruthie promised to take care of everything. Ruthie had to go to Vermont and suffer the new wake and the candles and the hysterical behavior.

Bette, very depressed, was back for tests on *Mr. Skeffington* on September 21. John Loder and Paul Lukas were both tested for the part of the husband whose career as a businessman is flawed by his wife's extravagantly silly behavior. Fortunately, Claude Rains was chosen for the part. Haggard and worn by her long ordeal, Bette looked far from the beauty she should have been for the story when she reported for twenty-six changes of wardrobe tests. Her worst problem was the rubber mask which Perc Westmore made to show her drastic aging following an attack of diphtheria. The mask fitted tightly to her skin, which sweated under it and could not breathe properly.

Director Vincent Sherman told me: "There was the terrible problem of makeup for Bette. She had to get up at five o'clock in the morning in order to be on the set at nine. Perc Westmore, who was quite an artist in his field, had to put on the wrinkles layer by layer with rubber. By eight-thirty Bette was already fit to be tied. As she perspired under this rubber, her face itched. So late in the afternoon at five or six o'clock, by the time she got the rubber mask off, she wanted to dig her nails into her face. She was nervous and jumpy and uptight. I am sure that contributed a lot to some of the difficulties later. There were times when she just had to stop at five and said that she couldn't shoot any more. She said she was just going crazy with that thing on her face.

"There was one scene where she was lying in bed and her hair had fallen out. There was a furry wig she had on. It was a little on the reddish side and she was half bald. Well, when I came in and saw her that morning and looked at it—we didn't have time to test it—I was shocked. I said, 'My God, if I photograph her like that she'll look like a witch.' I told her, 'Gee, Bette, don't you think we're going a little too far with this?'

"She said, 'Don't you worry, Vince. My audience will take me in this kind of thing. They don't mind if I do this to myself.'

"I said, 'I don't know about your audience, but *I* mind it a little bit.' But she felt it was honest and real. I suppose to some extent she was right about that. Perhaps she was more right than I was, although I think I was more right in other places."

Bette would run into her dressing room again and again and beg Westmore and Margaret Donovan to get the horrible rubber mask off her before she went completely mad. She was still sick and exhausted after Farney's death. To the end of her life she would say that her relationship with him was the only perfect one in her troubled life.

Vincent Sherman said: "I used mirrors in the picture. I felt a woman as vain and self-centered as Fanny would always be looking in mirrors. I even had the art director put them downstairs. Eventually, instead of being reassured by her beauty, she becomes tortured by her looks. John Barrymore once told me he didn't count the number of speeches he had in a script. What he wanted to know was 'Who does the suffering?' For an actor that's sometimes more important than the size of the part.

"What the Epsteins were saying in this script, and what is said in the film is that 'A woman is only beautiful when she is loved.' *Mr. Skeffington* was a study of a charming, feminine woman who was self-centered, slightly superficial, but not a completely unworthy human being. One of the things that made Bette hesitate about doing the picture was that she didn't think she was a great beauty. In the normal acceptance of the work perhaps she wasn't, although I felt she looked lovely in the picture. We didn't concentrate too heavily on that so that it wouldn't cause any invalidity to the film itself."

One afternoon on the set, about three days into shooting, a very curious thing happened. A small boy asked to see Bette. It was assumed he was a fan and was told to come back some other time, but he insisted it was a matter of life and death. Bette came out to have a look. She was astounded to see him carrying Farney's briefcase. It had not been seen since the time of his death. Without explaining her interest, she invited the child into her dressing room. He told her he had picked the briefcase up from the sidewalk and confessed he had run off with it.

He opened it and showed her the contents without a word. There were numerous bottles of liquor. She was horrified. She had known Farney had been drinking heavily but she had not realized he was an alcoholic. The discovery of the bottles was never shared with anyone. She kept it a secret for many years.

There was a commotion on the set on October 15. Bette insisted upon having everybody in a dinner-party scene introduced by her, as the hostess, to each other. The Epsteins, as producers, pointed out that these introductions were not in the script and would be assumed by the audience to have taken place before the action began. Julius Epstein recalls that in the peculiarly high-pitched affected voice Bette selected to play the part, she said, "But a lady would never allow her guests to sit down at a table unless she had introduced them to each other."

"This is a picture, not a society clambake," Julius Epstein said.

Bette refused to eliminate the dialogue. The rows went on the rest of the afternoon. The next day, Bette played a sequence in which she arrived in Skeffington's office. In the script she would simply appear before Claude Rains's desk and make a scene. Bette added lines of dialogue when she entered the secretary's anteroom, told the secretary to announce her, stood impatiently while being announced, and then, on being admitted, made a lengthy walk across the set to the desk.

This unauthorized piece of business slowed the scene up unconscionably and the Epsteins flew into a rage. They told Bette she should play the scene as written. She refused. She pointed out that when a lady came to her husband's office she wouldn't enter it unannounced. The Epsteins pointed out that the secretary would know her and would simply glance up as she went in; that to show this transition was a complete waste of screen footage.

"But she's a *new* secretary," Bette explained.

"How do you know?" the Epsteins asked. The absurd and futile conversation went on without resolution.

There was a scene in which Bette sat in a café with Claude Rains and a child. Bette wanted to have Rains bring the child through the door, discussing her in the process. The production manager Frank Mattison sent a memorandum to the studio chief Steve Trilling who had taken over from Hal Wallis. It read: "She wants her name to be mentioned even when she isn't in the scene so no one can ever forget for a second she's in the story."

The Epsteins sent a memorandum to Trilling: "There isn't a damn thing that can be done as long as BD is the director."

By early November the production had slowed almost to a halt because of Bette's changes and additions. Mattison wrote to Trilling: "It sure is tough on a unit manager to sit by with a show where she is the whole band. The music and all the instruments, including the bazooka."

By November 12, everyone agreed that Bette was not only the director but the producer too. The Epsteins did something unthinkable, even unique in the history of Hollywood: Julius Epstein told me they walked off their own picture, abandoning it to the star, starting legal proceedings against the studio for denying their privileges as producers. They disappeared for an indefinite stay in New York.

Four days later, on December 3, Bette was suffering from an irritation of her right eye caused by makeup poisoning. She took a special solution in an eyebath, threw back her head, and emptied the solution into her eye. She screamed with agony. A pain lanced her head. She collapsed. Perc Westmore, who was standing nearby, rushed to her aid. Seizing a bottle of castor oil he washed her eye out. She was still unable to see in the affected eye. Paul MacWilliams of First Aid took her into the dispensary. He analyzed the eyewash. It contained a deadly fluid known as acetone, which could have blinded her for life. It could not have been an accident. Some member of the crew or cast, or, if Farney was murdered, the same person who had killed him had tried to put an end to her professional career.

To this day, the mystery remains unsolved. She was in the hands of eye specialists for over a week. By Christmas, the picture was three weeks behind schedule. Bette was doubly tense and distressed following the attempt on her sight. She quarreled with Sherman constantly. He hated the high-pitched voice she used and the exaggerated rubber mask. He also hated her constant interference with the writing and her ceaseless attempts to overbear him in the matter of the direction. Following Farney's death, she herself seemed to have become full of hate, violently intolerant of the slightest sloppiness, weakness, or incompetence. And yet, paradoxically, on January 21, 1944, she turned up for work, without explanation, not wearing her rubber face. It had been called for, and scenes had to be switched around to accommodate her.

Incredibly, the picture was still going in late February. Jack Warner and Steve Trilling decided it would never end. Warner said to Trilling one day, "Do you think she'll break shooting to come to my funeral?"

Steve Trilling replied, "Only to make sure they're not lying."

No sooner had Bette folded up with relief after five months of shooting (the picture was sixty days over schedule) than she discovered she would have to do the montage sequences wearing the mask again. She disappeared for a week before she could force herself to undergo the ordeal once more. Frank Mattison wrote a final note to Trilling:

"Thank God *Mr. Skeffington* is finally being put in mothballs."

Bette's behavior during *Mr. Skeffington* was the cause of a new serious breach with Jack Warner. Without Hal Wallis to act as a buffer and control the shooting, with the weaker Steve Trilling in charge, Warner knew nothing but total exasperation. As for the Epsteins, words could not do justice to their fury. They threatened to remove their name from the picture; and when it was released with numerous horrible cuts to compensate for the additions made against their wishes, they beseeched theaters and exhibitors to take it off.

Sherman was almost equally aggrieved by the results. When he saw the finished cut and realized just how extreme Bette's makeup was in the later scenes, he was reminded of nothing so much as a visit to the mummy room in a museum.

Sherman adds: "There are a couple of scenes I don't like. I don't like the ending after Claude Rains comes back and she discovers he is blind. Something went wrong that day. I never got that scene the way I wanted it. While Bette did a marvelous acting job all through the film, that scene was not as good as it should have been. But she was very tired."

Jack Warner never forgave Bette for her behavior during the shooting. For years he hoarded some of the memoranda from the production manager, Frank Mattison, such as: "I surely would not want to have my own money in any picture being made the way this picture is being made for Warner Brothers." And: "I am wondering if it would be possible to speed up the next Bette Davis picture by making it a Bette Davis Production, where she would understand that all these delays would cost *her* a little bit of money."

Bosley Crowther, all-powerful critic of *The New York Times,* launched an attack on the picture, condemning it and Davis's performance outright. He found the character of Fanny Skeffington insufferable, and Bette's performance excessively mannered. This seems unfair; the picture, and her acting, have great style and attack.

A few days after completion of production in the spring of 1944, Bette, maddened by Warner's arguments over the picture, asked for a release from her contract. Her request was bluntly refused. The Epsteins didn't speak to Bette for a very long time. She was depressed by the criticisms of her efforts, and scarcely recovered from these when she experienced a shattering shock: She learned at last the true cause of Farney's death.

Somebody told her that a few days before he died, Farney had been sleeping with the wife of a fellow worker. The man, huge and imposing, caught Farney and the girl in bed in a motel near Sunset Boulevard. There was a fight and the man struck Farney on the head with a lamp. Farney had only superficial treatment for the injury and the congealed blood was still on the wound when a combination of this new mishap and the earlier blow at the fall at Butternut destroyed him.

As Bette opened the paper hours after receiving this horrible news, she was riveted to a news story. It revealed that the man who had killed Farney had been burned to death in an air crash.

ELEVEN

Bette's only other work of the period was in *Hollywood Canteen* in which she appeared as herself, briskly running the entertainment for the troops and the mass serving of meals. She drove over from Riverbottom in Glendale for ten days of work in an exact replica of the canteen on Sound Stage Four at Warners. Reviews of the picture were bad, and a group of enlisted servicemen wrote a joint letter to Jack Warner calling the movie "a slur on the intelligence and acumen of every member of the armed services." The charge was justified; *Hollywood Canteen* was a dire example of mass self-congratulation as fifty Warner Brothers stars publicly patted each other on the back while bemused servicemen stood about gaping at their famous hosts and hostesses.

It was a difficult period. Bette had trouble trying to block Farney from her mind. Her two homes, Butternut and Riverbottom, reminded her constantly of her happy times with Farney. Every stick of furniture, the carpets, the drapes, colorings in their bedroom brought back the realization that she was alone. Ruthie remained a consolation and a driving force; she still, even at this stage of Bette's career, insisted on walking in front of her at premiers or first-nights. Now that Bette was rich, Ruthie's demands for expensive clothes, furs, and jewelry became more and more extreme. She fed off Bette with more determination than ever, and Bette, never forgetting for an instant that she owed much of her career to Ruthie's drive and conviction, never begrudged her mother anything. Sometimes the sheer pressure on Bette's purse irritated her in spite of herself. The bills poured in—in a stream which even threatened her income of over $4,500 a week.

And then, though again Bette never begrudged it, there was the emotional and financial drain represented by Bobby. Despite attempts in two marriages, Bobby was unable to achieve a balanced and comfortable existence. Though she was the last to admit it, she was still eaten by her jealousy of Bette's great career and by her own esthetic nature. She suffered from increasing dementia in which she became violent and had to be placed in seclusion. She was confined in a private mental institution whose costs were crippling. Bette was determined that Bobby would have the best of psychiatric care and she drained her bank account to bring this about. Bette's visits to Bobby in the home were agonizing. Patients would gape at Bette and imitate her grotesquely.

It was during this unhappy time that a curious episode took place. Joan Crawford, the neurotic star of MGM, had just signed with Warners to a contract that was to begin with a version of James M. Cain's *Mildred Pierce*. Crawford, many people thought, had been brought in by Jack Warner to threaten Bette's position as Catherine the Great of Burbank. The court began to divide into Crawford factions and Davis factions. For this reason, Bette was careful to avoid actually meeting Crawford.

She knew that the gossips would pretend they had quarreled, thereby aggravating an already charged situation. So she kept a cool distance, declining to comment in anything except admiring terms when directly challenged on the subject.

But Joan Crawford's attitude was different. For years she had repressed her lesbianism while tormenting her immediate family with a kind of twisted rage. She had fought against her nature because she knew that even an inkling that this sainted Witch of the West had feet of clay might have caused her downfall. She was admired, fawned on, but never really liked; she was too impeccable to be bearable. Her faults were smoothed down as neatly as the pleats in her immaculate skirts. Her heavy, slightly threatening animal furs and graven face had a daunting quality that defied friendship as strongly as enmity.

The safest procedure was clearly to grovel. Anything less abject might not win her imperial approval. To Bette, all this was nonsense. And yet she was deceiving herself; she, too, found irresistible the idea of being in command.

Crawford had for years nourished a secret desire for Bette. This greatest of suffering female stars admired this greatest of actresses sexually as well as professionally. As soon as she arrived at Warners, Crawford began sending Bette perfume, flowers, and letters, begging her to meet for dinner. No lovesick male in those happy, half-forgotten days when women were still wooed by men tried harder to seduce a beautiful woman than Crawford did in her pursuit of Davis. There is something odd, unsettling, and grotesque about this; over the years Bette has confided it to friends. Bette returned all the gifts with quick impatience and ill humor, thanking Crawford for her consideration and preferring to explain to the immediate circle that it was merely an effort of Ms. Crawford to bring about a truce in the studio conflict.

One night, according to a publicity man, Bette was asked to give a sudden broadcast for a particular charity. She refused, on the grounds that she had insufficient preparation. The publicity man went to Crawford and asked her to make a broadcast instead. Hurt by Bette's refusal of her, Crawford instantly agreed but insisted the broadcast be channeled into Bette's dressing room. Bette was asked to go to her room for an urgent meeting and drove over from Glendale only to find the deafening sounds of the Crawford broadcast played many times too loudly and surging through her room.

Fortunately, Bette's rebuffs finally worked and Crawford gave up.

Bette now wanted to be a mother (she had had, she told Mike Wallace on TV, more abortions). She was pushing forty. Clearly, she had no time to waste.

She spent much time at Laguna Beach, where Ruthie had a house and where her uncle Paul Favor was living with his family. There she met a twenty-nine-year-old Sunday painter called William Grant Sherry. He swept her off her feet. He was a good-looking, lean, hairy, dark man with a deceptively mild manner that disguised a fierce personality. He had been an unsuccessful boxer because he was too light and wiry and indecisive; and his painting was just fair. It consisted of marine landscapes and ordinary portraits.

In her memoirs, Bette portrays Sherry as bad-tempered, violent, frustrated, miserable. Yet it is hard not to sympathize with him. Bette's charm, energy, and enormous fame undoubtedly excited him. She in her turn needed him after her sufferings, her bereavement, her painful loneliness. He clearly sensed that need, and he was propelled into a relationship for which he was totally unready. Like Ham and Farnsworth he was obscure, struggling, trying for success; she was success personified. It was crushing to his male ego to know this.

Their romance began quickly, thoughtlessly; it soon became dark and threatening. Ham had been gentle and sincere and ultimately deceitful and desperate; Fransworth had been largely an absentee, and weakened by ill-health, he had never been deeply present in Bette's emotional sphere after the beginning. Sherry matched her in temperament and fire; he gave as good as he got, or more. He was physical and cruel and vibrant. He represented a melodramatic harshness in her life: lightning and thunder. She favored fire, it's true. But in the last analysis she wanted to dominate still. And Sherry, obscure and unsuccessful as he was, refused to be dominated.

Her friends disliked Sherry. Jane Bryan Dart says, "Marrying Sherry was the worst mistake Bette ever made." The writer Catherine Turney, a friend of Bette's, says: "I don't think he was at all right for Bette. I remember during their engagement he was a physiotherapist in Laguna. He was excited by the glamour of 'Bette Davis.'" The director Curtis Bernhardt said, "I think Bette quickly tired of Sherry. I remember a party once. He had been placed at her table—the stars' table. It was some studio shindig. He had, she felt, no right to be seated next to her and she ordered him and his place card to another table. He was ready to kill. When she danced with a man who *was* seated next to her, Sherry broke in and she refused to dance with him. When he became angry, she sat down."

The relationship was a catastrophe from the beginning. It was fortunate that in the endless quarrels and violence of their affair, Bette had the relief of making a film she wanted to do: *The Corn Is Green,* which she had so much admired with Ethel Barrymore on the stage.

She insisted that the performers Rhys Williams, Mildred Dunnock, Rosalind Ivan, and Gene Ross repeat their perfect performances from the New York production. She also demanded Orry-Kelly, who had left the studio, as the designer of her costumes.

Perhaps in part because of her unhappiness with Sherry, Bette flung herself with even more than the usual intensity into studying for the characterization of Miss Moffat, Emlyn Williams's noble schoolteacher in the Welsh village who encourages a young miner, played by John Dall, to go to Oxford and have a career as a writer. She was very much against wearing a wig which would age her and which the studio called for; she preferred to have her hair dyed gray and cut straight back, very short, like a skull cap over her head. She was excessively nervous about her appearance as an elderly woman, despite the fact that Perc Westmore's makeup was spectacularly effective. After two days of using her own hair, she suddenly decided she wanted to test with the wig; then she changed her mind and decided actually to include a shot of herself with the wig in the work of the day. Eric Stacey, production assistant, wrote to studio manager Tenny Wright:

> For your information, if this scene is made with a wig that is approved, it will involve a good two days of retakes at a later date. Mr. Chertok is trying to pacify [Miss Davis] and, as the director [Irving Rapper] said to me this morning, what she needs is a psychiatrist, not a director.

On July 3, Bette insisted on using the wig from that day on and reshooting the first eleven days of work, which was unthinkable in Hollywood. Jack Warner quipped to Rapper, "She flipped her wig!" At a charged meeting in Projection Room Five, Jack Warner, studio head Steve Trilling, Bette, and Eric Stacey ran the tests with and without the wig. Bette went over to Jack and said, "You see, I was right, wasn't I? The wig makes all the difference, doesn't it?"

Warner nodded. He told her: "Yes. The wig's a great improvement. We'll just have to retake the first twelve days."

She kissed him in gratitude.

Shooting proceeded uneventfully for just over a month. Then an event took place which suggested that perhaps, along with her other gifts, Bette was visited by second sight. About three in the afternoon of August 7, 1944, she was very nearly killed.

TWELVE

Bette was shooting the difficult examination scene with John Dall, who played the miner-writer, when she heard a noise above her head. A heavy steel cover for an arc light, high up in the flies above the sound stage, either fell or was pushed and came plunging down onto her head. If she hadn't been wearing the large wig that Jack Warner had approved and she had so strongly fought for, she would have been fatally injured. As it was, the wig cushioned the blow. She fell into Irving Rapper's arms and he said, "Oh, Bette, I never thought you felt that way about me!"

The next night, there was a big studio party, and Bette, despite a headache, attended it in good spirits. She went home to Riverbottom, feeling a little dizzy and sick; she woke on Monday morning feeling terrible. The studio memoranda show that no one was in the least sympathetic about her plight. The executives were annoyed that she had chosen a Monday to be ill when the actor Nigel Bruce, also in the cast of *The Corn Is Green*, broadcast a Sherlock Holmes radio show, making it impossible for him also to be filmed that day; theirs were the only scenes called for by the script.

By Tuesday, Bette was suffering from the results of concussion and her headache worsened. She became nervous and sick to her stomach, anxious that she might be stricken with the same brain disease that had killed her character in *Dark Victory* and that had helped to kill Farney. But even on her bed of pain she was adamant about one thing: She had insisted from the beginning that, despite the nerve-wracking expense and difficulty, the entire picture must be shot in correct time sequence because it was based on a play. So it proved impossible to shoot scenes for which she was not required, and, difficult though this was, the entire picture had to be closed down until its star came around. A typically irritated note from Stacey to Wright reads:

> We could get rid of two or three $75 a week singing miners by shooting the end of the picture immediately . . . But I promise you that Miss Davis would raise an awful lot of hell and I don't think it's worthwhile upsetting her for such a small item, since she is so much better on this picture than she's been on former pictures.

On August 11, still feeling a little groggy and barely able to sleep for fear of the effects from her injury, Bette struggled into work to finish the scene with Dall: the scene in which she presided over his examination.

Back on the set, Bette turned out to be unpredictable. She had asked for the cancellation of a scene in which she was riding a bicycle, because she had long remembered her accident in Britain in which she fell off a similar vehicle. Now, without warning, she decided to bring it back, which meant breaking her own rule and shooting out of sequence. At first, it proved to be impossible because of the schedule; but over everyone's dead body, she forced the scene in—and then fell off the bicycle.

Her quarrels with Irving Rapper were one-sided: *she* argued with *him*. In turn, he let fly at his assistant Bob Vreeland, screaming and yelling until Jack Warner asked him to stop. Later, he apologized to Vreeland, saying, "I'm sorry, Bob. Miss Davis is making me so nervous and upset, I'm almost ill."

No scene was achieved without savage arguing by Davis. A problem was John Dall. He was a homosexual who lived with his mother; they were known popularly as "the Dalls." Their devotion was the joke of Hollywood. They used to go to premieres together.

All this would have been irrelevant had it not been that Dall had an alarming tendency to swish in scenes in which extreme virility and masculinity were called for. Bette was completely baffled by Dall. Irving Rapper told me: "She and Dall were playing the very important scene when she tells him he must go to Oxford. He was sitting down, and I told him to twist his cloth cap in his hands to suggest indecision and tension. He was supposed to stand up and stride manfully out of the room. Suddenly, he rose and began swinging his hips and wiggling his fanny at Bette. She threw up her hands and said to me, 'This is impossible! We'll have to get another actor.'

"I said, 'Wait a minute.' I went over to John, who was red with embarrassment, and said, 'Next time you get up, think of the King of England and imagine the national anthem playing and *march like a soldier*.'

"John was a good sport. I called 'Action!' and watched his fanny nervously. It didn't swish, and the scene was fine."

Deliberate and heavily theatrical, *The Corn Is Green* nevertheless was an admirable showcase for Davis's talent. Her face, expertly aged by Westmore, had never been more expressive, nor had her mastery of movement and gesture ever been more vividly displayed. Supported by a strong cast, she attacked the role with tremendous style and relish; she was at her best in the examination scene—despite the fact that it was done in two halves, divided by her near-fatal accident—if accident it had been.

Certainly, there were people in the crew who hated her as well as those who loved and worshipped her. She was so demanding, imposing, seeking restlessly for what was best, that some people—especially Tenny Wright— couldn't tolerate it. Her outbursts of rage and her additions of pages to the script were upsetting even in perfectionist Hollywood.

231

With Bette, everything was work, work, work: a grim concentration on achievement, on professional brilliance.

In the last months of 1944, Bette's affair with Sherry failed to improve. But they still planned to marry in 1945. She had long wanted to make her own pictures, both to control the material and the director and achieve a tax deduction. In 1945, as World War II neared its end, several stars began to set up their own corporations to avoid the vastly increased taxes that the war had brought about. Characteristically, she decided to begin a career as a producer by offering not one, but two Bette Davises in the same picture: *A Stolen Life*, adapted from a 1930s British picture with Elisabeth Bergner about twins, one good, one evil, who were in love with the same man. It was a season for movies about twins: Olivia De Havilland, Bette's old friend, the following year appeared in *Dark Mirror*, in which she also played an evil and a good sister.

This was typical of the egotism of stars—that, not content with one of themselves in the movies, they wanted two. Bette often complained that she lacked strong leading men, just as she lacked strong husbands or lovers, but she certainly did not go out of her way to select a powerful actor for *A Stolen Life*. She tried Robert Alda, a dark, handsome Latin type, and dropped him summarily; she tried Dennis Morgan and found him wanting. Catherine Turney, the scriptwriter, and Bette together got involved in a cloak-and-dagger operation to sneak Bette's choice, Glenn Ford, into the picture. Turney remembers that "Glenn was just out of the Marine Corps and inexperienced. Bette and I enlisted the aid of a publicist, a very funny man named Harry Mines. He literally smuggled Glenn onto the Warners lot against Jack's orders, and when they found out we had tested him and sent him in to be signed up, all hell broke loose. Steve Trilling, the studio boss, insisted that we have Robert Alda, but Bette was adamant it must be Glenn." Finally, she was able to borrow Ford from Columbia.

Bette's production company was called B.D., Inc. She owned 80 percent of it; her agent Jules Stein owned 10 percent and Ruthie and Bette's attorney Dudley Furse owned 5 percent each. B.D., Inc., was to receive the first $125,000 of the net, then Warners the next $232,000. The net would be split dollar-for-dollar, Warners getting 65 percent and B.D., Inc., 35 percent.

Once again, Bette brought in Orry-Kelly to do her costumes. The production was complicated. "The studio was surprised and dismayed that Bette wanted to be her own producer," its writer, Catherine Turney, says. "They felt she couldn't handle all the major problems."

These problems included the astonishing total of thirty-six sets, a lighthouse constructed at Laguna Beach, three complicated scripts, and an appallingly difficult scene in a storm in which the bad sister drowns.

Worse still, there was the hair-raising problem of matching the shots in which one twin would light the other's cigarette or touch the other's hair. Herb Lightman explains how cameraman Sol Polito achieved what he wanted: "Bette lighting a cigarette for her twin was executed by having Miss Davis play the scene opposite a double who lit her cigarette and performed other actions at close range. Later, the double's face was marked out and Miss Davis's head literally placed on her shoulders."

In one scene, Bette had to make a complicated matching movement and she had to watch in the projection room her double in action with her. Due to a mistake, her head had not been placed on her double's shoulders. She found herself talking to a headless woman on the screen. She was horrified and turned away, covering her face in her hands.

Shooting began in the spring of 1945, Annoyingly, since this was her own picture, Bette fell ill with a mysterious virus and work was delayed for over a week. Then her face broke out in boils. It is clear this was due to the stress of handling production details; in competition, Glenn Ford announced that *he* had boils on his face—and disappeared for five days to recover.

Bette had several run-ins with the gifted German director Curtis Bernhardt. At one stage she sent a memorandum calling for his dismissal and then reinstated him with equal abruptness. On the other hand, she admired his strength of will. Bernhardt told me: "We began with a tremendous clash on the first running of her wardrobe tests. I thought they were dreadful. She would say, 'Isn't Orry's work wonderful?'

"And her entourage would murmur, 'Yes, it's gorgeous, darling.'

"I hated that kind of movie-star nonsense. After three costumes, I turned to her and said, 'Miss Davis, don't you think these costumes are too theatrical?'

"She replied angrily, 'How can you *say* that? I am *never* theatrical!'

"I was appalled at her dishonesty. I got up and started to walk out of the projection room. She stood up and followed me, right in the middle of the screening. 'Where are you going?' she shouted.

" 'Home,' I snapped back.

" 'What do you *mean* you're going home? These are the costume tests for *your* picture!' She was bursting with rage.

"I said, '*You* don't need a director. *You need a yes man!*' I told her to her face.

"We met eyeball to eyeball. And suddenly (she's a wonderful sport) she backed down. She said, 'You know, I think you're right!' And from that moment on she didn't argue with me about the costumes."

Bette had a great rapport with the charming and talented writer Catherine Turney whose script, with numerous touches by Bette herself, was breezy and vigorously entertaining. In many conversations with Bette, Turney built up the role of the good sister; the problem with the previous version had been that once the bad sister was drowned, the picture fell flat because the character of the good sister was excessively dull.

Bette and Catherine together instilled in the picture a strong and salty sense of the Yankee seafaring atmosphere of a seaport in Maine, with the aid of the director, recreating an authentic mood in a totally alien setting. The picture is perhaps closer to Bette's own world than any other she made. It has a wonderfully brisk and attractive sense of people living at full stretch, in beautifully accurate settings

234

thought out to the last detail in the ornaments: a ship in a bottle, framed in a window overlooking a white and sparkling harbor; a cozy fire on a winter's night with a kindly old man and a pipe to greet the wayward wanderer; light flickering on the ceiling of a summery room when the heroine recovers from near drowning.

Throughout the shooting, Turney says, "We had endless discussions in Bette's dressing room about every scene. It would sometimes make the crew very angry, because they didn't realize that good would come from these discussions. Curt agreed with us that we should show deep motivation in the characters. We kept nothing from the original picture except the scene in which the dog doesn't recognize the good sister, who is posing as the bad sister after the latter's drowning."

Much of the work came from the problem of differentiating between the twins. It was decided early on that Bette should have the same voice in each performance, or the impersonation of the second half would fail to make sense. There were subtle differences, worked out by Bette, Turney, and Orry-Kelly in the clothes the sisters wore: Kate, the good twin, wore drab clothes, unpretentious but pleasant; her sister wore fussy pretentious clothes. The biggest problem in the picture was the big storm scene. Bette and her double, Sally Sage, had to get into a boat that was equipped with wires attached to the bottom of a deep studio tank. The tank was filled with water whipped by tremendous wind machines that churned up fifteen-foot waves. It was the size of a large swimming pool. Not only did Bette and Sally have to cling to the yacht but Sally had to keep the back of her head to the camera for matching shots. In seconds, both were completely drenched. The sail kept flapping and the jib struck Bette on the head and threw her into the water. Although both she and Sally were good sailors, Bette, probably largely through nerves, became seasick. She sprained her ankle and struck her elbow violently. The shooting, with both actresses soaked to the skin and furiously thrown about, continued through three harrowing days. In the last shot Bette had to slide off the deck while her sister grabbed at her hand and the wedding ring slipped off her finger. The yacht accidentally capsized and Bette went down in the water. Her feet caught in the wires and she was unable to come up. She struggled desperately, convinced that she would drown in seventeen feet of water. At last she managed to get loose and, striking out powerfully, came to the surface with the aid of a frogman.

"I thought we had lost you," Bernhardt said.

"Why didn't you dive in and see?" Bette replied.

Fast-moving and energetic, *A Stolen Life* contained two of Bette's best performances. Some of the interviews given out by the director at the end of production were notably confusing. He told *The Detroit News*: "With Miss Davis's characterization, we were handicapped because we could never make Bette cross the room in front of herself. Always we had to have her walk behind her other image."

There is a curious parallel in the movie between the character of Karnak, the sullen painter who is rude to the heroine, insulting her while supplying paintings which she does her best to encourage, and William Grant Sherry. It is almost as though Warners created a mirror for a living person in a part played with scenery-chewing emphasis by Dane Clark.

At the end-of-shooting party, Sherry got into a quarrel with Glenn Ford, apparently (and quite mistakenly) jealous of him. Bette had absolutely no sexual interest in Ford, nor he in her; and in later years, they were to become enemies.

Bette married Sherry late in 1945. One would have thought that, given the miserable relationship, she wouldn't have made this mistake. More than once, they were seen fighting in public. Their behavior became the talk of Hollywood. Bette, who had always managed to control the press completely, was unable to stop the criticism that greeted her for marrying someone below her station. She admitted in her memoirs that Ruthie's and Bobby's opposition to the marriage drove her headlong into it. She claimed in interviews that Sherry signed an agreement before the ceremony stating that if and when the marriage ended, he would make no claims on her property. *Photoplay* commented acidly: "In other words, Bette Davis could try it out, and if it didn't work, it wouldn't cost her anything."

Bette and Sherry left for a honeymoon in Mexico in November. On the way Sherry threw her out of the car. In the hotel when they arrived, he threw an ashtray at her head. It was a dire warning of what lay ahead, but there was one consolation. Soon afterward, Bette became pregnant. Bette was always grateful to Sherry for that!

THIRTEEN

At the beginning of 1946, Bette severed two links to the past. She sold Riverbottom and Butternut within a few weeks of each other, and moved herself and Sherry to a new rented home in Laguna. It was a handsome house, smallish as Bette liked houses, perched on a cliff on Sleepy Hollow Lane overlooking Woods Cove with a striking view of the ocean from every window. The entrance hall was oak paneled, and Bette hung British sporting prints on the walls. In the library, very small and cozy, she packed the crowded shelves with her favorite books. She brought in a desk, typewriter, and leather chair to make it into an office. The living room faced north—ideal for Sherry, who was addicted to Rembrandt's north light. He stood his easel by the windows overlooking the ocean, and filled the four walls with his sea- and landscapes and still lifes, and a winter scene of Butternut with a large red barn and trees hung with icicles. Bette's favorite rocking chair, coffee table, lazy Susan, antiques, all came from Riverbottom. The dining room was up a flight of stairs; it was furnished in walnut. At the front of the house there was a porch of the kind Bette loved, which embraced the entire facade over a terrace turned into a flowery rock garden. There were pools to swim in between large rocks, and a barbecue patio. A huge four-poster bed filled the bedroom, just leaving space for a couple of sticks of furniture.

Bette was busy preparing the nursery and baby clothes that winter. She spent hours dreaming of future projects: a version of Edith Wharton's novel *Ethan Frome;* and *The African Queen,* with James Mason, a picture lost years later to Katharine Hepburn. But all too many evenings were spent in violent quarrels, so that finally, miserable and contrite, Sherry went to a psychoanalyst. His cure consisted in a sudden burst of wifeliness; when Bette came home, he, in the words of Louella Parsons, "would have her dinner ready for her, bring her slippers, press her dresses, draw her bath, give her massages." She found this unbearable and, after pretending politely to accept it, exploded. She regarded these duties as her prerogative; Sherry was usurping her by taking them on.

She wanted Sherry to be her equal, financially, professionally, and in temperament and personality. But this dream of a liberated woman had no chance of realization— and, once again, one wonders if, had she attained it, she would for a moment really have wanted it. Given her ego, she probably could not have endured matching competition. Yet on the other hand she hated the fact that Sherry had very little success as an artist, that, like Ham and Farney, he was somewhat weak, that it was impossible for him to keep up with her financially, and this tortured him. Her friends' and family's dislike of Sherry began to seem not so unreasonable to her. But at least her pregnancy bound them together up to a point—until once more Sherry would lose his temper. It was a season of partings and rejoinings, sudden departures of either partner, and above all the constant gnawing hate that destroys as it consumes. There was no basic respect between the couple, no tenderness; even in their passion there was a kind of hatred. It was the worst period of Bette's life to date, more tormenting even than the most miserable times with Ham. She should have been a joyful expectant mother, bathed in a sense of well-being despite the inevitable problems that accompany pregnancy. But she was not happy. Once more she was heading for a breakdown; in her late thirties, she felt and looked ten years older.

In this dark period, Bette tried to buoy herself up with a new picture which she began with decidedly mixed feelings. Given the title *Her Conscience*, which troubled Bette, it was fortunately changed to *Deception*. Because of Bette's condition, it quickly became known in the studio as *Conception*.

Based on a play that had originally been filmed with Bette's idol, Jeanne Eagels, as *Jealousy*, *Deception* reunited the principals of *Now, Voyager*—Bette, Claude Rains, Paul Henreid—with the director Irving Rapper. Bette had to study the piano for a scene at a reception following a wedding; she trained carefully under the tutelage of Shura Cherkassky, her hand movements matched for some of the more difficult passages by Norma (Mrs. Richard) Boleslavsky. A problem in the action was that Bette, with her odd streak of physical cowardice, had to fire a gun; she had had to do so, of course, in *The Letter*, but on this occasion she was more troubled emotionally and tried desperately to have the shooting scene changed. The dialogue seemed to her exceedingly pretentious and heavy, and her part was a nuisance; she had to play a congenital liar, a tearful, neurotic woman. But at least she was back in Jeanne Eagels's shoes again.

The story was absurd. The mistress of a famous composer is visited by her former lover, a cellist who has been confined in a concentration camp. She has to tell lie piled on lie to deceive the amorous revenant that she is not involved with the composer. The composer gives the concentration camp victim a cello concerto to perform, intending to destroy his belief in the woman the night following the performance. This rigmarole was very aggravating to the industry censor Joseph Breen, who wrote to Jack Warner: "From the standpoint of the Code the major difficulty seems to be that this past relationship is not treated as sin; there is no voice for morality; there is no punishment for either of the sinners; and the general flavor is almost one of condemnation for the whole situation." The script had to be extensively rewritten so that Bette's character ended the picture threatened with the electric chair after killing the composer at point-blank range. Presumably the cellist's

241

subsequent agony at the revelations of the trial was considered punishment enough by the Breen office.

From beginning to end the making of *Deception* was a nightmare, relieved only by Claude Rains's brilliantly exaggerated playing of the composer. Bette, more overwrought and hysterical because of Sherry's treatment than she had ever been, painfully conscious of the possible effect on her unborn child, and miserably self-conscious that her pregnancy condition showed, spent hours each day in her dressing room in tears while the production ground to a halt. Since there were only three significant characters, and she was on camera almost constantly, the picture was forty-six days over schedule, almost twice its planned period of production.

Shooting began over the continuing objections of Joe Breen in May. Bette was distracted from the first. She was thinking not only of her personal problems but also of her disappointment that Jack Warner refused to allow her to make the story of Mary Todd Lincoln as her next production. In breaks between outbursts of crying and fights at home, shooting the picture, and making the difficult, rain-swept drive along the coast highway to Laguna each morning and evening that damp spring of 1946, she somehow found time to rush off long letters without punctuation—written with telegram dashes instead of full stops—to Jack Warner, who was on vacation in Hot Springs, Arkansas. The letters were chock-full of demands and requests, ideas and themes, for the Mary Lincoln story. During a troubled weekend in Palm Springs, she wrote that she understood Jack's fear of biographies, "but to me this is a story of so many women—not just a figure out of history—it is a story of any woman who believes in her husband and pushes him ahead." She went on that this was a story of a woman who was the power behind the throne, a theme "apt to be box office," that the character had a wonderful combination of Scarlett O'Hara and a *Back Street* woman; she cited the success of Katharine Hepburn in *State of the Union*, about the wife of a presidential candidate, "and anyway stubborn Davis is asking you to think more about it—I am so truly

242

sure someone in the theatre will do it soon—the Theatre Guild has always been interested—or could I do it as a play? . . . Bye for now—Bette."

In the first week of production of *Deception*, on the night of April 30, 1946, Bette was driving home to Laguna when a car swung out of a bend in the road without warning. In extreme distress after a harrowing day of shooting and nights of quarreling with her husband, Bette panicked and swerved off the road, crashing her auto in the process. The car was smashed and she was knocked unconscious. Somebody picked her up and drove her to her home where she collapsed completely. She awoke the next morning with a blinding headache; again she had a fear of sharing the fate of the heroine of *Dark Victory*. She managed to pull herself together sufficiently to call unit manager Al Alleborn in person to say she wouldn't be able to work on Saturday. She had a dizzy spell the following morning, and studio representatives called, not to ask her how she was feeling, but when she would return to work. This upset her fiercely and she called her physician, Dr. Wilson, telling him she felt seriously ill.

Wilson came over several times. He took X rays in the house with his nursing team so Bette would not have to undergo the ordeal of encountering a crowd of fans at the local clinic. He told her, in a scene reminiscent of the diagnosis scene in *Dark Victory*, that he was gravely worried about her condition. There was some evidence of a hemorrhage and possibly a fracture in the skull casing. He told her she must remain flat on her back without moving for several days. Wilson was alarmed to see blood trickling from her mouth down her chin; evidently she had suffered damage to her jaw which was to show up in an illness six years later.

Deception's producer, Henry Blanke, and Irving Rapper drove down to Laguna that weekend. Sherry, afraid Bette might die, was in a state of nerves and exhaustion, deeply sorry about his behavior—like a child who had suddenly regretted an impulsive action. Bette was too dizzy and hazy to do more than nod at her visitors; she felt nau-

243

seated and was terrified of the possible results of a further set of X-rays.

Yet, astonishingly, and with iron professionalism, she managed to pull herself together to go to work on May 8. Precisely how this miracle occurred is a mystery, but presumably her condition was not .as serious as everyone thought. However, the dizzy spells came back and she was off work again for several days. She was so run-down that she contracted a series of colds and some of her lines had to be dubbed. By May 25, she was in bed again, with a severe case of intestinal flu, a strep throat, and a fever of 101. Dr. Wilson gave her a heavy dose of penicillin; he said on no condition would she be able to work for several days. Wilson told her that the accident in the car and her insomnia because of Sherry had worn her system down to a danger point and that the damp air of Laguna was bad for her with her chronic throat weakness. But she shook her head speechlessly, a thermometer in her mouth, when he advised her to move. Bobby and Ruthie were nearby, as well as her Uncle Paul and cousins, the Favors, and without them there was nothing in life.

Due to the loving care of her mother and sister, and the remarkable Dr. Wilson, Bette managed to struggle back to work again on June 13. But the studio head, Steve Trilling, who had once been the casting director, was unsympathetic, reflecting as he did the tough Jack Warner's slave-driving attitude to the stars. Under doctor's orders, Bette had asked if she could come in at 10:00 A.M. each day to allow for the long drive from Laguna and sufficient time in makeup to cover the marks of grief and sickness in her face—a task which, to judge by the finished film, her devoted Perc Westmore notably failed to accomplish. On June 22, Trilling suddenly arrived on the set during a break in a difficult scene and called Bette aside. In earshot of other members of the cast—an unforgivable sin in Bette's eyes—Trilling asked Bette loudly if she would please come in at 9:00 A.M. and work till six each day because the picture was over budget and over schedule. Bette said to Trilling, according to a studio memorandum,

"I had an understanding with Jack Warner that I would start at ten A.M. and leave at five. Some days, I've worked longer hours just to please him. But if I work from nine to six each day"—she started to cry—"I won't be able to take it. I'll get sick and cause a shutdown again."

Suddenly she dried her tears and said sharply, angrily, "If Jack Warner wants me to change the arrangement agreed to, why doesn't he have the courage to tell me so himself? Why does he send *you* to tell me? A picture like this needs a lot of rehearsing! Jack knew what he was in for before we started! And they keep adding dialogue! I have to stay up at night learning lines for the next day! And they're long, difficult lines!" Now she started warming up in earnest. In full hearing of the entire company, she shouted, "You, Steve Trilling, have a lot of nerve, coming down the set during a shooting day! Discussing me shooting at nine instead of ten each day! And when you *know* we are working and I'm trying to concentrate and I'm about to go into a scene five pages long with difficult, complicated lines!" Bette pulled off her gloves and threw her hands to her face, sobbing so violently that the tears started through her fingers. Everyone was astonished; but typically of hard-bitten Hollywood, no one ran forward to comfort her. Steve Trilling went pale, turned on his heel, and strode off the set shaking his head. Bette called her maid. "Bring me some soda!" she exclaimed. Several of the crew were heard to laugh; they were tired of her tantrums and just wanted to get on with the day's work so they could get home to their wives or girl friends before sundown.

Bette walked back on the set and played her emotional scenes with an excessive emphasis, repeating lines unnecessarily and smoking far beyond the demands of the script. Her genuine emotional condition gave an extraordinary raw power to her playing when it was not downright hammy. She said nothing to anybody and went home in silence. She went straight to bed and called her agent, Lew Wasserman. She refused to speak to anybody from the studio and remained home for three days in a state of complete exhaustion.

Warner was furious that Bette had made a spectacle of herself with Trilling. Devoid of the courage that would have brought about a direct confrontation, he sent her a telegram instead, which read as follows:

DEAR BETTE: I AM AT A LOSS FOR WORDS TO EXPRESS MYSELF AFTER HAVING LEARNED OF THE TURMOIL THAT EXISTED LAST SATURDAY AFTERNOON WITH RESPECT TO THE PRODUCTION OF YOUR PICTURE. YOU MUST NOT LOSE SIGHT OF THE FACT THAT YOU ARE IN A PROFESSION THAT CALLS FOR CERTAIN FULFILLMENT OF MORAL OBLIGATIONS TO SAY NOTHING OF LEGAL ONES. YOU ARE TAKING THE WRONG ATTITUDE TOWARDS OUR COMPANY AND ME PERSONALLY ON THIS WHOLE MATTER IN THAT YOU WOULD CREATE CONDITIONS THAT ARE NOT FAIR TO OUR STUDIOS. WE ARE NOT RESPONSIBLE FOR THE WORKING HOURS UNDER WHICH THE INDUSTRY IS MAKING ITS PICTURES. WE HAVE DONE EVERYTHING IN OUR POWER FOR YOU, BUT NOW YOU ASK US TO CHANGE THE WORKING HOURS WHICH I FIND WE CANNOT DO AFTER HAVING HONESTLY TRIED, WHICH WAS OUR DISTINCT UNDERSTANDING WHEN I DISCUSSED THIS WITH YOU IN MY OFFICE SEVERAL WEEKS AGO. AM SURE YOU REALIZE OUR RAPPORT WAS RADICAL DEPARTURE FROM OUR NORMAL STUDIO OPERATIONS AND IF WE CONTINUE IT WILL CREATE A COMPLETE CHANGE IN OUR PRODUCTION METHODS AND PROVE VERY COSTLY TO US. I IMPLORE YOU AS A FRIEND AND BUSINESS ASSOCIATE TO USE YOUR GOOD REASONING. AM SURE IN THE LONG RUN YOU WILL REALIZE WHAT YOU ARE DOING NOW IS NOT THE PROPER THING AND AM ASKING NOTHING UNREASONABLE FROM YOU. SINCERELY,

JACK WARNER.

This telegram, to which Bette did not respond, marked the beginning of a gradual but increasingly steep decline in her relations with her old boss. The brutal fact was that her pictures were not making the enormous profits of previous years, that a new and tougher industry was less indulgent of the behavior of the old-time stars.

On June 24, 1946, the unthinkable almost happened: A member of the legal division sent a telegram to the production manager which was to be rephrased and delivered to Bette in Laguna, placing her on suspension for absenteeism. At the last minute Warner panicked, and the telegram was never sent.

Back at work at the end of June, Bette slammed into her dressing room in a fit of rage over rewritten dialogue and severely injured her finger. The pain was excruciating and the nail smashed and black. It didn't help her when Al Alleborn chose that moment to tell her she was seriously threatened with suspension.

With her finger in a bandage supplied by Perc Westmore, Bette stopped the shooting for the first time in her life on June 29 and demanded that the entire crew including the producer and director and other players gather around her. Extremely distraught, she said, "Many of you have been on pictures I have made previously. There are certain things you should know. You see my finger is badly hurt. The studio seems indifferent. I am appalled that the crew has been called in to work every day I've been off sick when Trilling *knew* you would be wasted because I couldn't come in. It shows terrible lack of consideration for you. I hate being put in a position like this. When Trilling and Warner make it seem my fault the crew is called in every day, when they know it's impossible for me to come to work."

Jack Warner was upset by this sudden labor meeting— the first of its kind in the history of Hollywood, the first time a star had presumed to complain about her employers to a crew. So what if Davis was the queen of the lot and earning eight thousand dollars a week? She had no business to criticize her betters!

The rift between Bette and Warners was never to heal. It was probably just as well that she gave birth to her child soon after the picture's disastrous previews and shattering reviews.

Bette underwent a cesarean operation on May 5, 1947.

The child was a very pretty, big girl of ten pounds, ten ounces. Bette lovingly named her Barbara, after Bobby, and called her from that moment on "B.D." Always extreme in her emotion, Bette became ecstatic over the child and for a time her relationship was cemented with Sherry. For a time, they were happy. There can be no doubt that, intensely family-conscious like all New Englanders, Bette had never cared as overwhelmingly for any human being outside of her mother and sister as she did for the strapping B.D.

Bette immediately took a year off work, over a grudging Jack Warner's complaints. Motherhood absorbed her torment and nervous strain and for a period at least she was reasonably serene. Her health suddenly improved; she had great fun entertaining columnists she normally despised. Louella came to coo relentlessly over the child who somehow survived the presence of this witch at her cradle; Hedda descended like a bird of prey in a feathered hat to bless the newborn. Bette was magnificent, sitting up in a bed jacket against large New England pillows and displaying her gurgling offspring to these alarming visitors.

Becoming a mother at almost forty had its risks, but Bette had triumphed over them. She began to live the life the fan magazines had been busily inventing for her. She took B.D. for dips in salty rock pools; waved Sherry goodbye when—shades of Arthur Farnsworth!—he went to flying school; joined him, family, and friends at weekend barbecues; took in movies and summer theater; filmed B.D. in home movies with Irving Rapper–like expertness; and in her own words undertook a regime of darning socks, sewing on buttons, and "doing what any family does—a family that is sufficient unto itself— the only really important thing for everyone in the world—the one thing really worth striving for. . . . I cannot ask for more than to have life continue as it is. I have my family—my work—I can look the world in the eye. I am happy."

But this idyllic dream state could not last. Bette told friends in anguish that Sherry had fallen in love with the baby's nurse, a young and attractive woman. Whether or not this was the case, it created great friction between husband and wife. Sherry returned to psychiatric sessions, which brought on further anguish.

During those painful months of recriminations and fears and quarrels, Sherry became intrigued by a novel about a sensitive young navy man, planning to be a priest, and a nervous spinster poetess in New York. Sherry, perhaps trying to compensate for the misery he had caused Bette, urged her to take on the story. Trying to please him, she agreed, though she was worried about the property. To protect herself, she asked her friend Catherine Turney, whose writing she much admired, to make the adaptation.

A New York theatrical director, Bretaigne Windust, was brought in to make the picture, because of his intimate knowledge of the New York social milieu in which the story was set. Bette kept writing notes through the spring of 1947 to Turney, who was in Manhattan, saying such things as, "I am very rested and very ambitious to do something really outstanding—and I don't feel this, the way it is, answers the requirements." Turney wrote and rewrote, but the script, finally called *Winter Meeting,* was never completely satisfactory. One of the problems was that Richard Widmark, who would have been ideal in the part of the priest and who gave a brilliant test, was felt by the studio to be too closely identified with his part of a giggling villain in the picture *Kiss of Death.* Instead, Trilling cast the wooden and awkward Jim Davis (who, until his death, had a leading role in today's TV series, *Dallas*), who was hopelessly outclassed by his namesake. The script was filled with yards of dull talk which irritated Bette; Sherry, who influenced the choice of Jim Davis and the acceptance of the final draft, proved to be quite mistaken in his influences.

The picture was a dull and uninspiring experience to make, received bad reviews, and lost a fortune. Nevertheless, it is in many ways one of Bette's more interesting pictures. Cleverly made, photographed with great artistry, it is at times a sensitive and moving study of loneliness and lack of fulfillment—rare themes in motion pictures. And Bette's performance was finely and delicately drawn, conveying a subtle sense of pain behind the confident surface.

In counterpoint to the anguished story of sexual deprivation there is the sharply witty characterization of snobbish New York social life, enlivened by the acid portrait of an effete Manhattanite by the excellent John Hoyt.

Although *Winter Meeting* was preferable to the overheated *Deception,* the picture proved to be the catastrophe of Bette's career. Jack Warner's impatience with her over her behavior on *Deception* would have been replaced by forgiveness if *Winter Meeting* (for which she can be held responsible) had been a commercial hit. But the delays in *Deception,* the long absence following the birth of her child, and now this fatal mistake in production destroyed his confidence in her as an asset. By 1948, her career at the studio was already doomed.

Her next picture, a comedy called *June Bride,* barely broke even, and Bette was, despite a brisk appearance, far from pleased with the shooting. Although she appeared in fan magazines praising the brilliance of her co-star Robert Montgomery, she disliked him intensely. Possibly her hatred of Montgomery is the reason for her exceptionally mannered comedy playing, notably lacking in sympathy and warmth in the love scenes.

One pleasure of the shooting—perhaps the only one— was that Bette formed a new friendship. She very much liked the young actress Betty Lynn, who played the bride of the story. They have remained close to this day.

Nineteen forty-eight was a watershed before a disaster. Barely able to tolerate her marriage, still finding satisfaction in her daughter, Bette spent much of the time trying futilely to get the Mary Todd Lincoln story and *Ethan Frome* off the ground. Unable to do so, she had to settle, early in 1949, for an absurdity called *Beyond the Forest,* a novel written by Stuart Engstrand, who, perhaps after reading the reviews, walked into a lake and drowned some days after the book appeared.

In *Beyond the Forest,* Bette played a small-town housewife who yearns for the big city—Chicago. Against a background of smoke-belching mill chimneys not unlike those which defaced the sky in Bette's birthplace of Lowell, Massachusetts, Rosa Moline is tormented and repressed: an American Emma Bovary. Bored with her sensible, down-to-earth husband, she becomes embroiled in a steaming affair with a macho businessman who later turns her down when she throws herself at his head. The plot involves a forced miscarriage, seductions, violent arguments, and arrivals and departures in heavy rain, all accompanied by the hothouse rhythms of Max Steiner's score. In the last scene, Rosa, half-dead, wanders distractedly toward a train, winding up, in a dramatic demise, firmly on the wrong side of the tracks.

The director was King Vidor, the most gifted craftsman Bette had worked with apart from Wyler. Yet Bette was unable to relate to the sober, subdued, and warmly human man. He was neither subservient nor overpowering: he was in a class by himself. She couldn't cope with his serious, controlled intelligence. And she overcompensated for the weaknesses in the writing by assuming a fantastic guise. She wore a long black wig, garish makeup, and ugly print dresses, and used all of her most extreme vocal and physical mannerisms in a rather desperate parody of herself. It was the beginning of a definite change in her approach to acting: a kind of exaggeration of all the elements that distinguished her as a performer.

As so often before, Bette was infuriated by the hypocrisy of the Breen office. When she visited an abortion clinic in the picture to get rid of an unwanted child, Jack Warner on Breen's instructions removed the clinic sign and put up another with the word *psychiatrist* painted on it. King Vidor says, "I don't think that fooled anybody. It was still obvious that she was trying to get rid of her baby."

Vidor recalls countless problems with Bette. He says, "One day we were doing a scene in which Joe Cotten, who plays her husband, a doctor, had given her a prescription in a small bottle. She picked the bottle up in disgust and threw it at him. I felt she threw it too weakly: I could see

251

she liked Joe. Her gesture was far too lacking in the necessary anger. I said to her, 'Bette, try it again!' She refused."

Bette was infuriated that Vidor overrode her in the gesture. She was not accustomed to being told what to do in so severe a manner. Tragically, she didn't realize that already her position was in danger, that she should not have dared to "cross" a famous director in this difficult period of her career. No longer box-office, she was no longer indispensable. It was her fatal mistake that her usual sense of realism failed her then.

She clashed with King Vidor again a day later. He says, "The only other point during the shooting which might have bothered her was a scene where she was dancing with [the actor] David Brian, who played the macho businessman. And there's this technique that's been used since the advent of sound—and it's still used—when you shoot a couple dancing they speak their lines when their faces can be seen. After one take that we did I said to Bette, 'I want to do it again, because when you swung around to speak your line you weren't facing the camera.' In fact, he was such a big fellow, David Brian, that she was completely covered. Today I wouldn't think anything of it, but this was the way things were done then. People were used to seeing the actors' faces when they spoke. So I said to Bette, 'Let's time it better so that they can see your face when you talk.'

"And Bette said, 'Oh, my *God*! Haven't they seen my face enough?' She went on in a loud voice, much louder than mine.

"So I said, 'That gives me a good idea. Let's do it again and fix it so they can't see your face at all.'

"She said, 'That's an excellent idea.'

"I told her, 'Keep your face hidden down there.' That must have burned her up something awful. And that's how we did it, so we couldn't see her face at all."

Bette called her agent, Lew Wasserman, and a meeting was held next morning at the studio, rather oddly on the set itself, between Wasserman, Bette's lawyer, and the studio's legal people, headed by Roy Obringer. She told the assembled group she refused to work that day. Word of this was brought to Jack Warner, who insisted on seeing Bette immediately. As it turned out, she was already on her way to his office. She stormed in and said, very loudly, "Jack, if you don't get another director, I want to be released from my contract. It's him or me!" Warner looked her straight in the eye. "Okay, Bette, it's you!" he said.

She froze for a moment, unable to believe what she was hearing. Then she stormed out. Warner was delighted at the opportunity to cancel Bette's contract. King Vidor says, "It took him fifteen minutes to draw up the papers and have her sign them on the set. But it says a great deal for her that she took the news after almost twenty years at the studio that had made her great without carrying on about it. She cooled off suddenly and did the rest of the picture like the pro she was. Suddenly, I saw the stuff she was made of. I lost all dislike of her."

The realities were there. Bette's pictures were more costly to make than those of other stars. They were not doing well at the box office. That was all that mattered in Hollywood. She was let go without a tremor.

From earning $10,000 per week or an average of $144,000 per picture, she found herself with nothing. Taxes and the cost of sustaining several people had left her far from the rich woman she should have been.

The day Bette left Warners after some thirteen years, having earned millions for the studio, nobody, from Jack Warner down, came to say good-bye. There was no farewell party. She sat on the bench with the grips and ate a box lunch. Then she drove home.

FOURTEEN

Within ten days of the disastrous press screening of *Beyond the Forest*, Bette filed suit for divorce against Sherry. It was agreed that Bette should have custody of B.D. with visiting rights by Sherry; that Sherry should not take B.D. out of the county of Los Angeles without Bette's written consent or outside the state. In a bitter passage in her memoirs, Bette says she had to pay Sherry alimony. By May of 1950, it was all over.

By another of those unappealing ironies that marked her career, Bette made as her next picture *The Story of a Divorce*, a bitter account of a collapsing marriage.* The film was directed by Curtis Bernhardt at RKO, and was Bette's first picture away from Warners in almost two decades. Intelligently written, harsh, and lacking in major compromises, *The Story of a Divorce* was much superior to Bette's recent vehicles at Warners. Bette ended it in a dark mood. Sherry was threatening to kidnap B.D. Convinced co-star Barry Sullivan was having an affair with Bette, Sherry burst into the sound stage one day and attacked Sullivan. Sullivan, a gentle, quiet man, struck back nervously; Sherry threw him to the floor. Then Sherry ran out, to face a damage suit and the final stages of the divorce.

Bette's character in the picture had to appear as fifteen

* It was later retitled *Payment on Demand*.

years old in one scene—a major challenge for a fortyish actress. She carried off the deception with amazing expertise. It was one of her finest performances, at its most striking in the scene in which, grim and determined, the wife attends a meeting to discuss alimony. The greed and cruelty of a detective, the heartlessness of lawyers, the sterile atmosphere of the house where the couple quarrel, all are admirably realized. The direction is consistently intelligent; there is no attempt to soften the pitiless ambition of the central female figure.

At the end of shooting there was a party which Sherry barged into. Bette had specifically excluded him from it, knowing he would cause trouble. He strode onto the set and dragged Bette from a table. She told him to leave at once and not come back. Barry Sullivan came over and said, "Why start trouble again? Why don't you have a sense of humor? The company's worked very hard and everybody's trying to relax." Once more Sherry took a swing at Sullivan; Sherry was dragged off by studio police.

During the last week of production, Darryl F. Zanuck, boss of 20th Century-Fox, got into a serious jam. He had cast the comedy-drama *All About Eve* with Claudette Colbert in the part of a temperamental star based on Elisabeth Bergner, a character who is threatened by the emergence of a younger actress. Colbert injured her back skiing in Switzerland and Zanuck needed a replacement. He approached Davis with some unease. He had quarreled with her violently over the administration of the Academy of Motion Picture Arts and Sciences during the brief period when she had been president. At first she didn't take his calls. But he finally reached her and explained that the picture was already starting to shoot in San Francisco and there was no time to waste. He rushed the script to her by special messenger; she read it at one sitting, fell in love with it, called Zanuck back to say she would immediately go ahead, and Zanuck rushed off to dinner with director Joe Mankiewicz.

The part of Margo Channing was perfect for her. Roy Moseley, a friend of Bette Davis's, describes the circumstances on which the plot was based: "Bergner was appearing in *The Two Mrs. Carrolls*, and a young actress playing a small part came straight to Bergner to say she would be quitting. And Miss Bergner said, 'Why?'

"And the young actress said, 'Because I'm not good enough, not good enough to be with you. You're so magnificent!' Bergner persuaded the young actress to stay on. The young actress was Irene Worth. The difference is, of course, that Bergner and Worth have remained friends to this day. There was an emulation, but not in an evil sense."

A little-known fact is that the part of Margo Channing was originally written for Gertrude Lawrence. She was actually signed to play it. But in the drunk scene where "Liebestraum" is played on the piano, Lawrence insisted on singing with it. Joe Mankiewicz refused to allow this, and Lawrence backed out.

Bette traveled to San Francisco in a state of great excitement, eager for work in her best picture in years. Although she didn't much warm to Mankiewicz, finding him self-opinionated, wordy, obvious, and much too slow at work, she was lost in admiration for his ability as a writer. She was also, with her customary professionalism, delighted to be surrounded by actors of equal importance, fine players like George Sanders, Thelma Ritter, and Anne Baxter; she welcomed and thrived on the vigorous competition for the audience's attention. And of course she was accepted at once with enormous enthusiasm into the acting company.

For years Bette has denied that she based her performance of Margo on any particular performer. But there is no escaping the fact that her hairstyle, gestures, movement, and sometimes the voice completely reflect Tallulah Bankhead. Mankiewicz almost certainly directed Bette as Tallulah without even telling her.

Mankiewicz has said of Margo Channing in an interview that he reduced her age from over forty-five to forty in making some adjustments to Bette's character:

> Forty years of age. Four O. Give or take a year the single most critical chronological milestone in the life of an actress. *Look*, I knew these women. I'd been in love with some—I'd worked with many of them. In

the late 1930's I'd watch them roll into Paramount and Metro at six-thirty in the morning on their way to hairdressing and make-up. Drive in usually with the top down, their hair all blown by the wind, no lipstick, their own eyelashes, wearing anything from a poncho to a polo coat—and I'd think Percy Westmore should be arrested for so much as touching a powder puff to their loveliness. Well, by the late thirties they were driving with the top up. Then, in the forties they started wearing scarfs. And by 1950 large hats. The pancake was getting thicker, the make-up took longer . . .*

The day before beginning work, Edmund Goulding, who had directed Bette in *Dark Victory*, called Mankiewicz at the San Francisco hotel and said, "Have you gone mad, dear boy? How could you hire such a woman? She will destroy you. She will grind you down to fine powder and blow you away. You are a writer, dear boy. She will come to the stage with a thick pad of long yellow paper. And pencils. She will rewrite everything. And then she, not you, will direct. Mark my words."**

But no problems awaited Mankiewicz of this kind. Despite her reservations about his character, she told him straight out, "I am neither Lady Macbeth nor Portia; I'll play either at a drop of a hat, anywhere. If I make a horse's ass of myself on the screen, it is I—me—Bette Davis—who is the forty feet by thirty feet horse's ass as far as they [the audience] are concerned. Not the writer, not the director, the producer, or the studio gateman—nobody but me. I'm up there as a representative horse's ass for all concerned. I made up my mind a long time ago, if anybody is going to make a horse's ass out of me, it's going to be me."

* Kenneth L. Geist, *Pictures Will Talk: The Life and Films of Joseph L. Mankiewicz* (New York: Charles Scribner's Sons, 1978).
** Ibid.

Mankiewicz admired Bette enormously. He has consistently praised her. He told his biographer:

> On the first day of shooting, I was marking Eddie Goulding's words. I had my antennae deployed to pick up possible storm warnings. Miss Davis arrived on the set fully dressed and made up, at least a quarter of an hour before she'd been called. Bette didn't even glance at the set. She lit her cigarette and opened the script . . . Bette was letter perfect. She was *syllable* perfect. There was no fumbling for words; they'd become hers—as Margo Channing. The director's dream: the prepared actress.

Cameraman Milton Krasner recalls that shooting the picture was a completely happy experience. Delighted with the script and ideally cast in every instance, the company relished the filming, and its relish shows on the screen. The picture expertly hits off the overheated, witty, dangerous world of theater people even while it glamorizes that world quite legitimately to appeal to public taste. One's only serious question is whether cynical, finely tuned people of this kind, alert to the presence of ambition and deception in their midst, would for an instant have accepted Eve, the relentless phony young actress, as one of them. Her line of fake sentiment seems false—too false to be accepted. And for all Anne Baxter's cleverness, it is hard to believe that an untried actress could suddenly emerge to fame and fortune with little more than cunning and chutzpah, and a capacity to imitate greatness. It is a misfortune that Eve's first theatrical triumph takes place off-screen.

By contrast, the acting and writing of the other parts is consistently convincing. Bette got along well with Celeste Holm, who played the cool, dignified writer's wife in expert contrast with Margo's tantrums and storms. Bette told me, "That scene in the car. When her friends maroon Margo in order to give Eve a chance. I couldn't have played it if I hadn't had Celeste with me. She was so perfect. And we were sweltering in our mink coats! It was *hot* in Hollywood and here we were pretending it was winter!" By contrast, Celeste Holm has not been as flattering about Bette. She complained to Mankiewicz's biographer Kenneth L. Geist that Bette and the romantic lead, Gary Merrill, spent all their time together and rudely ignored everyone else in the company.

This is unlikely.* But it is true that Bette found Merrill attractive, that he was powerfully drawn to her. Like Sherry, he was a man with a strong temper; he was extremely virile, hirsute, with an odd combination of a caveman physique, a carved all-American face, and a nimble, witty, challenging mind. Drawn always to very physical men who were unpretty and rugged, Bette was captivated by Merrill. Of all her husbands, she almost certainly cared for him most deeply. He was her match in temperament if not in talent; her match in his drive and fierce commitment to his profession, his intelligence and understanding. They should have been happy together.

By the time the picture was finished shooting, Bette was deeply involved with Merrill. It was an impassioned relationship, as impassioned as any Bette had known. And once again she was blinded by her strong physical drive toward domineering, extremely masculine men, blinded to the fact that the price she would pay would be in a direct challenge to her power. She committed herself to Merrill within only two months of their meeting. The divorce with Sherry was rushed through on Independence Day; Bette's independence lasted for only twenty-four days. One would have thought she would have wanted to draw breath, to enjoy a calmer life as a famous, highly individual woman for at least a little while. But instead she impetuously eloped with Merrill to Mexico, married him in late July, and flew with him to New England for a quick honeymoon.

* And Ms. Holm had forgotten these remarks when she appeared to give tribute to Bette at the AFI Life Achievement Awards in 1978.

At first she and Merrill managed to make a go of it. She had had more in common with him than she had had with her previous husbands; like Ham and Farney he knew the same places and people in New England, where he had lived in his early youth. Although she had striven almost too strenuously to interest herself in Ham's conducting, Farney's aircraft design, and Sherry's painting, these occupations were somewhat alien to her, creature that she was of show business. She was far more interested in discussing pictures and picture people than in trying to follow a musical score, an aircraft blueprint, or a seascape design. Merrill was steeped in show business. He was charming—an aggressive, self-conscious, hard-driving actor of talent who at that early stage was not yet conscious that he wouldn't make it to the top flight of stardom. Davis's and Merrill's lives moved in similiar circles. Ruthie and Bobby, and the Laguna Favors, all felt that Merrill came at least within distance of Bette's professional position and that he wasn't open to the suspicion of using her.

Along with her new marriage, which filled her with a great optimism, Bette knew a great triumph in the success of *All About Eve*. Her performance as Margo Channing, at once funny, sentimental, and powerful, attracted the highest praise she had received in years. Her acting was the result of years of technical refinement; above all, the development of a sharp and knowing worldliness honed fine by experience. Nobody who had not been part of the theater could have played with such understanding of the theater. No actress who was less than great could have made one believe in Margo Channing's greatness. Margo Channing and *All About Eve* represented the peak of Bette Davis's career. It is sad and unjust that she didn't receive the Academy Award for which she was nominated, but she was almost consoled by the New York Film Critics Circle Award and the San Francisco Film Critics Award.

As always in Bette's life, nothing ran smoothly. It would have been the joy of her life if Merrill could have been with her in the fake Oriental interior of Grauman's Chinese Theatre on November 9, 1950, when she saw *All*

About Eve from beginning to end for the first time. But he had been sent by Zanuck to Germany to make *Decision Before Dawn*—ironically, since that picture was directed by Bette's former lover, Anatole Litvak. And shortly afterward Bette had a quarrel with another of her former flames: Howard Hughes. He owned RKO, and he wanted to change the ending of *The Story of a Divorce*, along with the title, which became *Payment on Demand*. Bette was upset when Hughes destroyed the ending of the picture. The last reel was supposed to show that the wife in the story was as relentless as ever, confronting her future without hope. Instead the ending was softened and made ridiculous. Bette argued with Hughes in vain, their close feeling permanently fractured, their powerful mutual attraction long since forgotten.

One would have hoped that Bette would have gone from *All About Eve* to another triumph—but a disastrous professional mishap occurred instead.

The English screenwriter and producer Val Guest had written a script, *Another Man's Poison*, from a heavy, melodramatic stage play. He had designed the movie for Barbara Stanwyck, but a problem arose. Val Guest says: "Stanwyck was all signed and fixed for it, and one of her understandings if she came here to do it was that we would pay her fare to Rome to see her husband, Robert Taylor, and she could spend Christmas with him, and then come over to do the film. She went to Rome to surprise him, while he was shooting *Quo Vadis*, and she *did* surprise him—having an affair with somebody else. And from Rome she called me to say, in tears, 'I'm sorry. My whole life is in shreds. After all these years we've been married! I've got to go right back home and arrange a divorce. I'll have to bow out of the picture.'

"So I said, 'Work is the best thing you can do at a moment like this.'

"But she replied, 'No, no.' She had to go back to California.

"So there we were with a picture, a unit, a studio booked, and no star. What could we do?"

As so often before, Bette was second choice. Douglas

262

Fairbanks, Jr., who partly owned the picture, sent the script to Bette, who inexplicably liked it. She evidently saw a chance for her to co-star with Merrill; perhaps this overrode her better judgment. The story cast her as a thriller writer having an affair with a handsome young engineer in a house in Yorkshire. Her husband is a convict who comes back unexpectedly and she poisons him. The rest of the story involves a series of absurd events including attempted murder—and an impersonation of quite extraordinary implausibility. In the last scene Bette accidentally swallows a brandy glass full of poison, laughing uproariously when she discovers she is the victim of her own lethal dosage.

Just before leaving for England, Bette and Merrill adopted a pretty baby girl, Margot, who at that time seemed to be a normal child, giving no indication of the tragedy that lay ahead. Five-day-old Margot appeared to be perfect; she underwent the mandatory medical examination without a problem. Bette, who had been advised not to have any more children herself, adored this sweet creature, and adopting Margot bound Bette and Merrill very closely together. B.D. was three years old and Margot was presented to her as a "wonderful surprise." While B.D. closed her eyes, Bette put Margot in the child's lap. B.D. opened her eyes and squealed with joy.

Bette, Merrill, Bette's maid Dell Pfeiffer, B.D., Margot, and two nurses sailed to England aboard the *Queen Elizabeth* on December 1, 1951. They arrived after a rough crossing in freezing winter weather to be greeted by a hostile press, rationing, harsh postwar austerity, and an England that was far removed from the prosperous country Bette remembered, perhaps unrealistically, from the late 1930s. The press was so vicious—dubbing Merrill "Mr. Bette Davis"—that she threatened to go straight back to America when the *Queen Elizabeth* returned.

She arrived at the Savoy Hotel in a temper to face a disagreeable press conference. She wasn't feeling well and looked haggard and worn—which the press photographers exploited cruelly. Maybe because of the extreme openness and depth of her emotion, and an increased tendency to let her health go, she had aged very suddenly and looked

263

much older than she did in *All About Eve*. Few reporters failed to note this.

As a result, her insecurity was enormously increased. Val Guest, who went to the Savoy to talk with her, says, "She was very uneasy. She had struggled and got to the top at forty-three and viewed anyone she didn't know as the person who was going to undo many years of stardom and slogging. I tried everything, foul means and fair, to win her confidence. At last I did. She showed a toilet sense of humor, she was loud and boisterous, but even then there was a problem: She had no sense of humor about herself. She took herself seriously to the point of excluding humor. Because 'herself' was her career."

Irving Rapper was imported as director. Robert Krasker was chosen as cameraman. Bette was nervous about working for the first time with a British cinematographer. Conscious of her appearance—she looked older than her years—she was afraid of a realist who wouldn't protect her as her favorites Haller and Polito had done. She had reached an age at which the cameraman was as essential to her as the makeup artist, and considerably more important than the director, since she could be relied upon, at least in this instance, to do much of the directing herself.

She agreed to Krasker's selection on the interesting ground that he had won an Academy Award. Val Guest continues: "She would *only* have an Academy Award-winning man. She insisted on having photographic tests done with him before we started production. Bob was not a 'glamour' photographer, but a very fine, harshly accurate cameraman. We all went in to look at the tests. Everyone was terrified of Bette. She didn't dole out warmth that day. The lights went down and the tests came on the screen.

"I could see Bette was very unhappy about her haggard appearance. Suddenly she snapped open a cigarette lighter, lit up a cigarette, and asked, with an acid edge only she could manage, 'And for *what* did this man get his Academy Award?'

"Bob had won if for *The Third Man*, which was shot in a war-torn Vienna. And someone at the back of the projection room said, in answer to her question, and very loudly, 'For shooting ruins!'

"There was immediate chaos. Bette yelled out, 'Put the lights on! Stop everything! Who said that?' No one owned up, needless to say. She stamped out. But afterward, more tests were done, and she was pleased. She was a sport. She kept Krasker on."

Work began at Walton Studios. It was miserable from the beginning. Bette realized she had been insane to do the script in the first place. She argued constantly with Irving Rapper, and virtually controlled the shooting, insisting on rehearsing scenes over and over again, dismissing an anxious camera operator who explained the difficulties of a staircase shot with a sharp "I don't know about that. It's *your* problem!" She tended to fluff her lines, overplayed some scenes, and underplayed others. She smoked forty cigarettes a day, and as many as sixty during particularly strenuous days. At one stage, after completing a staircase scene, she was so exhausted she lay at its foot without being able to get up. She called her male romantic lead, Anthony Steel, "a beautiful prop," which infuriated him. When they played a love scene on a bank, they rehearsed over and over again, and finally Bette said, "Look, just let me do it. Do nothing. Let me do it." She wound up on top of him, completely blocking him from the camera.

The cast and crew took off to the Yorkshire moors and had to sleep on couches in farmhouses. One night everybody gathered in damp and chilly conditions, feeling thoroughly depressed, before a radio to hear the Academy Awards. Screwed up to an extreme of tension, Bette quipped cheerfully, pretending not to care whether she won or not. The rain beat down outside. The announcements droned on and on.

Everyone expected to hear tremendous news. When the words, "And the winning actress is . . ." came over the air, Bette jumped up. At the words *Judy Holliday* she sat down abruptly. She gave the performance of her lifetime in front of the others, lying with consummate bravery:

"That's *good*! A *newcomer* got it! I couldn't be more *pleased*!" Not a soul believed her.

Bette stayed at a place called Greatfosters near London. A consolation of the shooting of the picture was that she enjoyed the hotel and Merrill proved to be very affectionate. Once more, as she had done in the late 1930s, she loved the English people. The Elizabethan atmosphere of the hotel—the family occupied a wing—fascinated her and sometimes at night she poked about, looking for ghosts and secret passages in a humorous childlike mood.

Bette was enormously relieved when *Another Man's Poison* was completed and the Merrills could set sail for America (Bette still hated flying) on board the *Queen Mary*.

On the way back, in heavy weather, Margot seemed to cry excessively. But still Bette had no inkling of what was to come.

Another Man's Poison was a critical failure and scarcely broke even at the box office. It was a film so embarrassingly bad as to be virtually unwatchable today. Bette returned to California in a surprisingly good mood, delighted with B.D. and Margot, enjoying her role as a mother, still convinced Merrill was right for her. She and Merrill decided B.D. and Margot needed a baby brother, so they adopted a little boy, naming him Michael Merrill.

The family, after a brief stay in Malibu, moved into a large ugly house in West Hollywood and Bette and Merrill began reading scripts. Merrill received the first offer: Zanuck sent him the screenplay of an omnibus picture, *Phone Call from a Stranger*, in which he would act the survivor of an air crash. Bette insisted on playing the small part of a crippled woman injured in an underwater swim. Zanuck was amazed she would want to do what was in essence a bit part, and this may have been a mistake in her career. Her performance was very fine but many people felt she was slipping; the signs of a declining career were ominous. After the triumph of *All About Eve*, there had been nothing more than a melodramatic failure and a small part in an episode picture. And now came a depressing example of

Hollywood hackdom: *The Star*, the story of an actress down on her luck, reduced to selling lingerie at the May Company, arguing with a hard-bitten family, and driving about drunkenly through the Beverly Hills settings of her former glory. A weakness had begun to show itself: poor judgment of scripts, the downfall of many performers. At first she had thought the script of *Another Man's Poison* was good, but at least she became disillusioned when work started on the picture. In the case of *The Star* she continued to admire the script until the end of shooting and still admires it. And she made the mistake tactical as well as professional, of acting a failed performer: an open invitation to critics who said she was all too visibly a failure. Several reviewers seized on the publicity flimflam for the production ("The orchids . . . the furs . . . the diamonds that were the star's were all gone now . . . and nothing remained . . . but the woman!").

The picture was directed by Stuart Heisler and co-starred the large and rugged actor Sterling Hayden, a man of many talents flawed by a streak of intellectual pretension. Shot cheaply in twenty-four days, the picture's chief merit was that it gave a seedy, authentically grim view of Hollywood in the 1950s.

Bette clashed with Stuart Heisler on the first day they met. Heisler said: "I got into the damnedest wrangle with her about the script. I said, 'These writers, for chrissakes, they're silly. All they're doing is pussyfooting you.'

"And she said, 'What do you mean? I like those little touches.'

"I said, 'They don't mean a damn thing. You've got a subject here that's got guts in it. These little things they want you to do, Christ, they'll ruin the whole picture. Just throw the whole thing out of the window.'

"And she went into the goddamnedest scene and I thought, 'Oh, shit, this is it.' Anyway, we went through the script and I kept telling her, 'That's no good, that's no good, that's throwing time and effort away.' At the end, she shrugged and gave in. I loved her for that and we never argued again."

Heisler shot almost the entire picture in first takes;

Bette enjoyed the challenge. Her keen mind ensured a degree of realism, particularly in an ugly scene in which the actress is dismissed from the lingerie counter: a bitter moment evoking those days before customers in department stores were reduced to helping themselves from the racks. But not even she could save the poverty-row atmosphere of the picture, with its gray, grainy images. *Time* magazine said that Bette was "down to her last thousand tantrums," and today the picture looks that way. It is unfortunate that while eagerly accepting the script of *The Star*, Bette turned down the screenplay of *Come Back, Little Sheba,* William Inge's play about a drab housewife that would probably have won her major critical acclaim. Again, her fatal lack of judgment let her down.

During the shooting of *The Star*, Bette formed a new friendship that would last the rest of her life. There was a scene in which a child, the star's daughter, Natalie Wood, was to fall in water from a pier. Stuart Heisler wanted to throw Natalie in; the little girl was terrified, and cried hysterically. Bette heard Natalie's cries, came out of her trailer, picked Natalie up, and said to Heisler, "If you make Natalie do this, I'll walk off the picture. Who do you think she is? Johnny Weissmuller? You mustn't do this kind of thing to a little child." Heisler backed down and Bette took over the direction of the scene.

In the summer of 1952, Bette began to think of returning to the stage. Somebody came up with the idea of her following Judy Garland into the Palace in New York, playing scenes from her pictures and singing various numbers. Fortunately, this ghastly idea was never realized. Instead she was approached to appear in a scarcely more inspiring format, in an absurd musical revue called *Two's Company.* Vernon Duke came to her house in West Hollywood and played the tinkly score, which contained not a single memorable number. And Bette's disastrous judgment drove her into another catastrophe.

She made a mistake as serious as undertaking a show that called for singing and dancing, neither of which she could manage with more than minimum competence. She also refused an understudy, which meant that severe pres-

268

sure was put on her not to be absent for a single performance.

Bette had for some time had dental problems. But, obsessed with work and career, she didn't have the patience (or perhaps the courage) to face a dentist. The poison from an infected tooth drained into her system without her knowing it and caused her to feel tired and ill much of the time. Moreover, the awareness that she had rendered herself literally irreplaceable made her weary and strained. She and Merrill moved from West Hollywood to New York and she went into tough rehearsals. She wound up exhausted by her commitment and intensity, by forcing her voice when she had no singing ability and stretching her forty-four-year-old body to the limit in order to manage complicated stage movements. Her lack of a basic calisthenic training program each morning through her life and her fondness for smoking and alcohol told on her severely. She had forgotten that a stage star has to have the physique of an athlete in order to stand and move about for hours at high pressure night after night.

Two's Company opened in Detroit in October. She went on the stage completely wrung out, feeling seriously ill after a night without sleep in which Merrill had in vain begged her to relax. She had to go onstage in the opening scene in a large magician's box. It was airless, cramped, and hot, and Bette, when she burst out of it suddenly felt giddy. As she sang a number called "Good Little Girls," the lights began to swim in front of her. Just as she entered the third chorus, she blacked out. The audience screamed as she fell forward, jarring her chin. Merrill rushed to her side as the curtain was rung down and said to her sharply, "Get up, Bette, get up!" She was grateful for the instruction. She struggled to her feet and walked out front to deliver the memorable quip, "Well, you can't say I didn't fall for you!" Incredibly, she willed herself with Merrill's help to complete the performance, which involved several complicated musical numbers and some dance movements. She had never been more painfully aware of the pressure of knowing that she had to go on because people had bought tickets to see her, and that her replacement by an understudy would result in the play closing and the disappointment of her former mentor, the producer John Murray Anderson, to whom she owed so much.

With fairly good reviews, the show proceeded to Pittsburgh and Boston. Bette cut the opening song from the show; superstition got the better of her. When she arrived in New York in the icy December of 1952 the poisoned tooth had severely weakened her system. And added to the physical illness was a psychosomatic one: the sickness of fear that she would let herself and everybody else down, that she would not return in triumph to Broadway; that she would not be the big Broadway star everyone would expect after *All About Eve*.

She was so ill she was unable to attend rehearsals. John Murray Anderson had put in a great deal of work in changing the show at the last minute. She had to go on without being able to prepare for changes.

She struggled through opening night, imitating Tallulah Bankhead, Jeanne Eagels, a hillbilly singer complete with briar pipe, a tenement dweller, and a torch singer. The reviews were, on the whole, bad. Brooks Atkinson, who had so warmly encouraged her at the outset of her career, wrote, "No one should be surprised to discover that her severe performing is on the elementary side—colorless and monotonous. She has never had a chance to learn the sharp techniques of musical acting." The critic of the *New York World-Telegram* took a more mixed view:

> Her dancing is likely to consist of hip rolls, marching and none too steady lifts by a whole corps of male partners. Her singing is deep, husky, very articulate and rhythmic, but not very musical. In sketches she can do almost anything better than whip off a laugh line. But . . . Miss Davis is electric, as she always has been on the screen . . . Somewhere along the line you are dazzled and in the end awed.

Bette was devastated by most of the reviews; she was convinced the critics were inspired by snobbery about Hollywood stars. However, she was cheered by the packed houses, and the show ran successfully on her name to predominantly gay audiences through the long winter into 1953. But the infection continued to drain into her neck and shoulders, causing pain that was often very severe. In early March she had to be injected daily by Dr. Stanley Berman at New York Hospital with penicillin and pain-killing drugs to get her through the performances. She managed to survive a special benefit for actors. But after the Sunday-night performance she was rushed to the hospital where Dr. Berman extracted the infected tooth. Examining the jawbone, Berman discovered what he had feared most; that she had osteomyelitis, a disease of the bone that was very rare in adults. He told Bette she would have to have a major operation in which the diseased tissue would be scraped from the jaw. The show was closed immediately and the road tour canceled.

Walter Winchell ruthlessly lied to his public that Bette had cancer. Propped up miserably in her hospital bed, Bette read this lie in Winchell's column and fired off a demand he retract at once. He did—and published her telegram along with the retraction. But many people still believed she was mortally stricken. It would be three years before she recovered completely. And a worse suffering lay immediately ahead.

FIFTEEN

During the run of *Two's Company*, Bette's distress had been increased by the strange, unsettling behavior of little Margot. The child had continued crying all night even at the age of two, sobbing hysterically and sometimes throwing her bedclothes on the floor. Margot took an exceptionally long time to adjust to her new parents and would alternate excessive affection with unexpected bouts of hostility. Ruthie warned Bette that similar indications of mental and emotional imbalance had been found in Bobby when Bobby had been a little girl.

Merrill and Bette tried their utmost to deal with the troublesome child. Their marriage was unstable, insecure; they were capable of shifting from charm to violent anger and hostility with scarcely a warning. Yet they did their best to create a normal home for Margot in the face of the painful realities of show business, with its basic insecurity and enforced domestic moves—drastic threats to the stability of any household.

It soon emerged that there was a worse problem than simply a severe emotional disturbance in Margot. In the period following *Two's Company*, the Merrills moved to Witch Way, a large house, rather gloomy in winter months, situated high up over the ocean at Cape Elizabeth, Maine. They embarked on life in their new residence with enthusi-

273

asm, remodeling, refurnishing, working on the garden, and keeping a succession of servants in a dither of excitement followed by joyous anxiety.

One afternoon, Bette has written, when she was paying a visit to her neighbors, she rashly left three-year-old Margot on her own in the automobile. As Bette emerged from the neighbors' house, she was disturbed to see that Margot had angrily stripped off all her clothes on that chilly day and flung them into the drive. The neighbor's wife made light of this, but Bette felt a stab of unease. And when, a few days later, Margot again flung off her clothes and threw them through a window, Bette realized something serious was wrong.

Nights began to prove unbearable. Margot would not just cry, but suddenly jump to her feet and scream like an animal, almost cracking the bars of the crib. Every effort Bette and Merrill made to have her settle down proved futile. Often the Merrills would be up all night struggling with Margot—doing everything possible to make her relax.

One morning Bette came into the playroom. She had, some weeks before, given Margot an adorable kitten, and had been worried because Margot seemed indifferent to the pet. On this occasion Bette was pleased to see Margot fondling the creature. As Bette opened the door a look of hatred distorted the child's face. Margot squeezed the terrified animal's throat until it began to choke. Bette screamed with horror; she came perilously close to striking Margot across the face. She snatched the kitten from her—and began to cry from desperation and exhaustion after a week virtually without sleep.

Still recovering slowly from the painful operation on her jaw and the distress caused her by the column items suggesting she had cancer, Bette came as close to a nervous breakdown over Margot as she had since Farney's near death from pneumonia and her frantic air flight to him in 1943. Often her quarrels with Merrill came about because they vented on each other an anger that sprang from frustration, an anger that it was not in their decent natures to vent on the child.

Bette and Merrill tried to encourage B.D., Margot, and

Michael to play together, so that Margot would feel she was a member of a family that loved her and wanted to protect her. But B.D. found it difficult to sleep with Margot and was given a separate room.

A horrifying episode took place in the summer of 1953. During a hot late afternoon, Michael and Margot were playing together when Margot suddenly pulled Michael's hair out by the roots with a strength astonishing in so small a child. Bette heard the screams and came running. The two children had disappeared. Almost vomiting, her stomach in knots, Bette ran all over the house, looking for the children. Then she heard a scream from the bar. There was a sound of shattering glass. Bette opened the door. She felt dizzy for a moment at what she saw.

The floor was strewn with broken cocktail glasses. Michael was covered with blood. Margot was watching him as he bled from many cuts on his shoulders and arms. Margot held a piece of broken glass in one hand.

Bette broke down completely. Fortunately, Merrill proved to be a tower of strength in this agonizing moment. He cleaned Michael's wounds and soothed him. It was obvious, Bette wrote in articles and told in interviews over the years, that Margot needed professional help. Bette and Gary took Margot to New York's Presbyterian Hospital for tests.

Waiting for the results of the tests was an appalling experience. Bette was worn out physically and mentally when she went in with Merrill for a meeting with the doctors at the end of a week. They explained to her that the child wasn't merely displaying symptoms of dementia. She was also brain-damaged and must have been from birth. Her I.Q. was 60 and would probably never improve. The damage was incurable.

In this desolate moment the doctors tried to provide some hope. They told Bette and Merrill that Margot could at least be given some degree of training to enable her to adjust better to her surroundings. Infinite care and patience would help. It was a question of the child being sympathetically controlled. Normal people and things would drive a retarded child into desperate anger and frustration.

The doctors asked Bette if Margot seemed to have unusual strength for her age. Bette explained that Margot actually threw heavy chairs and tables out of windows without injuring herself.

The doctors advised the Merrills not to continue having Margot at home. It was obvious that centering an entire life around a sick child would ultimately and most seriously affect Bette's health. At forty-six, the suffering that her always excessively nervous temperament endured through Margot had aged her still more. Her shockingly haggard appearance alarmed Ruthie and Bobby so much when they came to visit that they insisted on Bette returning Margot to the adoption agency on the grounds that the child had been illegally supplied.

Bette violently disagreed. Her motherly instinct made her want to devote herself utterly to giving Margot some degree of light in the hell in which Margot lived. But Gary, her family, and the doctors finally overrode her obstinate and well-intended objections. They persuaded her to take Margot to an institution known as the Lochland School on Lake Geneva in northern New York State. Florence Stewart was the director, a genius in the field of retarded children.

The Merrills drove to Lake Geneva in agony of mind at parting with Margot and submitting her to an alien environment. But as soon as they saw the Lochland School, which they had feared would be a grim institution with guards and high walls, they were deeply relieved. The school was in a converted nineteenth-century mansion with a new brick schoolhouse on the grounds and many oak and elder trees shading the smooth green lawns that rolled down to the nearby lake.

They were even more pleased when they met Florence Stewart. A warm, lovable, but firmly disciplined woman, she exuded good sense and efficiency. She took the Merrills and Margot to meet many of the retarded pupils, showing how they were taught coordination, peaceable cohabitation, and various crafts that could control their extreme nervousness. The children were given special clothes, which, though attractive, were as effective as straitjackets in preventing them from leaping from their beds and causing themselves injury at night. Miss Stewart explained that the first essential for a retarded pupil was for her to feel she could contribute something to the world; that she was not a useless near-animal whom people barely tolerated; that she must be constantly praised because retardation brought with it a profound, inborn inferiority complex.

Bette and Gary didn't immediately decide to leave Margot at the school. They needed some time to think about it. They drove back to Maine. As they made their way along a leafy country road, Bette suddenly burst into tears. The idea of sending her beloved daughter away proved too much for her. But with her usual common sense, the New England pragmatism that overcame the more hysterical strain in her nature, Bette pulled herself together and realized her tears were selfish. Her mind was made up. Merrill was greatly relieved. A week or so later, Bette, again fighting back tears, her vitality very low, dressed Margot in a little sailor suit and Gary flew the child back to school.

Bette was constantly in tears after Margot left—wondering if she could endure much more. But she rallied and, with Margot gone, began to enjoy some desperately needed sleep. She learned not to call the school too often; to control her overwrought nature and let the teachers get on with their training of Margot. She could visit Lochland; and in the summer and at Christmas Margot came to visit, showing signs of improvement but still unable to control her rampant, terrifying hostility.

Bette's life should have been completely peaceful during this period of semiretirement. But even though she was inactive, recovering through late 1953 and into 1954 until at last she began to feel strong again, Merrill had to go on working for the sake of his career. And here was another problem. It was a torment to this driving and ambitious man that all the way from the heights of *All About Eve* he was suddenly reduced to motion pictures of surpassing mediocrity like *A Blueprint for Murder, Witness to Murder,*

The Black Dakotas, and *The Human Jungle.* The worst blow of all was that at thirty-eight his contract at 20th Century-Fox was summarily canceled. Sometimes he would fly with Bette, B.D., and Michael, Bette hating every minute of the air journey, to hole up in a Los Angeles hotel, trudge through weeks of futile shooting, and at the end have a sense that his career might be over. To anyone like Merrill, this was nothing short of a catastrophe. He would slam his fists on walls or tables. Sadly, Bette told court judges later, he took to drinking, trying to drown his disappointment in the traditional and futile manner in alcohol. The marriage somehow kept going, perhaps more because of love of B.D. and Michael and concern for Margot than anything else. The misery the Merrills endured over Margot was a binding factor.

For the sake of sanity, Bette needed to work again and it was Darryl F. Zanuck who came to the rescue. He found a script which would, he felt, restore her to the top: *Sir Walter Raleigh,* later retitled *The Virgin Queen.* She liked the script, which dealt with an older and more subdued monarch than the ferocious figure of *The Private Lives of Elizabeth and Essex.* The problem was that Merrill was in a TV series in New York and there would have to be a separation. But the couple agreed that this mightn't be a bad idea. The ordeal with Margot and the quarrels had made living together increasingly painful in recent months. For every cookout, lobster picnic, or beach visit, for every evening of laughter and family games, each could count at least a dozen traumas and turmoils that year.

Once more, in February 1955, Bette found herself back in Hollywood. CinemaScope had come in, temporarily revitalizing the industry but reducing motion pictures to watery versions of the stage. Because of the peculiar demands of the wide screen, performers found themselves compelled to learn full scenes, to make exits and entrances without the protection of clever cutting, and to meet the requirements called for by Broadway or the West End. Needless to say, this was no problem for Bette, but she resented the ugly bluish tints of DeLuxe Color and the clumsy CinemaScope cameras.

She was also suffering from an old problem that was aggravated by middle age: the extreme sensitivity of her pale blue eyes to both indoor and outdoor powerful light; and her delicate skin which, still missing the top layer after her burning incident as a child, freckled and scorched in scenes calling for direct sunlight. *The Virgin Queen*'s cameraman, Charles G. Clarke, remembers, "The stronger the sun, the deeper the shadows, and the great problem with lighting exteriors is filling the shadows. Bette didn't like the bright lights too much. She kept saying to me they were too intense for her. And she thought she knew something about cinematography and lighting. A couple of times she'd try and tell me my job, but I don't put up with that kind of business."

Clarke remembers a particular incident: "One thing I recall was when we were working in a courtyard. It was supposed to be an English courtyard. It was an exterior, naturally. And when I'd finished lighting it, she demanded that the whole thing be diffused. That meant breaking for lunch and having the grips come in and hanging and stretching these diffusers all over the set. I think her main reason for demanding that was just to show that she was the star. If it had been necessary to use diffusers, I would have done it in the first place. That cost us a couple of hours."

Bette's quarrels with Clarke had to be refereed by director Henry Koster, who had made his name with the Deanna Durbin pictures. On one occasion Bette was seated on a bed, her hair shaved back, in an ugly red wig, feeling terrible. Clarke took what seemed to her an unbearable amount of time setting up the lights and moving the camera on instructions to his operator toward the bed. Suddenly, unexpectedly, she exploded against the infuriated Clarke and production stopped for over an hour while the savage words flew to and fro.

Bette's regal behavior, appropriate to her role, upset the entire unit. The brutal fact was that she no longer occupied the supreme position in Hollywood that would justify behavior acceptable at Warners in her heyday. Marilyn Monroe was the queen of 20th Century-Fox, not Bette Davis.

This fact was often and painfully brought home to her. But Zanuck, surprisingly in view of his ruthlessness, was very supportive, gave Bette extraordinary license—and a dressing room almost comparable with Monroe's.

The picture lacked the physical splendor of *Elizabeth and Essex*. It was a somewhat dowdy production, drab and pedestrian, and the public notably failed to respond at the previews. The result was that the studio virtually threw the picture away, and it lost money, a sure sign that Bette's star was rapidly fading.

Back in Maine, at the house called Witch Way ("Because a witch lived in it," Bette used to say), the Merrills continued their uneasy, spiky marriage. Their separate schedules (Merrill was still making second-grade thrillers) and their temperaments did not lead to any increase in comfort and ease. Bette tried to occupy herself with new scripts; at last she found one she liked, written by Daniel Taradash and Elick Moll; *The Library*. The picture had been written in 1951, when Joe McCarthy and his redbaiting was at its height. It was a story directly antagonistic to McCarthy's point of view, about a librarian accused of left-wing commitment. The story included a ritual burning of books.

Mary Pickford originally was supposed to come out of her retirement of nineteen years to make the picture. But she was annoyed when a headline in the *New York Herald Tribune* announcing her comeback was headed "Life Begins at Fifty-Eight." And within days of her committing verbally to the project, the right-wing forces closed in on her. The ferocious Hedda Hopper called her and asked her if she had gone out of her mind, wanting to appear in a "Red motion picture." Pickford panicked that she would be identified with the left wing and backed out. The very right-wing Barbara Stanwyck and Irene Dunne were approached, but of course declined. Liberal Bette Davis was fourth in line for the part and accepted it immediately.

Daniel Taradash and the producer Julian Blaustein flew to Maine to discuss the script with Bette. She was so determined to make it, felt it was so important, that she took a very small sum of money up front against a percentage of the gross. But no sooner had she agreed to go ahead, feeling that the part of an embattled librarian would be a wonderful opportunity for a big performance, than Harry Cohn, boss of Columbia, decided the McCarthy era was ancient history and no one would want to see the picture. It was only when producer and director agreed to make the movie for no money and a profit share that he agreed to go ahead.

Bette began shooting the movie, retitled *Storm Center*, in the suffocating August of 1955. It was shot in the pleasant small town of Santa Rosa, California, where Hitchcock had made *Shadow of a Doubt*. Bette enjoyed Santa Rosa, the warm and friendly people and the pleasant setting with its tree-lined streets and lack of pressure. But as always there were problems; her nerves began to fray as the shooting went on.

A major headache was the child actor Kevin Coughlin, who later became a casting director. Good at the reading, crying convincingly on cue, he never cried again. Taradash says, "His mother was on the set, and it would make me sick because she would take him away and pinch him to make him cry on cue but it failed to work every time."

Bette, in spite of her love of children, became impatient with Coughlin and irritated by Taradash's incapacity to direct the child. She talked of "amateurism." She was also infuriated because local women's club leaders beseeched her with letters warning her that the film was subversive and that for the good of herself and her children she should walk off the picture. There was one gruesome experience during the shooting, followed by a surprise. Taradash says: "One day, Bette had a day off. We were shooting a scene in which Kevin Coughlin and some of the neighborhood kids discuss communism. They wandered along a street with small residential houses. As we passed a front door, a hag with wild hair jumped out and screamed: 'I told you motion-picture people I didn't want you around! Now you get the hell out of here or I will call the police!' She screamed on and on and on.

"My God, I was terrified! I said to the assistant director,

'Didn't you get permission from all these residents? Didn't you get releases? You should have given them fifty dollars apiece.'

" 'Fifty dollars!' the harridan shrieked. 'You're out of your ever-loving mind! Think that would buy me off? You're crazy, the whole lot of you! I'm calling the police right now!' And then suddenly the hag pulled off her gray wig and stood there holding her sides with laughter. It was Bette!"

At times, Bette changed from joking to toughness. Taradash told me: "She *can* be tough. She had worked with Willie Wyler, who would often make actors and actresses do ten, fifteen, twenty takes without telling them why. There was one scene that I did with her when you could see the title of the book, *The Communist Dream*. It was a close shot of her as she's replying to the city councilman. I wanted it framed so that you could see the title of the book as she talks about it. It was a long speech and she did the take perfectly. But the camera operator whispered to me that the aperture was set so that the book could not be seen. So I asked him if he changed the position of the camera a bit, could he get the book in without any trouble, and he said yes.

"So I said, 'Bette, I'd appreciate it if we could do it once more.'

"And she said, 'Why?'

"I didn't really want to tell her the truth, so I said, 'I don't know why.'

"And then she said, 'Well, in that case I'm not going to do it!' She said, 'If you can't tell me what change you want, there's no point in doing a scene over for no reason.'

"I said, 'Bette, I really don't know, I just have some kind of a feeling we ought to do it again.'

"I didn't want to tell her the reason, because I was afraid she would blow up and say, 'If I can be a pro you can be pros too, and if you want something in the shot, then get it in the shot.' So I said, 'I really don't know, I just feel we can do it better.' I tried to be as vague as possible: 'I just can't articulate it, Bette.' Finally I said, 'All right, Bette, if you don't want to do another take, then we won't do it.'

"And then she said, 'Oh, all right, go ahead . . .'

"The irony of this story is that I discovered later that the first take turned out to have a negative scratch on it. So the second take was wonderful for two reasons: We got the book in, and there was no scratch on the negative."

Bette was very lonely during the shooting. She missed Merrill in spite of their differences—there were rumors that they had actually separated, rumors which were unfounded but still unsettling. Moreover, some of the crew were having affairs with people in the town or flew their wives in; the producer and director were too busy to escort Bette to dinner or cocktails at night. They were preoccupied with preparing the pages for the next day's work. She usually ate dinner alone.

Back in Hollywood, Bette was given the star dressing room. One day she heard a noise from the wall next to her dressing table. She was astonished when the wall flew open and Harry Cohn walked in. He began to make an obscene gesture. She snapped in her best frost-and-fire manner, "How dare you come in here. Get out immediately and don't dare come back!" Suddenly sheepish, the all-powerful studio boss turned on his heel and disappeared. Later that day, Bette told a studio executive of this alarming apparition from the woodwork. He said, "Oh, Bette, I wouldn't flatter yourself too much. He hadn't been told they moved Kim Novak to an even bigger dressing room last night!"

Storm Center was as worthy as it was dull, and notably failed to set the box office on fire. Bette felt her hopes dashed; she was slightly revived by being offered the leading role in Paddy Chayevsky's *The Catered Affair*—and along with it the chance to rent Fay Bainter's attractive house at Malibu.

The Catered Affair was made at MGM and directed by Richard Brooks. Bette played a Brooklyn mother, overweight, gray-wigged and unattractive, but with great warmth and charm. Bette was fascinated by Brooks, an appealing and handsome man's man: sure sign that her marriage to Merrill, with its endless conflicts of ego and schedules, was now in even worse trouble. But Brooks was not similarly drawn to her, and this created a measure of tension during the shooting. In one conversation with Brooks, she made a curious indirect reference to Wyler. Brooks recalls: "One day, after we'd been shooting a day or two, we were sitting around. I was lining up a shot and she was sitting in a chair beside me. She said, 'Do you think it's going to be all right?'

"And I said, 'I think we're getting into it.'

"She fell silent and didn't say anything. And I said, 'You know, probably every director you've ever worked with has been in love with you.'

"And she said, 'Really? Why?'

"I said, 'I don't know why. But that could happen. You're a very sensual woman.' She didn't say anything. I went on: *Jezebel, Dangerous, Marked Woman, Little Foxes*—in all those pictures you can see the love that your directors had for you. I don't know if any of those loves were consummated, but I can see it on the screen.'

"And she said, 'You can?'

"And I said, 'Yeah—it's up there.'

"She said, 'You're crazy.' She then said, 'Name the pictures where you think it was consummated.' So I named a couple. I'm not going to tell which ones. She said, 'You really think you can see it up there?' And then she said, 'Well, we could have been great together—but I was a coward.' "

Brooks remembers that there was a difficult scene in which the housewife played by Davis had to come apart under the pressures of arranging her daughter's wedding. She had to start sobbing as she left the parlor, walk down a hallway, and enter a bedroom—then completely break down. The husband (Ernest Borgnine) was in the kitchen swilling beer. "I asked Bette not to lie on the bed sobbing as the script indicated," Brooks says. "I asked her to sit on a chair, put her arms on the bed, lay her head on her arms, and just sob her heart out."

Brooks explained the scene to Bette. She asked him, looking him straight in the eye, "What kind of crying are you talking about?"

Brooks got the impression that she had so vast a repertoire of emotion she could turn on tears instantly at any

284

degree of intensity that was called for. He told her, "From the belly. I don't just want to see tears in your eyes. Your whole life is falling apart."

Bette told him, "Fine. I'll do it. But I can only do it once. Can you get it in the first take?"

Brooks told her, very honestly, that he wasn't sure. For two hours he laid out the scene in terms of camera movement so that the camera could follow her all the time in one continuous take that wouldn't have to be shot again. The camera could not be mounted on tracks because Bette might stumble. Finally the camera was mounted on a three-wheel dolly. When he was ready, Brooks said, "Are you okay, Miss Davis?"

She had spent the whole two hours in deepest concentration. She replied, "I won't say anything. I'll just nod to you when I'm ready." Five minutes later, screwing up her emotions, she nodded. Brooks shot the scene perfectly; Bette built the emotion from the first sob to the final storm of hopeless tears. It was one of her best moments on the screen.

There was another strong moment at the end of the picture. The husband and wife are left alone in their depressing apartment. All of the poison of their many quarrels has drained out of them and now they are left with nothing except four walls and little or nothing to say. At last they go to the church for the daughter's wedding. A lovely touch has the father start to get into the taxi ahead of the mother and then remember his manners and open the door for her. Bette's laugh at that moment had to be a combination of sheer amusement, resignation, and an understanding of her husband's reality. Brooks says, "One laugh told it all. She stopped as she got into the taxi and she looked at him and the look was wonderful. She was of course so supreme a professional that she instinctively knew where the camera was even though she couldn't see it. Her laugh was so joyful, it ended the picture perfectly. What an actress she is!"

Much of the performance was modeled by Brooks on his mother. Bette wanted to know what his mother was like. Brooks said, "She suffered all the time."

Bette asked, "What kind of suffering?"

Brooks told her, "My mother would just put her hand on her heart and say constantly, 'You want to make me suffer? You want to do this to me?'" Bette understood instinctively what he meant. Brooks comments, "Bette *became* my mother. I almost fell apart! Although she wasn't trained in a Method way, she was a Method actress in a sense. Her capacity for invention was amazing. She reached for the essence of a scene. She knew how to transmit feelings. It's instinctive with her."

The mother in *The Catered Affair* remains one of Davis's towering peaks of achievement. She subdued all of her mannerisms and affectations in order to give a harsh, uncompromisingly realistic performance that no doubt compensated her for not doing *Come Back, Little Sheba*. She went to Brooklyn and bought cheap dresses off the rack. She watched neighborhood women and caught an Irish-American intonation in their voices to perfection. To this day Brooks remains overpowered by her. Years later, when he was directing Geraldine Page in *Sweet Bird of Youth*, he wanted Miss Page to walk down a Hollywood staircase with the style and command of a great motion-picture star. Miss Page had been told by a vicious acquaintance that she was a fool to consider herself attractive, that she was all too well cast as a faded beauty who had to buy sex from a gigolo. This so seriously affected Geraldine Page that she was unable to play the staircase scene correctly for the director. In a fury she asked Brooks, "What the hell are you talking about? What does a movie star walk like?"

Knowing she would be offended, Brooks told her not to be, and advised her he would be rushing the print of a picture to her so that she could see the way to walk downstairs like a star. This was, of course, a blow to any actress's pride but Miss Page staunchly endured the thought of being given lessons. She went into a screening room and suddenly *A Stolen Life* came on the screen with two Bette Davises walking downstairs! Fortunately, Geraldine was a sport. She went straight to Richard Brooks and said, "It was wonderful! Don't say another word. I know exactly how to play the scene." And she did.

It is unjust that Bette did not win an Oscar for *The Catered Affair*. And it is unfortunate that *Storm Center* was released so soon afterward, out of sequence, because it proved to be ineffective and dulled the impact of the much finer picture.

In 1957, Bette spent as much time as possible visiting Margot. The child was still at Lochland School, and Bette described her slight progress in an article entitled "It Could Happen to You." She wrote: "For example, you can tell an average child for maybe one week—don't forget to brush your teeth. It took almost a year to teach Margot to do it. Lacking coordination, it is difficult for retarded children to learn to dress themselves so that clothes must be provided with oversized buttons at first. They walk slowly, they dress slowly, they start out and forget where they are going. They require infinite patience and no parent can possibly give them this most rigorous of over-and-over training in the world."

By contrast with Margot, B.D. turned out to be a happy and well-adjusted child. She grew very tall and big-boned, a strapping youngster who could take Bette on anytime in an argument and win. Bette loved her intensely and devoted herself to her and made sure her daughter had the best education possible. She had a strong rapport with B.D.; she often had her on the set to watch her work. But she was relieved in a way that B.D. seemed to have no ambition to be an actress herself. Perhaps B.D. had seen too much of the misery of it.

In the late 1950s, Ruthie lived in Laguna, still in the grand style to which she was accustomed, costing Bette a fortune with her bills. Bobby continued to be in and out of sanitariums, and the cost of B.D.'s schooling, Ruthie's high living, and Bobby's expensive nursing homes was crippling. The pressures were severe and often made Bette ill; she had to carry so much on her famous shoulders, and all her money was running away. But she was happy to give herself and her income to her dependents.

Bette worked in television in the early months of 1957.

She told Cecil Smith of the *Los Angeles Times* on March 19, 1957: "I had to get into the medium eventually. I had to find out what this new thing was. And now that I'm in it I love it. Simply love it! Such wonderful economy. They're making films the way we used to make them. Back twenty-five years ago when I began. Movies have become so enormously wasteful, so time-consuming. The thing that happened in the movies—the technicians took over. Now television's giving back that acting to the actors again. We used to make six, eight pictures a year. So these television schedules—rehearse two days, shoot three—don't terrify me. I like them." But she was afraid of live television; she panicked over the difficult costume changes in Playhouse 90's "If You Knew Elizabeth" and, for the first time in her life, actually backed out of giving a performance. Claire Trevor ultimately played the part.

Her best opportunity in years came early that summer; she was offered the important role of the mother in *Look Homeward, Angel*, adapted for the stage by Ketti Frings from the novel by Thomas Wolfe. The play was good, she admired the book, and she was looking forward to working with such practiced performers as Rosemary Murphy, Hugh Griffith, Arthur Hill, and Anthony Perkins . . . when yet another shocking, unexpected accident occurred that marred her life.

In June, Bette moved into a new house in Brentwood. A Mrs. Clark, a real estate saleswoman, took her to see the house, owned by Mr. and Mrs. Ronald Buck. Merrill was working when Bette, alone, explored the house with her customary thoroughness, neglecting only to open a door to the basement. Indeed, she wasn't told there was a basement; seeing a particular door, she assumed that it led to a closet. She moved in on June 29, 1957. She noticed the previously hidden door; she could tell from the jamb that it opened inward; she pushed the knob, took a tiny step forward, and suddenly felt the ground give from beneath her feet. She plunged into black space and felt agonizing pain as she hit a hard stone floor. She fell at least twenty feet, and lost consciousness. When she came to, she felt excruciating pain in her back and in the right hand she had instinctively thrown out to block the fall. Later she found out that the door opened over the top step of the stairs which was about nine inches wide and seven inches below the level of the hall floor. There was no landing at the top of the stairway and only a tiny sill. The stairway was less than four feet across; it had cement walls at its side and no handrails.

The pain was so acute she was unable to move. When someone finally came to her rescue, she could not walk and had to be placed on a stretcher and rushed to the hospital. She had broken her back and was very lucky indeed that, unlike David Niven's first wife, who was killed by a similar accident, she had not been fatally injured.

She sued Mr. and Mrs. Buck; the real estate woman Mrs. Clark, who had failed to show her the door; and Lelah Pierson, the real estate agent employing Mrs. Clark. Five years later Bette was awarded a verdict of $65,700.

It cost her most of that amount in hospital fees and lost work, as well as the heartbreak of losing *Look Homeward, Angel* to the admirable Jo Van Fleet. The hospital expenses, the costs—which she never begrudged—of maintaining Margot and giving B.D. and Michael the finest schooling, her several moves, and the problem of maintaining the life of a star on drastically reduced income severely drained Bette's financial resources. Almost fifty, she was very far from a rich woman and had to work, despite the agony that followed the severe and dangerous surgery on her shattered spine. It says much for her New England constitution that she wasn't permanently crippled; but she was never free of recurrent back pain for years afterward.

Incredibly, given her condition, only six months after her accident, Bette appeared in a thriller on television called *The Cold Touch* in which she had to make her way along a high building ledge in high heels. And then another weird incident happened.

Merrill and she had patched up their fractured relationship. Their mutual humor and shared interests helped them overcome their existing hostilities, and they also shared the joy of seeing B.D. and Michael grow up strong, healthy, and handsome children. After staying several months at Laguna with Bobby, whose mental health had much improved, Bette moved into the Chateau Marmont with Gary and began working on a pilot for a series called "Paula." The night between rehearsals and commencement of shooting, some faulty wiring or perhaps a fallen cigarette caused the bedroom drapes to burst into flames in the middle of the night. Smoke enveloped the sleeping Merrills' room in heavy clouds. They were awakened by a scream from a woman down the hall and staggered from the room, choking. Fortunately, they escaped unharmed. But it had been a close call.

SIXTEEN

Cameo roles are often considered death for major actors. But Bette was anxious for money in the spring of 1958 and was very glad indeed to receive an offer of $50,000 for two days work at Versailles, France, as Catherine the Great in *John Paul Jones,* an adipose epic in which she would speak several lines in Russian. Accompanied by B.D. and Bobby, she traveled to Europe on the S.S. *Independence;* she was perhaps glad of the separation from Merrill. She also had another script in her suitcase. She was to go on to England to make *The Scapegoat,* by Daphne du Maurier, in which she had been cast as a monstrous, cigar-puffing morphine addict confined largely to her bed and playing mother to Alec Guinness. She decided in advance she would adopt the "Japanese" rice white makeup she had used in *The Little Foxes,* and a costume from that picture, let out a little for her now fuller figure.

Shooting the brief sequence from *John Paul Jones* was not a pleasant experience. The director, John Farrow, Australian husband of Maureen O'Sullivan, was ill-tempered and directed Bette with a leaden hand. The producer, Samuel Bronston, was in severe financial straits and every conceivable corner had to be cut in the production. Farrow asked Bette to play her part on a single note of voracious sexual intensity, and this irritated her, but, undoubtedly, the movie queen in her vibrated to the challenge of portraying what Farrow insisted on calling "the Queen of all the Rushes."

With a loud sigh of relief Bette, her sister, and daughter took off for a vacation in Italy. Tourists froze in their tracks as Bette swooped down on the Vatican, swept through the Sistine Chapel, and trudged around St. Peter's; the Italians adored her, and noted in the press her volcanic enjoyment of everything she saw and everybody she met.

The Latin atmosphere, with its noises, enthusiasms, and extremes of emotion, suited Bette perfectly. After a trip to Milan, she flew with Bobby and B.D., in the finest of humors, to England.

Bette had high hopes for *The Scapegoat*. The director, Robert Hamer, had made the famous Victorian black comedy *Kind Hearts and Coronets* with Alec Guinness, and Bette felt that the combination would work again. But from the beginning it was obvious to her that it would not.

Although she herself enjoyed drinking—but sparingly, because alcohol went quickly to her head—she hated people who were incapable of controlling their intake of liquor and she felt particularly uncomfortable with alcoholics. Even at the first meeting with Hamer, she realized he was suffering from severe alcoholic degeneration. The production chief, Sir Michael Balcon, assured her that Hamer had promised he would lay off drinking completely if only he could direct Bette Davis. But she spent the entire length of shooting wondering anxiously whether Hamer would keep his word. And she was bothered by his evident incompetence, his attacks of shaking, and his disagreeable atmosphere of someone aching for an indulgence he dared not allow himself.

The truth was that, though Bette could not have known it, Hamer was actually dying during the production. In fact, he barely outlived it.

Sir Alec Guinness says: "Bette Davis behaved throughout with impeccable professionalism, and, of course, we were all thrilled to be working with her. But she allowed none of us to get to know her. I invited her to dinner several times, and she never responded. It would have been a much more enjoyable movie if we had got along better.

"She acted admirably, of course, concentrated, forceful, and formidable, with a fine sardonic wit. But I feel she was affected by being overdressed; and the settings in which she played were dizzy with distractions: hundreds of roses, eye-catching bric-a-brac, rococo serendipity of every description. Not only did she not trust the director, she was suspicious of me. I don't know whether she thought I was going to try to take scenes from her, which wouldn't have been possible anyway, but I was prepared happily and rightly to sit at her feet, as it happened. I was proud to have worked with her and sad that she didn't seem to have enjoyed working with me."

The cameraman, Paul Beeson, recalls: "I first met Bette Davis ten days before we started shooting the picture for the makeup tests. I was nervous at first, very young, and she disconcerted me because she started to tell me what makeup she would wear and precisely how she would like to be photographed. This was hard for me to accept but I was polite and said, 'Will you let me do the tests the way I see them, and if you don't like them, tell me?'

"She said, 'Fine.'

"I realized she was a good sport. She liked a direct honest approach. She hated dishonesty. She went to see the tests and said simply, 'We're on the same wavelength, Mr. Beeson.' And that was it. No more trouble."

Bette rather enjoyed the experience of being in bed during the entire production. She would sit cross-legged, pretending to be lying down, and smoke furiously between takes, stubbing out her cigarettes in a large marble ashtray hidden behind the pillows. Once, the pillows caught fire and a small column of smoke began to form behind her head on camera. Robert Hamer threw up his hands in despair and the scene had to be started again.

The famous director Anthony Asquith visited the set one day. He was a fan of Bette's who always wore a jump suit. Nobody told Bette he was visiting. She noticed him out of the corner of her eye and during a break said to Hamer, "I don't want to make a fuss, but would you please ask that workman in the jumpsuit to move out of the way?" Asquith, crestfallen, nervously disappeared.

B.D. was Bette's joy during the picture. Every time a scene was finished, B.D., aged twelve, would plop herself down on the bed and give a long, serious critique which often ended in both mother and daughter bursting into laughter. Hamer became irritated by this, and also by the fact that Bette flatly refused to allow her stand-in (whom she called, in this instance, a "lie-in") to take over when the lights were being set up. She was so comfortable in her cozy position she had to be practically dragged out in order to satisfy union requirements.

Beeson grumbled constantly about her makeup. He says, "She wore this terrible white stuff. Most black and white makeups were yellowy pancake but this ghastly white stuff prevented me from lighting her correctly. She apparently wanted to accentuate her eyes but she looked like a kind of talking mask."

Everyone disliked the picture. Daphne du Maurier says, "I felt the performances of both Guinness and Bette Davis were bad. I wanted her to play the role I had devised with zest and vitality but she had neither. I was so disappointed with her I can't even remember if I met her. I've just blanked the whole thing out. It was a disaster."

There is no need today to question Dame Daphne's opinion. Bette returned to Hollywood for nothing more exciting than an episode of "Wagon Train"; fortunately, an unexpected opportunity came up immediately afterward: a series of readings of Carl Sandburg's poems, with Gary Merrill, and the program arranged by the accomplished Norman Corwin.

Bette had always admired Sandburg. She had known him chiefly for his poem "Fog." Corwin and Sandburg sent the package, including the full selection of poems under the heading of *The World of Carl Sandburg,* to the Merrills in Maine. Bette and Gary saw this not only as a chance to do something worthwhile, but perhaps to recement their shattered marriage, since a long tour was called for across the country. But after her first enthusiasm, Bette was tortured by anxiety that she would not be able to sustain a stage performance; that, once again, she could not have an understudy; that her old problem of laryngitis might flare up; and that standing for hours at a stretch might prove serious in view of her recently broken back.

Her first insistence was that she meet Sandburg. They hit it off immediately. At eighty, Sandburg was an irresistible, sexy old charmer, filled with a vitality almost equal to her own. He made her ashamed (shame was not normally a word in her vocabulary) of her own fears and tensions about growing older and her inhibitions in several directions. He was like a rock: secure, decent, and noble. Not for the first time, Bette realized how different the life of a literary man or woman with a solid body of achievement was from the frightened, insecure life of a performer on stage or screen.

For the Merrills's convenience, Corwin and Sandburg agreed that the show should be rehearsed in Portland, Maine, the nearest city to Cape Elizabeth. Screwing up her courage, and inspired by Sandburg, Bette learned the script in record time and plunged enthusiastically into work. After so many years of speaking the dialogue of hack writers, she was thrilled by the experience of working with an artist. She said to Sandburg during a break at the theater in Portland: "We don't have 'great words' anymore. *Your* words are great." The evening in which the verse was showcased was exhilarating in that it called for twenty-five speaking parts in two hours. Bette said later, "It was like playing the full range of every part I'd ever done, in fragments, during one evening."

The problem was that, despite the excellence of Bette's performance, which inspired Merrill to give the best acting of his career, the show was not quite the commercial triumph hoped for. In spite of this the tour was perhaps the most satisfying experience of Bette's later career. A special pleasure was the Hollywood opening in March 1960, with Ruthie in the front row. Bette was overjoyed to find an audience of her peers loudly delighted with her acting.

A curious episode took place in a small town. There were two spinster sisters who had spent their lives worshipping Bette Davis. The idea of seeing her in person threw them into a state of excitement. They arrived, chattering and laughing, and sat transfixed when Bette made her appearance on the stage. Suddenly, one of the sisters put her hand to her chest. Moments later she died of a heart attack. She was taken out of the theater. But her sister refused to leave, stood up, and insisted to the Merrills that they continue the performance. At the end there was an ovation and the old lady was asked to come on the stage. She said, "I adored this performance. And my sister would have too if she hadn't died two hours ago!"

Undermining the pleasure the tour gave her was the unhappy fact that Bette's marriage to Merrill finally foundered. One would have thought that, bound together in a mutual professional success, working on the most worthwhile show they had done in years, the unhappy couple would at last have found a new lease on life in their relationship. But perhaps because of the constant proximity of hotel rooms and dressing rooms, without the slightest surcease from each other's egos, they did not.

In the spring of 1960, Bette filed suit for divorce. The Maine and California divorce documents, followed by court records of the subsequent custody battle, have a raw, disturbing quality. Merrill agreed to pay B.D. and Michael $250 a month each for child support and one half of Margot's special school fees; Bette got the station wagon and Merrill the Mercedes; Bette waived all alimony except for a token of one dollar per year. The reason for this was that the matter could be kept open and renegotiated if Merrill's earnings suddenly increased. He agreed to keep up the insurance policies on the family and home in return for Bette agreeing to release all interest in Merrill's property other than their co-tenancy in Witch Way at Cape Elizabeth.

It was a calm beginning to a custody battle over Michael Merrill that would drag on for years.

Merrill left the show. Many people who would have come simply to see the famous couple were no longer interested. Others were dissatisfied by the replacements—Barry Sullivan and, later, Leif Erickson. The opening in New York at the Henry Miller Theatre on September 14, 1960, had mixed reviews and failed quickly. The gay audience that would have rushed to see Bette in almost anything was rapidly absorbed. After four weeks *The World of Carl Sandburg* closed.

Bette blamed Merrill's absence for the failure of the production, and in his memoirs Sandburg provided a series of excuses—including the occurrence of a Jewish holiday—that rivaled in complexity his most intricate verse. None of this worked: *The World of Carl Sandburg* was, quite simply, too intellectual for the commuter audience that had kept Broadway alive since World War II. At the end of the tour there was a consolation prize: The show was very successful in North Carolina, where almost a quarter of a million high school students saw it before it finally emerged in Flat Rock, where it appeared in its author's home territory. Despite the tragedy of the divorce from Merrill and the strain of the trip, Bette never forgot the joy of playing to young students from one end of America to the other, in all weathers from brilliant sunshine to lashing Gothic storms. The tour was a summit of her life.

She was financially very hard up when it ended. She still had to pay for Ruthie's expensive life-style, with endless new clothes and new furniture, as well as a substantial allowance; Bobby's psychiatric treatments and occasional visits to the hospital when she had setbacks of mental and physical health; the rapidly increasing charges for Margot's schooling; the normal schooling of B.D. and Michael; and her own expenses as a star. She was very nearly broke again in her early fifties because of the financial sacrifice of paying out constantly and being paid very little for the Sandburg readings. Normally, given her New Englander's dislike of discussing her private life, she would have turned down at once the offer made that year by Howard Cady of Putnam's to work on a memoir. But she couldn't afford to refuse the offer. She had just rented a house in New York and was grateful for the advance against royalties.

Bette needed a ghost writer. She asked almost everybody she knew whom they could recommend. A friend of hers, Kaye Ballard, recommended Sandford Dody, who combined an agreeably sophisticated personality with journalistic skill. Ballard was convinced Dody would be perfect for the task.

Ballard was appearing at the Blue Angel nightclub and it was arranged for Bette to meet Dody there. Bette arrived with the lyricist Fred Ebb, whom she admired enormously; and she enjoyed Dody, whom she found admiring and relaxed, rather like a big rabbit. She was fascinated by his *outré* hats and turtleneck sweaters, toothy grin and crinkly humorous eyes.

They lunched at her house on East 78th Street and began to sketch out plans. Dody describes their working relationship in his memoirs, *Giving Up the Ghost*. He says that at first everything worked out well. But soon there were arguments over the division of profits and royalties and the credit Dody would receive. She asked to see a sample chapter and he declined, saying, "I think, Bette, it's a little unseemly for me to audition at this point in my life." She shrugged and accepted his decision.

They met day after day in the winter months of early 1961, starting work at 10:00 A.M., toiling in the library on chintz-covered chairs in front of a cheerful wood fire until six. Plucking cigarettes from pottery hens and matches from slop bowls, Bette paced about eagerly, remembering everything she dared, until, Dody wrote, "The room looked like an opium den at Walden Pond."

Soon, Dody was calling her Bette Dervish. The story of her life became convincing as she built a matchstick castle of largely familiar information. It was difficult for her to probe into areas of her life she would have preferred to have left dark. It was harder still to include a stranger in the intimacy she had so carefully kept from reporters all of those years and at times she deliberately softened the truth, particularly about her husbands. And then, when she did become rash and bold and told the harsh and ugly facts of so much of her life she cut them summarily—according to Dody—when the manuscript was completed.

The writing continued over several months. Merrill dropped by and hit it off well with Dody; Merrill seemed unconcerned about so much of his life being exposed. He probably knew Bette's New England sense of propriety would eliminate the more unflattering passages.

Oddly, Bette and Merrill were happier together at this time than they were to be afterward and than they had been since their first year together. Or it may simply have been that they were giving a performance worthy of *All About Eve* or *The World of Carl Sandburg* in front of an official biographer.

Dody recalls pleasant evenings with Bette, her dental surgeon Stanley Berman and his wife, Gig Young, Elizabeth Montgomery, and other friends. And yet, all along, there was the sense of discomfort any writer of talent must feel in rendering himself subservient to the profound egotism of a star. It was a question of flattery, cajolery, easing out secrets, playing under the great performer and never imposing one's self—of being, in short, a courtier.

Perhaps fortunately, work was interrupted when Bette had to go to Hollywood to make *A Pocketful of Miracles* for Frank Capra. This stupid movie, which showed no trace of Capra's legendary genius, was a remake of his earlier *Lady for a Day*. It was a Damon Runyon story about a drudge called Apple Annie elevated suddenly to riches.

Once again, Bette had been last choice for the part. Shirley Booth had been offered the picture, but after seeing *Lady for a Day* she cried and said through tears she could never hope to equal the great May Robson in the original part. Helen Hayes accepted it immediately but for complicated reasons withdrew. Glenn Ford co-starred with Davis and at first was pleased. But they clashed from the first day of shooting.

Bette's chief reason for taking on Apple Annie was that B.D. wanted her to. She was terrified of making her Hollywood comeback as a miserable hag; she was convinced that comments would be rude in her old hometown. They were. Several backbiters remarked that she could now play this kind of role without makeup. There was a tremendous quarrel over Bette's dressing room. It was normal for star dressing rooms to be adjoining. But Bette claimed in interviews that Glenn Ford insisted that the actress Hope Lange should be his neighbor. Bette had to move to a smaller dressing room. Her rage was cosmic and she was restored to the correct dressing room. Worse trouble came when Glenn Ford gave an interview saying that, out of gratitude for Bette having put him into *A Stolen Life,* he had insisted she play Apple Annie in order to rescue her from obscurity. Capra said later, "Bette read Glenn's interview. She was mad as hell! She screamed at me, 'Who is that son of a bitch that he should say he helped me have a *comeback!* That shitheel wouldn't have helped me out of a *sewer!* I should never have come back to Hollywood! *I hate all of you!* And Apple Annie most of all! I must have been *out of my mind* to come back!' "

Glenn Ford detested Davis for these comments. He spent the rest of the picture treating her like a supporting player. Capra suffered from severe cluster headaches because of the tension between his stars and the behavior of everybody concerned. Bette's only friend on the picture was the very young Ann-Margret. Capra said years later, "It was all impossible. I 'lost' the picture right from the beginning. I realize now I should have understood Davis better. I didn't see that she was very sensitive, that she needed consolation and reassurance after so long away. I couldn't see that she was in fact vulnerable, living on her nerves. She'd only become a monster to take care of herself in a monstrous business. Underneath, she was a neurotic woman, deeply afraid and uncertain of everything except her genuis. Her armor couldn't be penetrated and the fact that I tried to get through it appalled her."

In New York after this experience, Bette plunged back into work with Sandford Dody, censoring much of what he had written in her absence but allowing some of it to be reasonably candid. Dody shrewdly observed in his autobiography: "She was used to candor to begin with, and was shrewdly aware that admitting, for instance, that she was a bitch was the surest way of convincing the reader that she was not."

During the months of renewed work at the house in New York, Bette was shadowed by the sudden death of Ruthie in the last days of shooting *A Pocketful of Miracles*. In recent years Ruthie had drifted partly out of her life, but the overwhelming influence of her mother on her career remained and would never be forgotten. Indeed, the best part of the book Bette wrote with Dody, ultimately called *The Lonely Life*, dealt with Bette's extraordinary mother.

In the summer of 1961, Tennessee Williams was determined to have Bette play the outrageous part of Maxine, the landlady in *Night of the Iguana*. So often fascinated and puzzled by homosexuals, Bette was intrigued by Williams and loved the idea of playing a bad-tempered slut. Dody wanted her to be the arid spinster writer's daughter in the play but neither Williams nor Bette agreed. They were probably right.

In the late summer of 1961, Bette waged a new war on Merrill. She had been granted custody of B.D., Margot, and Michael, with Gary allowed visiting rights. But suddenly she brought action against Merrill through her attorney Sidney Wernick in the State of Maine Superior Court, claiming that his conduct and behavior were detrimental to the children and he must not be allowed to see them again. She wanted the entire clause allowing such visiting rights stricken from the record of judgment of divorce.

This was a very tough action to take against a father. But Bette charged in a clear and unequivocal manner that she considered Merrill "drunken and disorderly" and "incapable of behaving properly in front of his family." She alleged that Merrill had become violently drunk in front of the children; had committed acts of physical violence against her; that his house in California was filthy and unkempt; that he was having an affair with a woman to whom he was not married; that he was irresponsible and neglectful; and that on Father's Day she had arranged a dinner for him to meet his family and he had arrived drunk and insulting and left without eating anything. She was, she told the court, particularly concerned that Margot, who had now moved from the school at Lake Geneva to a home at Spruce Creek, Pennsylvania, would be subject to danger from Merrill. Bette and Merrill quarreled more savagely than ever on the telephone or through their attorneys.

Sandford Dody struggled on with the manuscript. At one stage Bette canceled it completely, throwing Dody into a depression. He at last succeeded in finishing the book in the early fall of 1961, just as Bette began rehearsals for *The Night of the Iguana*. He was upset when the publishers decided not to give him joint credit as author; dashed still more when, before the book was published, Bette cut the manuscript, removing, he claims, the best passages without Dody's permission. Dody also says in his own memoirs that Bette wrecked his prose in rewrites which at times rendered it ungrammatical. It is unfortunate that his contract did not allow him right of final approval. The resulting book begins excellently, falters halfway through, and declines rapidly in the last third when discretion gets the better part of valor and the descriptions and comments on people, films, and life in general become disturbingly perfunctory and unpredictable.

The chief merit of the book is that it is stamped with Davis's personality; that despite the many excisions and shadings one still gets a sense of the humor, aggression, and raw vitality that propelled this great star to the top of her profession. It is Margo Channing's work—no doubt of it.

Night of the Iguana went into rehearsals in October 1961. After the ordeal of *A Pocketful of Miracles,* Bette hoped for a more joyful experience, but this was not to be vouchsafed her. She was not at her best at this time. Irritated by much of Dody's manuscript with its (as she felt) excessive intrusions into her privacy—privacy she had breached herself—and displeased with Merrill over his alleged drunkenness, she was hostile and bitter from the first day of work. She disliked Margaret Leighton, the very gifted, melancholy British actress who played the spinster in the production. She found Miss Leighton affected and mannered in the extreme, coldly ungrateful when Davis threw a cocktail party to welcome her to Broadway. And she had a fight with Tennessee Williams's famous agent of the time, Audrey Wood.

Convinced that Patrick O'Neal and Margaret Leighton were ganging up against her, nervous and overwrought as always when she had to play in the theater without an understudy, Bette opened in the play in Chicago in November. There were problems from the beginning with the writing; Tennessee Williams worked through the nights to fix the more problematical passages. Business was poor over Thanksgiving because exceptionally good weather drove many people out of town. The worst problem of all was that much of the audience was composed of Bette's loyal fans. They tended to applaud her every other line, "throwing" the other actors and sometimes bringing the entire play to a halt.

Worse problems arose in New York when the play opened there in December. The reviews were excellent and audiences far more substantial but the ill-feeling between the performers reached flashpoint. When Bette entered the stage at the beginning of the play, she was swallowed up every night in an ovation that spoiled the dramatic effect of the scene and that no persuasion on her part could prevent. There was a tension-ridden backstage meeting; everyone agreed that something would have to be done at once. Tennessee Williams devised another entrance but the same thing happened. It occurred night after night. Margaret Leighton was so maddened at having to come on without a single handclap after the storm of cheers for Bette, she didn't talk to her for the rest of the run.

At last Tennessee solved the problem. He had Bette make her entrance as the curtain rose and go straight to the footlights to take her call. Her first words as she walked on were, "*Hiya, Shannon!*" She had a cigarette in one hand and a drink in the other. She swung her hips and batted her eyelids and when some of the audience screamed and jumped up in a state bordering on ecstasy, she bowed, stepping completely out of character to do so. Only then was she allowed to give a performance without interruption.

As so often before, a large proportion of her audiences was gay, or composed of women's groups from out of town. The strain of making this artificial appearance at the outset of the show, the knowledge that these audiences would accept no substitute for her and that if her laryngitis flared up the show would have to close for a night or two, cost her much sleep and wore her down. At last, confronted by more dislike from Margaret Leighton both on and off the stage, she threw up her hands and walked out. She was exhausted and wanted only to rest in the country or, as an alternative, try Hollywood again.

SEVENTEEN

Just before she left the play, as it turned out, the producer-director Robert Aldrich had offered Bette the co-starring role in *What Ever Happened to Baby Jane?* It was a story about two former child actresses living in Hollywood in their late middle age. Aldrich, a big, brash former footballer, had hit on the gimmick of co-starring Bette and Joan Crawford in the production. His flair for publicity, crude but dynamic grasp of audience taste, and genuine fondness for the two stars resulted in a highly charged, highly sensational package.

Bette was uncertain at first whether she would play in the picture. Much as she needed a change of pace, she was uneasy about acting a grotesque role that called for bizarre makeup, wigs, and costumes and involved serving her rival actress a dead rat on a breakfast tray. She asked Aldrich to come to New York. When he arrived at her house, she said, "There are two questions I have to ask you. If you're honest with me and answer them correctly, I will do the picture." She looked at him very hard, puffing at a cigarette in her best one-woman firing-squad manner. "All right. The first question is: Have you slept with Miss Crawford?"

Aldrich paused before answering, and then he said, "Not for the want of Miss Crawford trying."

"Okay. I believe you. So I'll skip the second question,"

Bette said. The unspoken question, of course, was whether he would guarantee that he wouldn't favor Joan.

Bette left for Hollywood in a state of nervous tension. She had to return to her old studio after thirteen years to co-star with the woman who, she knew, both envied her talent and had been secretly in love with her. On arrival, somebody told her that Crawford had suggested her for the part. Although this statement was quite incorrect, she rashly believed it. Joan got what she wanted: Joan was now appearing with the actress she loved and envied.

Jack Warner decided to act the magnifico and gave an elaborate luncheon for Bette and Joan at the studio. Each spied on the other to see what they would be wearing. Joan was elaborately got-up in a vividly colored dress. Bette up-staged her by wearing plain black.

Warner did his best to make his two former stars feel at home. Yet it was a far cry from the old days, when Bette could rewrite most of a script and enjoy a two-month shooting schedule which would stretch to three if she wasn't feeling well. Aldrich was not subservient, fastidious, or delicate in his dealings with the stars. He took them on like boxers. He didn't waste a minute with flattery. The entire picture was shot in twenty-one days like a B picture which, except for its baroque surface, it actually was.

But Bette, with her tough professionalism, flung herself into the part at its own level, reworking the rice-white makeup she had used in *The Little Foxes* and *The Scape-goat* and using black kohl around her eyes in an imitation of the silent stars. Her blond ringleted wig and bizarre puffed-sleeve dresses were cleverly thought out.

Robert Aldrich remembers: "Joan and Bette didn't fight at all on *Baby Jane*. They behaved absolutely perfectly. They never allowed an abrasive word to slip out. They didn't try to upstage each other."

Bette was aggravated by the fact that Joan resumed her wooing of Bette, sending her gifts of shoes, handkerchiefs, and costume jewelry. Bette sent her a note asking her not to continue, saying that she didn't have the time to go out and choose something for Joan in order to reciprocate. As a result, Joan, frustrated once more, changed from an admiring fan to a savage enemy. She took her hate out on her unhappy adopted daughter Christina. She became a kind of monster. She constantly acted toward Bette in the manner of a cold nouveau riche society woman toward a fallen aristocrat turned lady's maid. Bette became infuriated with Joan's pretentious posturing and empty, meaningless politeness. She longed for a quarrel with words and fur flying. But Joan brushed off her occasional rude remarks with saintly condescension.

As it turned out, both Bette's and Joan's performances were in every way very fine. They created touching and convincing characters instead of mere grotesques. The last scene, in which Bette drags a dying Joan Crawford to the beach, was exceptionally well played and directed. The film sustained an effective nightmarish mood, crude and unsentimental, that entirely suited the Hollywood setting.

Relations between Bette and Joan did not improve after the picture was finished. Bette gave interviews discussing "we two old hags" in the picture and Joan rushed her a note, immaculately typed on pale blue stationery, saying "Dear Miss Davis. Please do not continue to refer to me as an old hag. Sincerely, Joan Crawford." Bette laughed and threw the letter away. It was obvious to her that Joan Crawford was utterly devoid of a sense of humor.

Perhaps as a gag to help promote the picture, perhaps because she was genuinely frantic for money, she borrowed $75,000 against her 10 percent of *Baby Jane*. Bette took out a famous ad in *Variety* on September 21, 1962. It read:

SITUATION WANTED, WOMEN ARTISTS
Mother of three—10, 11, & 15—divorcee. American. Thirty years experience as an actress in Motion Pictures. Mobile still and more affable than rumor would have it. Wants steady employment in Hollywood. (Has had Broadway.)
Bette Davis, c/o Martin Baum, G.A.C.
References upon request.

The general view in Hollywood was that this indicated that Bette Davis was finished. It therefore backfired as a joke. Fortunately, the excellent reviews for both *Baby Jane* and her memoir, *The Lonely Life*, followed by *Baby Jane*'s huge commercial success made nonsense of her enemies' remarks. She left for New York on November 2, to begin promotions for the picture; she was marvelous on the "Jack Paar Show," but lost her temper when fellow guest Jonathan Winters imitated her line, incorrectly attributed to the script of *In This Our Life*, saying, "Petah! Petah! Petah!"

She had to fly back to Los Angeles on November 15, because B.D., now fifteen, had gone into Cedars of Lebanon Hospital for a varicose vein operation. Bette stayed with her at the hospital each day and took care of her at home, as B.D. was unable to move her leg out of a straight position. Bette taped an Andy Williams television show and a "Perry Mason" show, and in mid-December appeared in court once again, demanding that Merrill not be allowed to see the children. Court records show that she repeated her charges that he was "drunken, physically violent, filthy, unkempt, immoral and in every way unsuitable as a parent." Gary Merrill denied all these charges. He swore that he had been denied rights of reasonable visitation quite improperly, that he was unable to reach her through his attorney, that Bette had deliberately influenced Michael against him, and that it was shocking a son should be deprived of the company of his father when he was growing up. He stated that Michael had stayed with him over Bette's complaints for six weeks that summer and that Bette had been unable to prove any misbehavior on Merrill's part during the vacation. He demanded that a court order be made forcing Bette to allow reasonable visitations.

Bette responded in court with a series of further and equally damaging statements. She said that Merrill had no suitable home in which Michael should be allowed to stay overnight. She asserted that his temporary home at Topanga on the beach was "cold, damp, and foggy" and that this would be "injurious to Michael's health." She charged that there was no one to take care of Michael, aged ten, and

308

that he wasn't given proper meals, or his clothes taken care of. She added that the building was in an area filled with "perverts" who "might molest a child," and she then proceeded to give a series of reasons why Merrill should not visit with Michael at Bette's home.

She described a call from Merrill from San Francisco that December 13,1962, in which, she said, Merrill drunkenly demanded Michael be put on a plane. She alleged that he had a hangover when he came to see Michael unexpectedly and that he dragged Michael from a party, making Michael cry. She said that he took Michael to a restaurant from which he had been previously evicted and that he got drunk in front of Michael. Furthermore, she asserted, he made Michael cancel an all-important football practice to spend a day with him. The charges went on to mention Merrill's allegedly drunken driving and threats if she decided to take the children to her old favorite resort of La Quinta for New Year's. Bette said that it was against Margot's interests to have Merrill visit her; that she was living with a private family in the East; and that Merrill excited her to the point at which she was seriously unsettled by him.

Merrill responded again. He said that the house on Topanga Beach Road was "well-heated" and that the area was "often warm and sunny in winter." He revealed that he had turned down a job on "The Naked City" television series to be with Michael. He denied that he had ever been intoxicated in the presence of Michael or had ever committed an act of physical violence. He admitted he had been annoyed when Bette prevented him from speaking to his son on the telephone from San Francisco but denied that he was drunk. He said that he did not take Michael from a football practice but instead offered to deliver him to it and in fact did so. He also on another occasion took him to a Notre Dame game at Michael's request.

He said he did everything in his power to adjust his schedule to fit in with Michael's; that he had not been drunk with him in the restaurant; that he had never driven a car when drunk and that to be deprived of his son was damaging to his well-being.

309

The hearings dragged on into January 1963. B.D., Bette's friend the director Allen Miner, and others appeared for Bette to testify, and Merrill's friend the actor Lyle Bettger and two others appeared for him. The court order was a shocking blow to Bette. The judgment was that Merrill be given far more access to Michael than hitherto. He was to have custody of Michael on alternate weekends commencing January 25, and he should have complete custody for the spring Easter school vacation, the first portion of the summer school vacation from June 7 through July 15, and the Christmas school vacation. Worse, if possible, from Bette's point of view was that Merrill was allowed to visit Margot with reasonable frequency providing she was not removed from her Home. There was a proviso that Merrill "must always be sober in the presence of the children" and "must not remove Michael from California without Miss Davis's consent. Bette's motion for attorney fees and costs was denied. She and Gary had to pay their own fees and costs.

In February there was the first weekend of Merrill's custody. But in the early evening hours of Thursday, Merrill's attorney received a wire from Bette, saying she would await further ruling of the court as to Merrill's visit. Merrill was upset, since the court order was clear at the moment. On Friday, at five o'clock, he arrived at Bette's house in Bel-Air to take custody of Michael. Bette refused to open the door. Merrill pounded on it angrily. She pressed the intercom button and said, very loudly, 'You shall not have custody or visitation of Michael now or ever!"

Merrill said, "May I speak to Michael?"

Bette replied, "You may not see him at all. I just told you."

Merrill said, "May I speak to him on the intercom or may I call him from a phone booth?"

"*You may not!*" Bette snapped back and the line went dead.*

Merrill drove in a rage down Stone Canyon Road and called his attorney. Two days later Merrill obtained an or-

* Conversation in Los Angeles Court House records.

der to show cause in re contempt, in which Bette was ordered to appear and show cause why she should not be adjudged guilty of contempt of the court order allowing Merrill custody. Bailiffs came to serve the order only to discover that Bette had fled to New York, leaving Michael with a friend, Barbara Barry, who had instructions along with the Black-Foxe Military Academy not to allow Michael ever to see his father.

Finally, Bette was forced to agree to Merrill visiting with Michael on alternate weekends.

To Joan Crawford's annoyance, Bette was nominated for an Academy Award for *Baby Jane* and Joan was not. On the night of the Oscars, both women had agreed to be presenters. Joan had solicited an agreement with all nominated actresses who could not be present that she would accept the award on their behalf if they won. Bette found out about this, and it disturbed her. But she was also sure that she would certainly win. Anne Bancroft's name was announced for *The Miracle Worker*. Bette, in a dressing room backstage, flinched from the shock of the news. And Crawford, chin held high, swept past her, turned, said "Hah!" to her face, and went onstage to collect the Oscar for Anne Bancroft.

Bette took off in a high dudgeon to Europe to promote *Baby Jane* there. She constantly called her friend Barbara in an uproar over the battle with Merrill. But she had a strong reason for leaving California. Joan Crawford had been asked to promote the picture but accused Bette of grabbing the better theaters at home and overseas out of the several hundred selected for personal appearances. Bette immediately offered to appear in all of the theaters. When she heard this, Crawford changed her mind, but it was too late. She had to sit out the entire tour while Bette did all the appearances on her own.

What Ever Happened to Baby Jane? opened in London in early May. Bette was miserable over the situation in California with Michael but she was excited by the feeling that the Warner people in England were pleased with the picture. There was no premiere. Ten days after the show opened, the *Evening Standard* ran a tiny box at the bottom

311

of the entertainment page, on a Tuesday evening. The advertisement read simply: "Warner Cinema, tomorrow, 8:30 P.M. Bette Davis."

A remarkable thing happened. A large crowd rushed the theater at two-thirty and packed it to capacity. They saw the movie three times so they wouldn't miss Bette's personal appearance. Another crowd gathered outside. At seven-thirty, Leicester Square had to be closed by the police.

At eight-thirty, *Baby Jane* finished playing. The cinema was plunged in total darkness. Even the house signs were turned off so that the only lights left gleamed from the exits. Three musicians played the theme tune of the picture, "I've Written a Letter to Daddy." Bette edged her way through the crowd in the dark and began to climb up to the stage, feeling her way with her hands. A spotlight had been cued to flash through the darkness and concentrate on the musicians, pinpointing her as the curtain rose. Instead, it swung around and focused on her behind as she climbed the steps. The whole theater dissolved in a turmoil of laughter. A moment later the spotlight focused on B.D.'s bottom; tall and imposing as a stretched-out Alice in Wonderland, B.D., aged fifteen, towered over her mother. (B.D. had played a small part in the picture.) The audience roared again.

It was several minutes before the manager succeeded in controlling the audience, which was beside itself with excitement and amusement. Bette played up expertly. She held a large piece of stationery and sang "I've Written a Letter to Daddy." When she finished the number, she threw the piece of paper into the air and the audience screamed. She chattered to the crowd and fielded questions; B.D. sang "What Ever Happened to Baby Jane?" in unison with Bette. When they finished, somebody rushed up to the stage with a gigantic bouquet of flowers. Instead of waiting for the flowers to be given to her, she marched over and collected the bouquet and handed it to B.D. This was a faux pas which brought another gust of laughter because at the same moment another bouquet was being brought up on the other side of the stage for B.D., who finished with two bouquets the size of herself.

312

Bette sang another number. She closed the proceedings with, "You don't know it, but you've all got a number underneath your seat. And when I give the command, I want you to all look for that number because the winner will be presented with a Baby Jane doll. On the command of three, you will look for your number. One, two, three . . ." Everyone bent over. And Bette found herself confronted with several hundred English bottoms. She said, "I've never seen so many fat fannies in my life!" There was another roar. And to her disgust the doll was won by a child. She had hoped to obtain a major laugh by having it won by a man.

When she reached the lobby, she was barely able to move. Her car was surrounded by a motorcycle squad. It took twenty minutes to get her out of Leicester Square, even though it was closed off to all other traffic.

Thrilled by her reception, more fond than ever of England, Bette flew to the Cannes Film Festival. She was accorded a royal reception, and accompanied Aldrich to the screening of *Baby Jane*, which she had never seen before from beginning to end. Perhaps because she had become so overexcited in London, perhaps because of her continuing fear of Merrill getting drunk and driving Michael on the freeways in Los Angeles, she was feeling exceptionally overwrought as the film unfolded. She was horrified at her appearance, which she had gone to such extraordinary lengths to attain. She burst into tears at her chalky, painted face and Aldrich turned to her in dismay along with several members of the audience. "I look awful," she wept. "Do I really look that awful?"

And Bette was dealt a blow from which it took a long time to recover. Because of her fear of Merrill visiting Michael, she had overreacted by being unduly protective of B.D. She was astonished when B.D., still so very young, went on a blind date with the young Jeremy Hyman, a nephew of Elliot Hyman, owner of Seven Arts. Bette thought nothing of the incident until B.D. told her she was in love at first sight. Bette was distraught. She felt that B.D. was much too young at fifteen to be in love with anybody.

Bette was at her lowest ebb. Michael was far too normal a boy to cling to a mother's skirts. Margot was lost in a world of her own. The traditional actress's fear of being left alone, accentuated in the case of stars, seized Bette by the throat. She told the following to a close friend, who passed it on to me.

In London, in a hotel room, she was so depressed she wanted to die. Then suddenly she caught a glimpse of her face in a mirror, distorted with grief and despair, and her New England horse sense took over. She burst out laughing at her melodramatic self. Her face laughed back at her from the mirror. Here was the great Bette Davis in the depths of despair! It was ridiculous. She must go on.

A good sport as always, Bette shot the bankroll to give B.D. an enormously expensive wedding reception at the Beverly Wilshire Hotel. She went through the ordeal bravely but it was excruciating for her to part with B.D. when B.D. was so young. She also felt B.D. should have waited until she was older before making so drastic a commitment.

As it turned out, Bette was wrong; and at least she had the good sportsmanship to admit it eventually. B.D. and Hyman made a complete success of their marriage. As late as 1981, they are still happily united.

In the weeks after the marriage, Bette had a private detective, Michael Parlow, follow Gary Merrill and Michael during their permitted weekends together. She was still trying desperately to prevent those weekends from continuing.

Detective Parlow's reports are in the court files. He dogged Merrill's footsteps carefully. He told Bette that on January 24, three weeks after B.D.'s wedding, Michael and Gary were staying at the Newporter Inn at Newport Beach. Parlow alleged that Merrill had left Michael alone in his room from 10:07 P.M. until the following day at 7:18 A.M. and that Merrill was drinking and partying all night in bars and private homes in the area.

The following weekend, Parlow asserted, Merrill left Michael alone again. And this continued on other occasions. There were evidences, Parlow claimed, that Gary drove

Michael on a public highway and ran through two stop signs and a red-light signal while drunk. Parlow also alleged that Merrill drank from morning till night and made love to a woman in the room adjoining Michael's. He also testified that Merrill had been loud, boisterous, and vulgar in Michael's presence while pretending to sell a coat to a woman from Chicago.

Parlow's statement was read in Superior Court of Los Angeles in an effort of Bette's to prevent further access. Merrill strenuously denied everything and stated that Bette had done everything for three years to harass him and to cut off his relationship with Michael. He said that he had had to come into court repeatedly to defend himself against "false, unsubstantiated charges against my character and reputation."

He again insisted he had been a good father to Michael, that Michael suffered acutely from his constant appearances in court when he should have been leading the life of a normal boy, and that whenever he had seen Michael he had "done everything to make him happy." He explained that he had often flown back from locations in New York, Puerto Rico, and San Francisco just to be with his son and that he would scarcely have gone through such sacrifice if he had not loved Michael.

He demanded that no further efforts be made to interfere with his loving relationship. Bette was almost out of her mind when, despite the detective's report, the court once again took the view that the son should not be separated from the father.

To pay for the expenses of B.D.'s wedding, Bette took $125,000 for the part of Susan Hayward's mother in *Where Love Has Gone*, a heavily overwrought version of the novel by Harold Robbins. It was shot in San Francisco and Los Angeles. Bette had to play a severe, haughty matriarch rather like Gladys Cooper's character in *Now, Voyager*. Almost from the first day, Bette, not always comfortable with strangers, intensely disliked Susan Hayward. She was infuriated by Hayward's haughty behavior and at one stage screamed "Take this wig!" snatched hers off, and flung it at Hayward. The director, Edward Dmytryk, says:

"Actually, Susan was scared to death of Bette. Susan was a very difficult person to know. She was very reserved, nervous, and withdrawn. Bette mistook that apparently for rudeness. They were exact opposites. And then, Bette upset Susan right at the beginning. Something horrible happened.

"It was right on the first day. I discussed an upcoming scene with Bette. What the problems were and how I intended to handle them. Bette said, 'Fine, that's great.' Then I went out, and, I was told afterward, Bette came on the set, she was talking to the crew, and she said, in full earshot of Susan, 'Fellows, hold everything. The whole script is going to be changed. And *I'm* going to do the changing.'

"Susan was horrified. She was so insecure she had to work with a script very close to its original draft that she had accepted to work with. And worse still, here Bette Davis would be rewriting Susan's lines! I don't think Bette really meant what she said. But Susan was convinced she did. She stormed up to the bosses at Paramount and said she wouldn't tolerate anybody rewriting her lines. The bosses said not a word of this script could be changed. And that was a disaster, because the script called for changes. It never really worked."

Throughout the shooting, Susan Hayward ignored Bette and everyone else and rushed off to her dressing room immediately after a scene was over, sitting alone and chain-smoking ferociously, feeling frightened and appalled by the challenge of Bette's talent even without a single line altered in Bette's favor. Excellent though she was, Susan Hayward knew she wasn't in Davis's class.

There was a problem toward the end of shooting. Dmytryk says: "The studio wanted Bette to do a scene where she suddenly goes mad. The picture was finished, and Bette knew the picture was complete without it, and she refused point blank. The executives tried to get me to talk her into it, and I said, 'I don't know how I can talk anybody into going mad for one minute on the screen.' They were insistent. They were thinking of the censorship at the time, in which somebody who was guilty of anything had to suffer and pay the price either by dying or going insane.

316

Bette said 'no,' and I respected her for it. The studio started legal proceedings but finally gave up. Because of Bette's steadfast refusal to do it."

Bette's performance in *Where Love Has Gone* was simply a static repetition of well-worn mannerisms: technique operating in a vacuum. But the money made life easier for her; the comfortable life she had become used to was a constant expense to maintain. For a time, Bobby came to work for her, but help was costly and the rental in Bel-Air painfully steep.

Money was again the motive that forced Bette to an astonishing decision in the summer of 1964. Incredibly, she agreed to co-star with Joan Crawford in another overwrought Robert Aldrich melodrama *Hush . . . Hush, Sweet Charlotte*. The script cast her as a suspected former murderess driven to the point of madness by her relentless relatives. Wholesale borrowings from several other pictures, unbridled confrontations, and a hodgepodge of horror-film elements scarcely supplied the basis of a worthy sequel to the entertaining *What Ever Happened to Baby Jane?*

Shooting took place in part in Louisiana. When Bette arrived at the hotel, Joan Crawford was sitting regally in the lobby with twenty-five pieces of luggage around her.

Bette said, "What *on earth* do you think you're doing?" And she added, "*Why* didn't you come down on the chartered flight with the rest of us?"

Joan said, "I'm waiting for my rooms. I *preferred* to come separately!" She spoke these words with an air of such insufferable haughtiness that Bette wanted to strike her.

Bette swept on to her suite. A few minutes after she had sat down and lit up a much needed cigarette, Joan was heard shouting and banging on the door. In a bad mood, Bette pulled it open abruptly. Joan almost fell in. She said melodramatically, *"Bette, something terrible has happened!"*

Bette, in no mood to be sympathetic, coldly asked her to sit down. *"What is it?"* she snapped, through a cloud of smoke.

"It's horrible!" Joan sobbed. "They've put me next to a

garbage disposal!" Bette resisted the obvious comment and went on smoking in silence. Joan stormed out.

Bette announced at the beginning of shooting that she wouldn't play a single scene with Crawford. This was virtually impossible since many of their scenes together were crucial to the drama. She said that the director would have to use over-the-shoulder shots using doubles whenever dialogue was involved.

This was out of the question and Aldrich refused. The tension between the two women was so extreme that Crawford developed a psychosomatic illness that was described officially as "an upper respiratory infection." After only three scenes, she disappeared into a hospital and wouldn't come out. When she finally did return, she was so fretful and nervous about Bette she would film for only three hours a day. She went back into the hospital again.

Bette was delighted. Miss Crawford's attacks of the vapors entirely made her days. Now she plunged enthusiastically into casting suggestions. Her first idea was to have Vivien Leigh. Aldrich sent an S.O.S. to Miss Leigh in London. Vivien didn't respond. Finally, a representative of the studio, 20th Century-Fox, called Miss Leigh who said icily. "I could just about look at Joan Crawford's face on a southern plantation at seven o'clock in the morning. But I couldn't possibly look at Bette Davis's!"

Unfortunately, this remark was relayed to Bette, who was not amused. She decided to hedge her bets by casting her old friend Olivia De Havilland. Aldrich flew to Switzerland to talk to Olivia, who had played evil women before, but who preferred herself in saintly impersonations. He had considerable difficulty persuading her, but the thought of working with Bette again overrode her doubts. She flew to America in September. The production had been closed down for three months.

Only one person did not know Olivia had been hired: Joan Crawford. Miss Crawford, still in the hospital, heard the news that she had been replaced on the radio. She threw a vase at a nurse.

Bette and Olivia enjoyed working together. They often

met after work, exchanging reminiscences of the old days—
the days of *It's Love I'm After, Elizabeth and Essex,* and
In This Our Life. Their biggest scene together was in a car
in which Olivia had to strike Bette hard across the face.
Bette, her physical cowardice showing, knowing Olivia's
professionalism, called Aldrich the night before the shooting and said, in her little-girl voice, *"Of course,* you're
going to use my stand-in, aren't you?"

Aldrich said, "Shit, what are you talking about, Bette?
You'll play the scene!"

Bette said, "Nothing in the world will make me do it.
Any more than I would with Crawford. Olivia—whom I
adore—has been waiting to slap my face for twenty-five
years!"

Aldrich said, "This is *insane,* Bette!" But Bette was adamant, Aldrich had to accept a stand-in. Olivia arrived on
the set only to be told that Bette would not be there that
morning because she wasn't needed! Olivia had to slap the
stand-in instead.

Bette's performance in the picture was remarkable. She
created a convincing picture of degeneration, of southern
nobility in ruins. She was at her best in the scenes with
Olivia and her old friend Joseph Cotten, and in one sequence she reached an extraordinary degree of intensity.
Seeing Cotten seemingly risen from a watery grave (a direct steal from *Les Diaboliques*), she is reduced to gibber-
ing on a staircase. Always at her best in staircase scenes,
Bette turned into a kind of Kabuki lion, writhing around
on the floor with a great mane of gray hair, moaning and
growling. A scene that could have been laughable became
moving and disturbing.

The writer Gavin Lambert accompanied Bette and Olivia De Havilland to a first preview of *Charlotte.* At the
end of the screening, Bette turned to Olivia and said with
terrifying sweetness, "Olivia! You were so good! Even
when I was off the screen you somehow managed to hold
the audience's attention!"

Perhaps fortunately, Ms. De Havilland's reply has not
been recorded.

There was no shortage of work after *Charlotte*. Bette was experiencing the pleasures of a comeback. She flew to England to make *The Nanny,* a pleasantly unsettling melodrama in which her cosmic rage was contained in starched white uniforms. She liked the script and looked forward to returning to London, where perhaps her largest audience of fans existed.

The picture was directed by Seth Holt, who died three years later of an attack of hiccups during the shooting of the picture *Blood from the Mummy's Tomb*. He was a big, cuddly, plump man with great talent, who suffered from poor health. Bette liked him from the first day she met him.

She was accompanied by a companion and friend, Violla Rubber, who had formerly been the manager-companion of Marlene Dietrich and a producer of *Night of the Iguana*. She also made friends with the actress Jill Bennett, who had an important part in the picture. Often, in the evenings, she told Jill that despite the bitter fight over Michael, she still felt a leap of affection when she thought of her first days with Merrill. Somehow, the hatred fell away and she remembered their good times together. But these feelings soon disappeared when, in the middle of production, she heard that Merrill had finally won the long struggle for weekend access to Michael.

Enjoying vodkas in her dressing room after work each evening with Jill Bennett, Bette gave her much useful advice. Jill Bennett says: "Bette told me, never see your rushes. You'll get depressed about how you look and you won't be able to do a thing about it. I always hated the way I look on the screen. Bette said she did, too. I didn't need any encouragement not to see the rushes. I loved Bette. She was real, gutsy, and *very dangerous*. Dangerous the way a star should be! And she told me something wonderful. She told me, 'Always make love to your props. To the furniture.' I told her I remembered that moment in *The Little Foxes* when she leaned against the door as though she wanted to kiss it. I often found myself making love to tea trays in pictures after that.

"One weekend, I had lunch with her at Grosvenor House. I bought her some yellow roses. She was waiting for me outside the elevator. No other star would do that. One night, we went to the greyhound races. She was got-up tremendously for the occasion. She looked at me and said, 'You look awful. Why are you dressed like that?' I had a plain linen dress on. I think a Mary Quant. It was summer. She said, 'You won't be a star if you don't look like one.' She was in sequins and she said, 'I can't go into the races with you looking like this. You'll have to walk behind me as if you're my secretary.' And I did. It didn't bother me at all."

The Nanny was a modestly successful picture. Bette gave an intelligent, carefully controlled performance based on various nannies she had observed. She even bought her own white uniform in order to give the part authenticity, dissatisfied with the one that had been offered to her.

Bette was entering a period calmer than any she had known. In her late fifties, she had no romantic entanglements except for a pleasant, undemanding romance with a wealthy publisher. She had sufficient money to live on and moved to a nice house in Westport, Connecticut, where she felt more at home than in the imitation New England house in Bel-Air. Although she wasn't particularly happy, she wasn't particularly miserable either. In her house, Twin Bridges—the address was Number One, Crooked Mile—she knew a measure of peace. The house was called Twin Bridges because it adjoined a stream that was crossed by two small bridges. She brought back the traditional furnishings that had crossed the country so many times—sixteen in all, by rough count. She had the round dining-room table, the dining-room chairs that (she liked to laugh about it) were actually commodes. The books and records, the antique chairs, the albums and scores from her pictures, the piano. Her favorite room, a tiny, cozy den, looked over the flashing stream.

She became more jealous than ever of her privacy. A lady called Ivory kept house for her; Michael came home on school holidays; B.D. and B.D.'s husband Jeremy were often there; and Margot would visit on birthdays and anniversaries and holidays. Bette, in jeans and denim shirt, with a crazy hat usually perched on her fair, gingery hair, took pleasure in keeping everything spic and span for these arrivals. She seldom saw Bobby, who once again was suffering from severe nervous problems. She corresponded energetically with her cousins the Favors in Laguna.

She worked sporadically through 1966, co-hosting *The Mike Douglas Show,* appearing in *Gunsmoke* on television and the *Milton Berle Show*. Then, in mid-1967, she embarked on one of the worst pictures of her career.

EIGHTEEN

The Anniversary was the story of a monster mother, one of whose sons is a transvestite, another a sad married man, a third a promiscuous character. Bette had to wear a patch over her left eye, which proved to be a constant irritation.

The picture was made for Hammer Productions, which specialized in low-grade horror films. Bette arrived in London determined to do what she could with the script. She quickly ran into problems.

She had no rapport with director Alvin Rakoff, nor with her fellow actress, the admirable Sheila Hancock. Miss Hancock says: "I had acted in the play of *The Anniversary* on the stage. I was acutely aware that Miss Davis wanted to replace me with Jill Bennett for the picture, and was annoyed because Jill wasn't available. I was terrified of what would happen when we started work. I was a working-class actress from the Royal Court Theatre and had no interest in the so-called star system. I wasn't used to venerating a star. I wasn't prepared for Miss Davis's great entourage and for the fawning attitude it had toward her. I was shocked when the producer, Mr. Sangster, gave us a lecture saying that Miss Davis liked to be treated *with great adulation....*

"In the very first scene, Miss Davis came down a staircase. It was quite uncalled for by the scene, everybody in the studio, technicians, the lot, was present, all those not working on *The Anniversary* as well as those who were.

And, as she made her descent, everyone clapped on cue. And she went back and did the scene again for the cameras. I was dumbfounded. I thought, 'This is rather silly.' It took me a while to realize this was the way Bette Davis was used to operating. She was a queen, after all."

Bette kept insisting the director be removed. She wanted the camera operator fired. She summoned producer Sangster to her dressing room. Sangster says: "I asked Bette, 'What's the problem?'

"She said, 'I don't like all this whispering. I'm working with an eyepatch. At the end of a take, it's very dark and I hear the operator whispering to the rest of the crew. I want to know what's going on. I ask, "Haven't I hit my mark?" I ask, "Haven't I hit a light? Have I covered somebody in a shot?" Nobody answers me. Neither Rakoff nor the operator. I just hear this terrible whispering, and a voice shouts, "Let's have another take." I ask, "Why?" And the answer is, "Just let's have another take!" '"

Sangster promised that all discussions would take place with her. Soon afterward, Sangster fired Rakoff.

Bette approved the hiring of director Roy Ward Baker, whom she had known because he had directed Gary Merrill in *Night Without Sleep*, a picture which sounded like the story of her life. They had met at the premiere of *All About Eve* in New York and had traveled together to Los Angeles on the train.

Bette and Baker hit it off. She admired his professional polish and he saw to it that she was expertly handled in her movements, handicapped as she was by the eyepatch. He found her interested in making the best picture possible. But the tensions with the camera operator and other members of the crew continued. Sheila Hancock says: "Bette Davis never had rows on the set. I just heard a lot of shouting from the dressing room next door. People kept getting sacked; there was an awful atmosphere. I heard her say once, very loudly, from next door: 'I *hate* a good atmosphere on a picture. Every picture I've done where everybody had been hail-fellow-well-met had been a total disaster and any film that had been miserable to make was a success.' I began to think maybe Bette Davis was making us all unhappy so that *The Anniversary* would be a hit."

Sheila Hancock had to screw up her courage even to speak to Bette. She watched her doing a take and said afterward, with typical British reticence, "That was pretty good."

Bette puffed at a cigarette and glowered. "*Pretty good?*" she snapped. "Well, at least, thank God, *somebody has said something*! The highest compliment I've had on this picture is 'Cut! Print it!' "

This bitterness persisted despite the change of director. Bette went home to her house in Elstree every night on the verge of tears from irritation, exhaustion, and the ever-maddening eyepatch. Fortunately, Violla Rubber proved to be supportive, checking the rushes, taking care of problems as much as she could. Bette even quarreled with her, and, not long after, they had a complete falling out.

The picture was a pathetic affair; but Bette, so often faulty in her critical judgment, rather liked it—she was clearly influenced by the fact that she was in every scene, that the movie was a showcase for her, and that Roy Baker, unlike Alvin Rakoff, was slavish in his devotion to her talents; she promoted *The Anniversary* wherever she could. But it did not emerge as a critical or commercial success.

She plunged into even choppier waters when, after a brief break at Twin Bridges, she returned to Britain once more to make *Connecting Rooms* in 1969. It was the story of a middle-aged lady cellist in a lodging house in London, who shares a life of poverty with a homosexual professor and a hustling pop singer. If this sounds like a recipe for disaster, it was.

The director was an unknown named Franklin Gollings, a friend of Irving Rapper who specialized in Americana. He had managed to snare Sir Michael Redgrave to play the professor on the basis that Bette would play the cellist; and Bette on the promise of Michael Redgrave as her co-star. Neither Redgrave nor Davis liked the script, but they wanted to appear with each other.

Once again, there were major problems in making the picture. Bette had approved the casting of the young Alexis Kanner as the pop singer. He was strong, vigorous, and very masculine, with a slightly mysterious undercurrent, and she felt he was ideal. But after seven days she realized she couldn't work with him. Disappointed in her first choice, she suggested to Gollings that Keith Baxter replace Kanner. Gollings talked to Baxter, who was unwilling to play the part because he was already well into his thirties and the singer as written was scarcely more than a teen-ager. Bette persisted nonetheless.

Flattered, Baxter turned up at her dressing room. Kanner, painfully aware of what was going on, still had to struggle through scenes. Using every ounce of charm she possessed, Bette managed to persuade Baxter to take over. He left in a glow of pleasure. She lit up and rushed into the producers' office. They told her bleakly it was too late: to much had been filmed with Kanner. Bette had to call Baxter with the bad news; her language can only be imagined.

Now she had to face the ordeal of getting Kanner up to her standards. She and Redgrave abandoned their caravan, shared because of the restricted conditions at the studio, so that Gollings could rehearse Kanner in there before every scene. Kanner was so inexperienced that complete privacy was necessary. It was a common scene at Pinewood to see Bette walking around and around the set, smoking furiously, because she didn't want to interrupt these crucial rehearsals.

She also had her problems with Gollings. He was suffering from a bad case of influenza and was taking antibiotics. One day he was driven to taking a Scotch because of his problems with Bette. The Scotch and the antibiotics resulted in his appearing groggy through the morning's work. Suddenly, in a scene between Bette and the actress Kay Walsh, Gollings passed out and lay on the floor in front of them! Some men arrived with a stretcher and carried Gollings out. Bette immediately took over and directed the rest of the scene.

Later, when the scene was finished, Bette said to everyone who would listen, "Never in all my thirty-five years have I heard of such a thing as a director carried off in the middle of the day." And someone else said, "That's a tall story, with Bette Davis around."

There was a night location scene in a square in Bayswater. Bette had to appear in a first-floor room of an actual flophouse. She was about to start her acting when a drunken woman, who had somehow found her way back into the building, yelled at her obscenely. Bette instantly responded in kind. Then she remembered her royal position and delivered a speech which went as follows: "Ladies and gentlemen. Will you kindly accept my apologies for my terrible lapse in manners, and for using such awful words in front of you. I do apologize to you. That person who spoke so rudely 'got to' me and I lost my usual self-control. I'm so pleased you're here, madam, and I do hope you'll stay!" The pronouncement over, Bette went on with the scene. The woman fled.

Wherever Bette went, she drew crowds. In one scene in *Connecting Rooms*, she had to play the cello for a line of people outside a theater waiting to go in. When she arrived, in a Rolls-Royce, shooting was held up for three-quarters of an hour as the crowd swooped on her. She filmed until 5:30 A.M. and the crowd still had not gone away.

A problem was that Sir Michael Redgrave was ill during shooting and, like the director, made the mistake of taking a drink. In one sequence he nearly passed out, and she had to carry him in her arms through the scene. Another night, at a subway station, she waited all night long with the unit and he didn't show up. He had been unable to find the director's telephone number.

Connecting Rooms was so bad it was barely even released. Incredibly, it won the Diana Award, a Belgian honor. The award was presented to Redgrave and Gollings at a club in Mayfair, London. Both forgot to mention Bette in their acceptance speeches.

Back in Hollywood, Bette appeared in Robert Wagner's TV series, "It Takes a Thief." Wagner was one of her favorite people: a handsome extrovert perfectionist with a fierce desire to improve the standards of television. She liked his toughness, aggression, charm, and energetic momentum through life. She still loved Natalie Wood, his wife.

She attended a tribute to Jack Warner in which two thousand members of the world's press enjoyed soup, squab, and ice cream on Warner Brothers' Sound Stage 6. She gave a generous speech, burying the sadness of her departure from the studio some eleven years earlier. In a gesture at once theatrical and touching, she asked for the audience to stand and give silent tribute to all those Warner Brother actors who had died.

She must have been painfully conscious of how much had been lost with the demise of a great studio when she became involved in a picture even worse than *The Anniversary* and *Connecting Rooms: Bunny O'Hare,* about a bank-robbing woman who steals to support her children. Once more, her misjudgment got the better of her. She thought that the script would allow her an agreeable change of pace.

She liked the director, Gerd Oswald, who had directed her in "It Takes a Thief." He wasn't afraid of her and she admired his tough approach. When she said to him, "If I make mistakes, tell me. Don't get scared of me," he had replied, "Don't worry. You bet your sweet ass I'll tell you!" And she respected him from that moment on.

Oswald flew from Hollywood to Connecticut several times to discuss the screenplay with her. She made many intelligent suggestions. She was pleased that Ernest Borgnine would once again co-star with her; she had liked working with him in *The Catered Affair.* But when she went on location in New Mexico her happiness, her always limited optimism, rapidly dissolved.

She had to get up at four-thirty every morning and sit for hours in the sun that, as always before, seriously affected her skin. She was bothered by nights of rain, snow, and sleet, followed by suffocating days.

Some scenes she had to shoot on the back of a motorcycle driving on dangerous mountain roads. She hated this, and many times felt like breaking her professional code and flying back to New England. But her will drove her through everything.

Gerd Oswald remembers: "Bette and Borgnine didn't get on very well. I wouldn't want to say they were jealous of each other, but they were both wanting to be on top of the situation. There was competition between them. It never reached the boiling point or anything like that. It was funny, in a way. One night, Ernie would come to me and sit with me and ask if a particular scene to be shot the next day could be steered in his direction. Next night, Bette would do exactly the same thing. Of course, I'm calling her Bette now, but none of us would have dared to do so then. She was 'Miss Davis' at all times. Even the cable boys who were still in their teens behaved as if they'd been in awe of her from the day they were born."

The harsh sun, the freezing nights, the competition with Borgnine, the impossible script left Bette totally exhausted. And whatever merit the picture had was destroyed when it was cut by the producers. Bette sued them, but finally she decided to let the case drop. It scarcely seemed worth it.

Bette returned to Britain yet again, the one place left where her stock was high, to film a melodramatic concoction called *Madame Sin* with Robert Wagner as her co-star. She had to play a strange half-Chinese woman who owns a large castle in Scotland: A female version of Fu Manchu taken from the bottom drawer of Gothic schlockdom.

Madame Sin was intended as a pilot for a television series. Much of it was filmed on the Isle of Mull, off the coast of Scotland. No sooner had production begun, than Bette had one of her inevitable accidents. She was at the local hotel when a bumblebee flew up the sleeve of her robe and stung her twice on the arm. She was allergic to stings and blacked out. When she came to, she found that her arm and mouth were severely swollen. The doctor scarcely cheered her by telling her that she was lucky to be alive at all, since the bee had stung her in an artery.

Some scenes were shot at Pinewood Studios. She stayed briefly at a hotel called The Compleat Angler, and later at a house in Ascot facing the racecourse. A Mrs. Bottoms, an Englishwoman who had worked for the Royal Family, kept house for her, as she had often done before.

There was a cottage on the grounds of the Ascot house. Liv Ullmann often stayed there. Miss Ullmann sat by her window for hours on weekends, hoping to catch a glimpse of Bette. One day, Bette's phone was out of order; she went to the cottage and rang Liv Ullmann's doorbell. Miss Ullmann was overwhelmed. They became friends at once.

The shooting was reasonably comfortable despite the fact that Bette had little rapport with the director, David Greene. But once again the results were barely tolerable, and *Madame Sin* was never developed into a series.

Ironically, Bette was asked to appear in a television special called *The Killer Bees.* She was approached by ABC's Barry Diller; she insisted on discussing the show with the director, Curtis Harrington. She told Harrington she liked the script, about yet another matriarch (who runs a clan in the Napa Valley and has mysterious command over swarms of bees). But she admitted she was terrified of having bees settle on her face. Harrington assured her the bees would be deprived of their stings. But she was fearful of a recurrence of the recent episode on the Isle of Mull and at the last minute backed out. Gloria Swanson took over.

Bette was distracted in the early 1970s by helping a fan of hers, Whitney Stine, put together *Mother Goddam,* a record of names, dates, and places, covering her career but omitting her private life and starting, rather oddly, in 1930, when she was twenty-two. To enliven the work, she filled it with rude remarks attacking her critics, correcting statements by her directors in a book of interviews,* dispensing praise and blame, and underlining or altering some of Stine's statements with acid good humor. This is perhaps the only biography that was ever published in which the subject contributed a running commentary on the material. Her remarks were in every way outrageous—more entertaining than the rest of the text. Clearly, she had succeeded in censoring everything even more drastically than she had done in the case of Sandford Dody and *The Lonely Life.*

It was a bad period but it was followed by an extraordinary and exciting new development. In 1974, Bette em-

* Charles Higham and Joel Greenberg, *The Celluloid Muse* (Chicago: Regnery, 1971).

barked on her most ambitious venture in the theater. This was *Miss Moffat*, a musical version of Emlyn Williams's *The Corn Is Green*, in which she had been so admirable under Irving Rapper's direction almost thirty years earlier. The director was Joshua Logan, about whom Bette had heard much from his former wife Barbara O'Neil, when she had made *All This and Heaven Too*. She had never actually met Logan.

Logan had come to her after failing to attract Mary Martin for the project. He went out to Twin Bridges with her agent, Robert Lantz, and the musical's composer, Albert Hague. Hague sat at her living-room piano and played the score. She listened intently, striking kitchen matches under the table, nodding vigorous approval through clouds of smoke. She liked Logan rather well. But she felt nervous with him. She, with Margot and Bobby and their suffering constantly present in her mind, was terrified of neurotic sickness in her presence, and she knew, as did most people in show business, that Logan was subject to severe nervous and emotional breakdowns. She was impressed by his portly charm, his keen intelligence, his brilliant reputation in the theater.

Back in New York after this meeting. Logan wrote Bette a most impassioned letter. He stated in it that it would be "the thrill of a lifetime" if she would star in his production. He promised her she would not have one worrying moment; that he would look after her in every possible way. Logan knew her fear of failure. He also knew her physical problems, her weak throat, aggravated by years of smoking, her attacks of laryngitis. He did not remember her fall downstairs or her subsequent severe back problem.

Bette was touched by the note and had twelve Xeroxes made of it. She put the Xeroxes in her handbag, her makeup case, her traveling luggage, and her pockets so that she would never be in a position where she couldn't read it. She wrote back to say that the letter would be close to hand at any given moment; she knew that if there were any trouble she would simply pull it out and say, "Josh,

331

read the letter you wrote me." The letter gave her great reassurance; it made her decide to do the show; it allayed her fears of the theater, of facing a live audience. And her fear of Logan.

She had met and liked Emlyn Williams, who had appeared in an important part in *Another Man's Poison*. She was delighted to renew their friendship and told him how much she admired his changing of the location of the story from Wales to the South. She was full of compliments for his portrait of the young would-be writer, who had now become a black.

Supported by Logan's admiration, in complete accord with Williams, Bette started preparing *Miss Moffat* with huge determination. It is possible she wanted to emulate her envied Katharine Hepburn, who had made such a splash in *Coco* on Broadway shortly before.

At first, Bette didn't approve the choice of Dorian Harewood as the juvenile lead. But she began to waver after she had seen him in a reading and rather uncertainly changed her mind.

She worked desperately at rehearsals, giving all of her talent to the intelligently written central role. Gradually, she grew used to Harewood, who belonged to a different world, and who had a belligerent modern uptightness along with his skill that she found difficult to handle. Above all, despite her enthusiasm, she was terrified, as terrified as she had been when appearing in *Two's Company* and *The Night of the Iguana*. And once again she had the painful realization that she really couldn't sing. This hadn't mattered so much in *Two's Company*, in which she had only been a parodist, a farçeuse; but on this occasion she would have to convey emotion in her songs. There was the dread knowledge that there could be no understudy for Bette Davis. And there was not the protection of the secure, comforting world of the old studio system. Everything—the show's whole success—hung on her. If she failed . . .

To judge by his memoirs, Logan was troubled by Bette's insecurities, and perhaps not entirely sympathetic to them. He was used to working with hard-core theatrical professionals who would take on anything at its own level. He was also upset by the fact that instead of half-singing, half-speaking the numbers, she wanted to sing them straight out.

Her psychosomatic fear and tension now combined with her old spinal problem to cause severe back pain that made working day by day excruciating. There is no doubt that the fear aggravated the sickness and forced her into traction after working for only a few weeks. Logan was impatient, and Bette was aware what a disaster it would be for him, Emlyn Williams, and the producers if she could not appear. She forced herself against her nerves and nightmares to come back to work just before the opening in Philadelphia.

The show was sold out for six months. Bette's audience of middle-aged and older women and gays had rushed to buy tickets. The tour already had been sold. The show was good despite some mishaps on the first night, but Bette was not quite at her best. She had stage fright and her voice was giving out as it so often had done before. She fluffed some lines and transposed others. Logan recalled in his memoirs that to his dismay Bette turned to the audience at one stage and said, "How can I play this scene?" She was complaining because Dorian Harewood, who was not yet ready to follow the cue, wasn't onstage. When Bette realized she had made a mistake, she turned to the audience and said, "I was wrong. I want you to know that. It wasn't his fault. Go back, Dorian, and we'll start over." Dorian Harewood, embarrassed and swearing, made a second entrance.

Logan says in his memoirs that on another occasion, a child in the show thought she was drying up and whispered her line to her. Bette, Logan asserted, snapped loudly in front of the audience, "Don't tell me my line! I know it! You're a naughty little boy!" The child started to cry.

Logan, watching in the wings, and later from the back of the house, was desperate. He felt he wanted to take a cruise to the end of the world. But the audience gave Bette a standing ovation.

333

A disaster followed. Logan had made a mistake and invited critics to the first night. The reviews were not good. According to Dorian Harewood, everyone panicked including Bette and Logan. Emlyn Williams began rewriting the show. Bette found she was rehearsing one version of the show in the morning, playing another version in the afternoon twice a week, and at night, and was constantly being fitted for new costumes between performances. Songs were put in, others were dropped. Logan was trying to sharpen the show in response to the critics' comments. Broadway loomed ahead. But Bette felt this panic was unnecessary. The show was sold out for six months. She had had six weeks of grueling rehearsals and surely minor changes would be enough.

Bette was used to the control she had over motion-picture scripts and shooting. In all the bad pictures she had made, mostly in England, during the past few years, she had obtained complete command of everything. The results had been bad, but at least nothing had been changed in the writing without her permission. Now she realized she had no control. She was being asked to read lines prepared in haste and entirely over her head. She began to go to pieces. Logan indicates in his book that he found her behavior intolerable; that her breakdown was inexplicable to him. But he didn't realize the full story of her long imperial progress through trashy material over most of a decade. Or how easily she could be scared by strong professionals like him, when she had worked only with mediocrities who were subservient to her will.

Inevitably, she broke down yet again. Whether psychologically or physically, or perhaps both, her system cracked and she took to her bed in severe agony and despair, deciding she could no longer continue. One morning, after she had given a perfect performance, the pain in her back became unendurable. Logan called an independent doctor who said that if she continued she would die. She was sixty-six years old and she was not in the best of health; her perilously weak nervous system was once again in disarray.

She was genuinely distraught that she would have to give

up. Logan clearly felt she had behaved mischievously and irresponsibly. But he simply hadn't understood her tortured psyche; that this attack of sheer terror and desperation had a hundred previous exemplars in her behavior over the years. It was part of her pattern. It was neither unusual nor capricious.

It is unfortunate that *Miss Moffat*, which might have been the crowning triumph of Bette Davis's career, instead put the nail in the coffin of any hopes she might have had of returning to the stage. Just as she swore she would never shoot on location again after *Bunny O'Hare,* so she swore she would never work in the theater again as long as she lived.

Miss Moffat was an ordeal of ordeals—and an almost equally severe one for Bette was reading Logan's account of it years later. She threatened a libel suit against Logan, then abandoned it. Evidently, she dreaded the prospect of having to relive the whole experience on the witness stand.

There were consolations. Despite his miserable childhood, torn between his adoptive father and mother, Michael Merrill grew up a well-balanced, healthy, intelligent, normal American youth. He followed in Bette's father's footsteps, showing a keen interest in law, and became, like Harlow Morrell, a successful Boston lawyer. He was the apple of Bette's eye. He married a girl called Chou-chou Rains, and the marriage was successful. B.D.'s marriage to Jeremy Hyman continued, despite all of Bette's fears, to be a great success. Bette's marital agonies, the long history of emotional conflict in the Davises and the Favors had at last, it seemed, worked themselves out in this newest generation. And in her children, and her grandchildren, Bette found cause for rejoicing. She would look up at big, imposing B.D. like a child looking up at its own mother. B.D. had a will of her own without her mother's emotional fragility. She had an imposing strength that seemed to hark back to Grandmother Favor. She was Yankee, all right.

B.D. and Jeremy settled down on a farm in New England where they raised cattle and chickens. Perhaps because of the storms of her childhood, B.D. wanted peace and safe harbor. Certainly, after an early fascination, she

335

had no interest in following the tormented puzzle of Bette's film and theatrical career in her own life. And Jeremy had no desire to emulate his successful family in the picture industry, with the constant strain, fears, and tensions that lay behind the supposedly glamorous front of a movie executive's life. He was well aware how quickly a Mercedes or a Rolls-Royce could change into a tumbril.

Bette followed a current fashion in the mid-1960s by touring in question-and-answer appearances. Her first show was at the National Film Theatre in London, under the direction of Roy Moseley. It was a sellout; many lined the streets to see Bette arrive. It was a Sunday afternoon; Max Factor's opened for her so that she could be made up before she faced the audience. She was cheered as she stepped out of the Rolls and the crowd carried her a foot off the ground. She entered at the back of the auditorium; it took her eight minutes to reach the stage. People were touching her, holding her back; they wouldn't let her go. At last they released her and she walked on to a standing ovation. She was very pleased when her frantic "They're Either Too Young or Too Old," from *Thank Your Lucky Stars*, was flashed on the screen. Too often, she had watched the picture on American television, only to discover to her disappointment that the sequence was missing.

She gave a show that effectively sustained her self-made image of brisk, no-nonsense, salty New England horse sense. It was one of her most sustained performances: not a hint of nerves, insecurity, guilt, ego fragility, or torment—all those things that had driven her to great performances. By seeming to be the public's image of her, she in fact became somebody else. This public Bette Davis was as much a *doppelgänger* as the good twin in *A Stolen Life;* she was "done with mirrors" like the performance of a great magician. She was that same alter ego on the stage, humorous, pulled-together, playing with even-handed skill to the gays and the straights, that she had delivered in a bright blue ribbon package to journalists for fifty years. Just as she

336

had always given the same interview, worked out from first word to last to disguise herself, so she had always given the same off-screen performance. And that night's was the performance of her lifetime.

After the lecture Bette went up the staircase into the Green Room for a champagne reception. Roy Moseley had specified (he knew what he was doing) that no film stars or celebrities of any kind would be present. She had the floor, and if anyone had tried to upstage her she would have wiped it with them. She unerringly occupied center stage. With her old theatrical knowledge, she gained maximum attention by seemingly being minimal. She sat on the floor cross-legged, surrounded by people who had to bend double over their drinks to talk to her. She announced, cleverly, in her little-girl voice, that she would stay only for half an hour, while firmly intending to stay for an hour and a half. The organizers begged her not to sign autographs before she left. She compromised by only signing copies of *The Lonely Life*, *Mother Goddam*, *The Films of Bette Davis*. Moseley carried her out bodily through the crowd; her feet hardly touched the floor. Out on Waterloo Bridge, crowds were gathered to get a glimpse of her. People had to be pushed off the Rolls; they were crawling on the roof. The chauffeur could barely get the door open, and when he did, it was almost pulled off its hinges. So many people crushed against Bette as she finally entered the car that her legs were bruised all the way up to the thighs.

Later, the publicist John Springer organized "Bette Davis at Town Hall" in New York. The first half of the program was film clips, the second questions and answers. Springer asked questions and more came from the floor. The audience, plentifully filled out with her gay admirers, enjoyed her hugely. Once more, she acted up a storm as her other self.

She toured with Springer—even going all the way to Australia to appear at the Sydney Opera House. She was astonished when out of the cavernous darkness of the concert hall a voice she hadn't heard in a quarter of a century asked her a question. It was Casey Robinson, author of several of her best vehicles at Warners, who had settled in Australia with his wife Joan.

The Australian tour was as much a triumph as Mary Astor's in *The Great Lie*. Bette reconquered England on a tour for the impresario Billy Marsh. A sour note was struck when Marsh came to see her at Grosvenor House in London and told her she would be at the London Palladium but that the upper circle would be closed. Bette took this as a personal insult. How dare Marsh bring Bette Davis back to England, and then not have enough faith in her that three thousand seats of the Palladium would be completely filled? She said that she positively wouldn't even enter the theater unless every single seat in it all the way to the rafters was sold. Marsh quailed before her wrath; he soon found that every seat was indeed quickly disposed of on the strength of her name. She made three appearances at the Palladium and could easily have appeared there twice nightly for a month.

One night somebody in the audience who knew a thing or two shouted out of the darkness, "Miss Davis, I'd like to have a wager with you that I can name the mystery man, the mystery romance in your life that you wrote about in your autobiography." She paused for a minute and looked up at the gallery. Thoughts of Wyler must have flooded into her mind: her refusal to name the one man who could have mastered her, who could have matched her in a marriage in terms of income and professional importance, who could have pitted his strength against hers, whose ego was if possible as colossal as her own. But she would still keep faith with her long-held secret. She paused, and said: "No. I *won't* risk the wager. You just *could* be right."

She brought the house down several times. This imitation Davis could emphatically laugh at herself in public. Somebody called out rudely, "Is that your real hair, Miss Davis?" And she lied expertly (she was wearing a wig that day), "Yes, it is. And these are my real eyes, my real teeth, and my real tits!" The crowd went completely mad and gave her a standing ovation on the spot.

From that moment on, Bette eschewed wearing a wig in public. She didn't need to, as it happened: her ash blond hair was always pretty, and looked fine when dyed auburn or even a reddish-gold. The only problem was it was rather thin and lacked body; it gave hairdressers a hard time, but the results of their labors were often strikingly attractive.

Bette realized she needed a personal hairdresser. In 1974 she hired, oddly enough, Joan Crawford's: Peggy Shannon. Peggy spent hours fussing over Bette's wigs, one of which was striped and made her look like a tiger. Peggy's was a rangy presence: six feet tall, with a mouth full of very large teeth, given to wearing Bermuda shorts over skinny legs or pants with boots up to her knees. Today, after seven years of employment, Miss Shannon still refers to Bette as Miss Davis.

Always, Bette was surrounded by successive members of her personal entourage, which included, at various times, a pleasant, intelligent young English male secretary, Vik Greenfield, the antiques dealer Chuck Pollock, Robert Wagner and Natalie Wood, the devoted Roy Moseley, her lawyer (the expert Harold Schiff), and her agent, Robbie Lantz. But Peggy Shannon, angular and resolute, was her most constant companion, succeeding such earlier female acolytes as her maids Dell and Ivory and the remarkable Violla Rubber. The test of staying with Bette was a capacity to determine her ever-shifting moods, to know when she needed honesty and when she needed flattery, when she wanted to be amused—or to argue. Her bursts of fury had to be weathered; her nervous actress's temperament called for gentle reassurance one minute, honest criticism the next. The big furnace had to be stoked so that the ship could sail on. She was a great star still: Margo Channing.

In the years since Merrill there had been no overwhelming, devastating affair of the heart. There were brief, unsatisfactory romances even in her fifties and sixties, but for her, clearly, the idea of a prolonged and painful relationship was totally intolerable. Like most stars, she didn't like being alone; but she grew more used to loneliness as she grew older.

The late 1970s were years of almost constant work. Television occupied most of Bette's time. She made *The Disappearance of Aimée,* about the evangelist Aimée McPherson. One of the great problems of shooting *Movie of the Week* was that allegedly Faye Dunaway, her co-star, who was ill, would keep everyone waiting for hours. Lilia Goldoni, who appeared in the special, says: "We were shooting in very hot conditions in Denver and it was excruciating to have the production held up day after day. At one time, seventeen hundred extras were crowded into an auditorium for a sequence in which Aimée Semple McPherson would address the crowd. Many of the people were unpaid: they just wanted a chance to be in a movie and get a free box lunch. Bette went out and did a show for them. Knowing their distress because of the five-hour wait for Faye without air conditioning, she kept them in an uproar with jokes and stories and sang 'My Heart Belongs to Daddy' and 'Dear Mr. Gable.' "

Bette appeared in a four-hour version of Thomas Tryon's *Harvest Home,* as an elderly dowager with supernatural powers, in long black dresses and a small starched cap like an Amish farm wife. On location in Ohio, a local witch coven took exception to her performance, pelted her caravan with stones, and threatened to set fire to it. She had to have police protection.

Harvest Home was done in a rush, partly because of the grueling schedules of television, partly because she had to fly off to Egypt to make *Death on the Nile.* The situation was so extreme that when some of her lines had to be looped, and when she was in Egypt, the impersonator Michael Greer matched her voice in the dubbing sessions.

Always fond of exotic locations, Bette had much enjoyed Australia and now responded vibrantly to Egypt. She reveled in her part of a haughty rich woman suspected of murder on a Nile cruise. She was paid an enormous amount of money and behaved like a dream, challenged by the formidable all-star cast. She was especially fond of Angela Lansbury, David Niven, and Maggie Smith. She was generous with advice to the young, handsome, but inexperienced Simon MacCorkindale. She was entirely in accord with the director, the disciplinarian John Guillermin.

Bette's behavior on *Death on the Nile,* cooperating, doing everything with consummate skill, indicated that at the age of seventy her fires might at last be banked, that she was finally achieving a degree of balance and calm. Yet at the same time, expert though her performance was, it lacked the nervous edge, the brilliance she conveyed at her best. She was in better form in two intriguing television specials: *Strangers* and *White Mama.* In *Strangers,* she was cast for once with an actress of almost comparable power: the extraordinary Gena Rowlands. She played a reclusive mother in a small town whose daughter returns after twenty years of absence. At first, there is a terrific antagonism; the daughter is determined to win the mother for a purpose that we don't know about. Finally, the daughter succeeds; there is a scene in a restaurant in which both actresses are at their best. The daughter tells her mother that the reason she needs sympathy and warmth is that she is dying of cancer. Here, the writing has a daring seldom found in television. Instead of bursting into tears and embracing her child, the mother reacts with bitter anger and revulsion. It was a scene that only an actress in full command of her powers could have carried off. It was one of Bette's finest moments on the screen.

White Mama, directed by the former child star Jackie Cooper, was less satisfactory: a rather too anemic study of a difficult, edgy, but sympathetic black boy and an old woman he befriends when she is threatened with eviction. But in one scene Davis is admirable. She returns home to her apartment of many years to find all of her furniture gone. The director shoots her from the back, so that her face cannot be seen. But the actress doesn't need a closeup. The body seems to be broken in front of us. It doesn't merely sag with disappointment and hopelessness; it is as though every bone has been shattered and splintered. It is a sequence that proves, once and for all, that Bette Davis today is as great an actress as she has ever been.

In 1978, Bette was given the Life Achievement Award of the American Film Institute. Jane Fonda, whose advent had created so many production problems during *Jezebel,* was the graceful mistress of ceremonies and many old friends turned up to pay tribute. Bette, looking healthier and more youthful than she had in years, was in tremendous form, peering quizzically or humorously at a succession of people she had known from close to the beginning as they spoke in praise of her before a crowd of her peers. Henry Fonda turned up to talk of his double date with her and Bobby and a friend of his long ago in New England; Geraldine Fitzgerald remembered her fear of Bette upstaging her in *Dark Victory*, and how that fear was assuaged when she found that Bette was completely unselfish to a young actress; Celeste Holm, all the way from criticizing Bette for being standoffish toward the rest of the company in *All About Eve* now had nothing but praise; and Bette responded to these and other speakers with great aplomb. She had hated the Ralph Edwards "This Is Your Life" on her some years earlier because of its surpassing silliness; but now she was overjoyed. After her many years in the wilderness, the industry had made her Queen Mother, and she rejoiced in the role.

As so often in her life before, reality disturbingly matched a screen invention. There was a strange, unsettling parallel with *Strangers* in the year of its making, 1979, when Bobby came to see Bette from her home in Phoenix, Arizona. At first, Bobby seemed better than she had in years and Bette hugged her tightly, delighted by her appearance and the absence of any drastic sign of nervous stress. But that evening, Bobby told her the truth: She had been stricken with cancer, and had only a few months to live. The shock was grievous. That unhappy woman had spent her whole life in and out of sanitariums or institutions or in the grip of disastrous marital relationships. Her failure to be an actress, let alone a star of Bette's magnitude, had eaten into her being. She was the most tragic possible example of sibling rivalry. Without exaggeration, one can say that Bette did everything in her power to make Bobby's life a decent and happy one. But it was a battle lost from the beginning.

And along with the anguish of watching Bobby's fatal illness, there was the perennial unhappiness of seeing Margot, who was now over thirty, still with the intelligence of a child of six, still confined in a home in the East, still talking to Bette with the same harrowing repetitions. Time had stopped for Margot; she was trapped in a hell which the constant attentiveness of her successive teachers could only partly penetrate. Visiting Margot would sometimes leave Bette feeling desperately weary in the spirit; but at least she knew that unlike so many mentally retarded patients, Margot didn't have to live her life out in brutal establishments with dangerous and violent inmates. Because of Bette's loving concern and great fame, Margot was assured of the best possible care. And that had to be Bette's consolation in her anguish.

Occasionally, Bette would hear from her men. George Brent turned up at a public appearance and she looked at him with the combined amazement and unease most people feel when they see a former mate. She wondered what she had seen in him all those years ago. William Grant Sherry's death was published at one time in the press; but in fact he is alive and well. Ham Nelson's family, before Ham's death in 1976, came to see Bette in a TV show.

For years, Gary Merrill occupied a lighthouse on the coast of Maine. He occasionally saw B.D., and Michael. He mellowed in late middle age and stopped drinking; after years he returned to the stage in an excellent performance in the Broadway hit revival of *Morning*'s *at Seven*.

Family ties remain. Bette spends as much time as she can with her cousins, the Favors, in Laguna. Interestingly, she is very close to William Wyler and his wife Margaret Tallichet. She is still very fond of her childhood friend Robin Brown, who lives in Connecticut, and of Betty Lynn, the diminutive former ingenue she had known since *June Bride*. Today, Bette's life is perhaps happier than it has been since her mid-thirties. She seldom goes to the theater or to movies. Once, when she went to a motion-picture theater in Weston, Connecticut, to which she had moved from Westport in 1978, she arranged for herself and friends to see the picture in the projection booth. Always embarrassed by attention when she was not on show, she has now become virtually a recluse.

343

Much of the time she spends at home, which at the time of this writing is a large apartment in the Colonial House, on leafy Havenhurst Avenue in West Hollywood. It is almost opposite an apartment building where she lived briefly before moving to the De Mille cottage she shared with Ham on Franklin Avenue in the first years of their marriage. Sometimes, her old sense of humor flares up: she greeted her closest friends on her seventieth birthday in blackface, carrying a banjo.

Particulars of Margot Merrill's personal tragedy are given in several articles by Bette over the years. I met Ham Nelson and talked with him about his marriage to the star.

In 1981, Bette's health has never been better. She is hoping to appear in versions of any one of a dozen scripts. She embarked tempestuously on a new, tell-all memoir with writer Lee Israel and as tempestuously canceled it. She is alive and well and emphatically Bette Davis. Could one ask for more?

AUTHOR'S NOTE

I owe a special debt of gratitude to Dr. Robert Knutson of the Department of Special Collections, Doheny Library, University of Southern California, who gave me access to the collection of Warner Bros. materials, which included day-to-day records of Bette Davis's motion pictures, minutes of all her conversations, a large selection of her letters to Hal Wallis and Jack Warner, her telegrams, and medical reports on her condition. The Warner files gave a very clear picture of her brilliant but troubled career at the studio in the 1930s and the 1940s.

I am grateful to Dr. Robert Gottlieb, of the Library of the University of Boston, whose collection of Bette Davis memorabilia, deposited for public access by Ms. Davis herself, is remarkable. It includes reviews of her stage performances, juvenilia, baby books, numerous notations by her mother and Uncle Paul, and impressive unpublished manuscripts by both, covering very fully the star's childhood, family background, and upbringing. The Massachusetts Historical Society has proved most helpful in illuminating Miss Davis's ancestral origins.

Robert Mundy conducted a number of interviews for the book. Others I conducted myself, many of them before the book was planned. Peter Lev did a fine job of research.

Gunnard Nelson supplied stills from his unrivaled collection.

In the matter of Bette Davis's bitter and protracted custody battle with Gary Merrill over Michael Merrill, I should like to say that the statements made in various court hearings by Ms. Davis about Merrill, and vice versa, do not reflect the author's own views. They are a matter of public record in the court files of California and Maine. George Brent discussed his affair with Bette at great length; he also told me of her relationship with Howard Hughes and William Wyler, and his account was confirmed by several friends.

The following people, some of them sadly no longer living, provided reminiscences that formed much of the texture of this biography. Among them were Eva Le Gallienne, Joan Blondell, Martha Graham, George Cukor, Marlene Dietrich, Frank McHugh, Wallace Ford, Miriam Hopkins, Louis Calhern, Brooks Atkinson, Blanche Yurka, Marion Gering, Sam Goldwyn, Rouben Mamoulian, Joan Bennett, Ray Jones, Carl Laemmle, Jr., Reginald Denny, John Boles, Doris Lloyd, C.J. Boyd, Darryl F. Zanuck, George Brent, Hal B. Wallis, Pandro S. Berman, John Cromwell, Henry Blanke, Jack L. Warner, Gracie Fields, Sir Gerald Gardiner, Mrs. Justin Dart, Irving Rapper, Edward G. Robinson, Olivia De Havilland, Robert Buckner, Jeffrey Lynn, Henry Fonda, William Wyler, William Dieterle, Geraldine Fitzgerald, Adela Rogers St. Johns, David Lewis, Sally Sage, Barbara O'Neil, Casey Robinson, Anna Sten, Mary Astor, William Keighley, Paul Mantz, Raoul Walsh, Paul Henreid, Max Steiner, Jules and Doris Stein, Herman Shumlin, Lenore Coffee, Janet Gaynor, Vincent Sherman, Minna Wallis, Julius Epstein, Curtis Bernhardt, Catherine Turney, Norma Boleslavsky, King Vidor, Anne Baxter, Milton Krasner, Val Guest, Douglas Fairbanks, Jr., Robert Krasker, Stuart Heisler, Natalie Wood, Charles G. Clarke, Henry Koster, Daniel Taradash, Richard Brooks, Ernest Borgnine, Geraldine Page, Paul Beeson, Sir Alec Guinness, Anthony Asquith, Dame Daphne du Maurier, Norman Corwin, Ernest Haller, Gig Young,

Frank Capra, Robert Aldrich, Christina Crawford, Allen Miner, Edward Dmytryk, Joseph Cotten, Violla Rubber, Jill Bennett, Roy Baker, Sheila Hancock, Jimmy Sangster, Sir Michael Redgrave, Robert Wagner, Gerd Oswald, Liv Ullmann, Curtis Harrington, and George Edwards.

BETTE DAVIS'S PERFORMANCES

STAGE

Cukor-Kondolf Repertory Theatre   Rochester   1928
The Earth Between   Virgil Geddes   1929
The Wild Duck   Henrik Ibsen   1929
The Lady from the Sea   Henrik Ibsen   1929
Broken Dishes   Martin Flavin   1929
Mr. Pim Passes By   A.A. Milne   1930
Solid South   Lawton Campbell   1930
Two's Company   Charles Sherman   1952
The World of Carl Sandburg   Carl Sandburg   1959–1960
The Night of the Iguana   Tennessee Williams   1961–1962
Miss Moffat   Emlyn Williams   1974

FILMS

Bad Sister   Director, Hobart Henley   1931
Seed   Director, John M. Stahl   1931
Waterloo Bridge   Director, James Whale   1931
Way Back Home   Director, William A. Seiter   1932
The Menace   Director, Roy William Neill   1932
Hell's House   Director, Howard Higgins   1932
The Man Who Played God   Director, John Adolfi   1932

349

So Big   Director, William A. Wellman   1932
The Rich Are Always with Us   Director, Alfred E. Green   1932
The Dark Horse   Director, Alfred E. Green   1932
Cabin in the Cotton   Director, Michael Curtiz   1932
Three on a Match   Director, Mervyn LeRoy   1932
20,000 Years in Sing Sing   Director, Michael Curtiz   1933
Parachute Jumper   Director, Alfred E. Green   1933
The Working Man   Director, John Adolfi   1933
Ex-Lady   Director, Robert Florey   1933
Bureau of Missing Persons   Director, Roy Del Ruth   1933
Fashions of 1934   Director, William Dieterle   1934
The Big Shakedown   Director, John Francis Dillon   1934
Jimmy the Gent   Director, Michael Curtiz   1934
Fog Over Frisco   Director, William Dieterle   1934
Of Human Bondage   Director, John Cromwell   1934
Housewife   Director, Alfred E. Green   1934
Bordertown   Director, Archie Mayo   1935
The Girl from Tenth Avenue   Director, Alfred E. Green   1935
Front Page Woman   Director, Michael Curtiz   1935
Special Agent   Director, William Keighley   1935
Dangerous   Director, Alfred E. Green   1935
The Petrified Forest   Director, Archie Mayo   1936
The Golden Arrow   Director, Alfred E. Green   1936
Satan Met a Lady   Director, William Dieterle   1936
Marked Woman   Director, Lloyd Bacon   1937
Kid Galahad   Director, Michael Curtiz   1937
That Certain Woman   Director, Edmund Goulding   1937
It's Love I'm After   Director, Archie Mayo   1937
Jezebel   Director, William Wyler   1938
The Sisters   Director, Anatole Litvak   1938
Dark Victory   Director, Edmund Goulding   1939
Juarez   Director, William Dieterle   1939
The Old Maid   Director, Edmund Goulding   1939

350

The Private Lives of Elizabeth and Essex Director, Michael Curtiz 1939

All This and Heaven Too Director, Anatole Litvak 1940

The Letter Director, William Wyler 1940

The Great Lie Director, Edmund Goulding 1941

The Bride Came C.O.D. Director, William Keighley 1941

The Little Foxes Director, William Wyler 1941

The Man Who Came to Dinner Director, William Keighley 1942

In This Our Life Director, John Huston 1942

Now, Voyager Director, Irving Rapper 1942

Watch on the Rhine Director, Herman Shumlin 1943

Thank Your Lucky Stars Director, David Butler 1943

Old Acquaintance Director, Vincent Sherman 1943

Mr. Skeffington Director, Vincent Sherman 1944

Hollywood Canteen Director, Delmer Daves 1944

The Corn Is Green Director, Irving Rapper 1945

A Stolen Life Director, Curtis Bernhardt 1946

Deception Director, Irving Rapper 1946

Winter Meeting Director, Bretaigne Windust 1948

June Bride Director, Bretaigne Windust 1948

Beyond the Forest Director, King Vidor 1949

All About Eve Director, Joseph L. Mankiewicz 1950

Payment on Demand Director, Curtis Bernhardt 1951

Another Man's Poison Director, Irving Rapper 1952

Phone Call from a Stranger Director, Jean Negulesco 1952

The Star Director, Stuart Heisler 1953

The Virgin Queen Director, Henry Koster 1955

The Catered Affair Director, Richard Brooks 1956

Storm Center Director, Daniel Taradash 1956

John Paul Jones Director, John Farrow 1959

The Scapegoat Director, Robert Hamer 1959

Pocketful of Miracles Director, Frank Capra 1961

What Ever Happened to Baby Jane? Director, Robert Aldrich 1962

Dead Ringer Director, Paul Henreid 1964

The Empty Canvas Director, Damiano Damiani 1964

351

Where Love Has Gone   Director, Edward Dmytryk
1964
Hush . . . Hush, Sweet Charlotte   Director, Robert
Aldrich   1964
The Nanny   Director, Seth Holt   1965
The Anniversary   Director, Roy Ward Baker   1968
Connecting Rooms   Director, Franklin Gollings   1969
(Released 1972)
Bunny O'Hare   Director, Gerd Oswald   1971
Lo Scopone Scientifico   (The Scientific Card Player)
Director, Luigi Comencini   1972
Burnt Offerings   Director, Dan Curtis   1976
Death on the Nile   Director, John Guillermin   1978
Return from Witch Mountain   Director, John Hough
1978
Watcher in the Woods   Director, John Hough   1980

(Since 1970, Bette Davis has appeared in television movies.)

INDEX

Abbott, George, 48
Adler, Luther, 147
African Queen, The, 240
Aherne, Brian, 148
Alda, Robert, 232
Aldrich, Robert, 305, 306, 313, 317, 318, 319
Ali, Mohammed, 15
Alice in Wonderland, 97
All About Eve, 16, 256, 261–262, 264, 266, 270, 277, 324, 342
Alleborn, Al, 147, 148, 172, 174, 243, 247
All Quiet on the Western Front, 69
All This and Heaven Too, 147, 162, 165, 166, 331
Anderson, Hugh, 42
Anderson, John Murray, 42, 43, 78, 270
Angelus, Muriel, 170
Anna Christie, 161, 165
Anna Karenina, 166
Anniversary, The, 323, 325, 328
Ann-Margaret, 300
Another Man's Poison, 16, 262, 266, 332
Arliss, George, 43, 78–80, 121
Asquith, Anthony, 293, 294
Astor, Mary, 170–172, 203, 338

Atkinson, Brooks, 56, 61, 270
Atlas, Charles, 13

Back Street, 242
Bacon, Lloyd, 125, 126
Bad Sister, 74, 75
Bainter, Fay, 283
Baker, Roy Ward, 324, 325
Balcon, Sir Michael, 292
Ball, Lucille, 43
Ballard, Kay, 297
Bancroft, Anne, 311
Bankhead, Tallulah, 15, 19, 143, 175–176, 178, 257, 270
Banks, Monty, 113
Barry, Barbara, 311
Barry, Philip, 143
Barrymore, Ethel, 192, 193, 227
Barrymore, John, 32, 89, 182, 216
Barthelmess, Richard, 82
Bartholomew, Freddie, 166
Baum, Martin, 307
Baxter, Anne, 19, 257, 259
Baxter, Keith, 326
B.D. *See* Hyman, Barbara ("B.D.") Sherry
B.D., Inc., 232
Becky Sharp, 142
Beeson, Paul, 293, 294
Behrman, Stanley, 299

Benchley, Robert, 67
Bennett, Constance, 204
Bennett, Jill, 320, 323
Bennett, Richard, 62–63
Bergner, Elisabeth, 256
Berman, Pandro S., 78, 92–94, 97
Berman, Stanley, 271
Bern, Paul, 80
Bernhardt, Curtis, 226, 233–234, 235, 236, 255
Best, Edna, 196
"Bette Davis at Town Hall," 337
Bettger, Lyle, 310
Beyond the Forest, 250–251, 255
Beyond the Forest (Engstrand), 250
Big Shakedown, The, 92–93
Black Dakotas, The, 278
Blanke, Henry, 100, 136, 171, 201, 202, 203, 243
Blaustein, Julian, 280
Blondell, Joan, 43, 132
Blood from the Mummy's Tomb, 320
Blueprint for Murder, A, 277
Bogart, Humphrey, 75, 98, 123, 125, 127, 131
Boles, John, 76
Boleslavsky, Norma, 241
Booth, Shirley, 299
Bordertown, 94
Borgnine, Ernest, 284, 328, 329
Boston Herald American, 30
Boyer, Charles, 142, 147, 166, 167, 191
Breen, Joseph, 103, 201, 241, 242, 251
Brent, George, 10, 81, 102, 104, 141, 143, 145–147, 152, 160, 163, 170, 172, 194, 343
Brian, David, 252
Bride Came C.O.D., The, 173, 174, 175
Broadway, 48–49, 53
Broken Dishes, 60–62
Bronston, Samuel, 291
Brooks, Richard, 283, 284, 285, 286
Brown, Robin, 86, 343
Bruce, Nigel, 229

Bryan, Jane. *See* Dart, Jane Bryan
Buck, Ronald, 285–289
Buckner, Robert, 133
Bunny O'Hare, 328, 335
Byers, Elaine, 185

Cabin in the Cotton, 82–83
Cady, Howard, 297
Cagney, James, 161, 174–175
Cain, James M., 224
Calhern, Louis, 54
Callam, Earl, 165
Cannes Film Festival, 313
Capra, Frank, 299, 300
Carr, Mary, 70
Catered Affair, The, 20, 283, 286, 287, 328
Centlivre, Susanna, 43
Challee, William, 56
Chang, A. A., 105, 106
Charm School, The, 52
Chatterton, Ruth, 81, 194
Chayevsky, Paddy, 283
Cherkassky, Shura, 241
CinemaScope, 278
Clark, Dane, 236
Clark, George W., 30
Clarke, Charles G., 279
Coburn, Charles, 189
Coco, 332
Coffee, Lenore, 171, 172, 202, 211
Cohn, Harry, 281, 383
Colbert, Claudette, 256
Cold Touch, The, 289
Come Back, Little Sheba, 268, 286
Comet Over Broadway, 138
Conn, Carl, 100, 156
Connecting Rooms, 325, 327, 328
Conroy, Frank, 40, 44
Conroy, Virginia, 42
Cooper, Gary, 97, 176, 209
Cooper, Gladys, 168, 193
Cooper, Jackie, 341
Cornell, Katharine, 168
Corn Is Green, The, 20, 192, 193, 227, 229, 231, 331
Corwin, Norman, 294, 295

Cotten, Joseph, 251–252, 319
Coughlin, Kevin, 281
Coward, Noel, 59
Cowl, Jane, 201
Cradle Snatchers, 54
Crawford, Christina, 307
Crawford, Joan, 224, 225, 305, 306, 307, 317, 318, 319, 339
Cream Princess, 102–104
Crews, Laura Hope, 50–51
Cromwell, John, 93, 136
Crosby, Bing, 97
Crowther, Bosley, 220
Cukor, George, 44, 48, 49, 54
Cummins, Oscar, 153, 156, 160, 164
Curtiz, Michael, 82, 127–129, 155

Dall, John, 227, 229, 230, 231
Dallas, 249
Damita, Lili, 156
Dangerous, 13, 94–95, 101, 102, 118–119, 284
Dark Horse, The, 81–82
Dark Mirror, 232
Dark Victory, 20, 143, 144, 145, 150, 160, 171, 198, 230, 243, 258, 342
Darrieux, Danielle, 142
Dart, Jane Bryan, 124, 125, 127, 163, 173, 198, 226
Dart, Justin, 163, 173, 198
Davies, Marion, 88
Davis, Barbara ("Bobby"), 10, 28, 31, 32, 34, 37, 39–40, 49, 55, 66, 71, 80, 85, 87, 100–101, 111, 114, 121, 124, 131, 138, 140, 143, 163, 165, 173, 212, 224, 236, 287, 291
Davis, Harlow Morrell, 12, 26–27, 28, 31–33, 56, 58, 70, 137
Davis, Jay, 184, 185–186
Davis, Jim, 249
Davis, Owen, 126
Davis, Ruthie Favor, 11–12, 23–51, 56, 57, 63–84, 87, 92, 102, 105, 114, 124, 131, 133, 163, 165, 173, 199, 212, 214–215, 223, 224, 226, 233, 236, 287
Day, Rosalie, 212
Death on the Nile, 340, 341

de Camp, Rosemary, 196
Deception, 127, 241, 242, 243, 250
Decision Before Dawn, 262
De Havilland, Olivia, 130, 188–189, 232, 318–319
De Mille, Cecil B., 87, 111
Denny, Reginald, 73–74, 75
Detroit News, 236
Dieterle, William, 137, 147, 149
Dietrich, Marlene, 49, 147, 196
di Frasso, Dorothy, Contessa, 209–210
Diller, Barry, 330
Disappearance of Aimée, The, 340
Disney, Walt, 210
Dmytryk, Edward, 315, 316
Dody, Sandford, 297–298, 300, 302, 330
Donovan, Margaret, 173, 198, 212, 216
Dracula, 69
Dreiser, Theodore, 28
Dr. Jekyll and Mr. Hyde, 142
Duke, Vernon, 268
Du Maurier, Daphne, 291, 294
Dunaway, Faye, 340
Dunne, Irene, 141, 191, 196, 202, 280
Dunnock, Mildred, 227
Duvivier, Julien, 205

Eagels, Jeanne, 49, 95, 168, 169, 241, 270
Earth Between, The, 55–56, 61
Eaton, Evelyn, 166
Ebb, Fred, 298
Edelman, Lou, 123
Eden, Anthony, 211
Edeson, Arthur, 102
Edwards, Ralph, 342
Einfeld, Charles, 103
Engstrand, Stuart, 250
Entwistle, Peggy, 37, 56
Epstein, Julius J., 212, 216–217, 218, 220–221
Epstein, Philip A., 212, 216–217, 218, 220–221
Erickson, Leif, 296
Ervine, St. John, 56

Ethan Frome, 240, 250
Excess Baggage, 52–53

Fairbanks, Douglas, Jr., 263
Famous Mrs. Fair, The, 44
Farley, James A., 103
Farnsworth, Arthur ("Farney"),
   13, 162–169, 173, 176, 178,
   181, 182, 184–190, 198, 210,
   211, 212–215, 216, 217, 219,
   221, 226, 230, 240, 248, 261,
   274
Farrow, John, 291
Fashions of 1934, 92
Favor, Eugenia, 23–26, 30–31,
   32, 33, 38, 61
Favor, John, 173
Favor, Rev. Paul G., 23, 24, 25,
   214
Favor, Ruthie. *See* Davis, Ruthie
   Favor
Favor, William A., 23
Feldman, Charles, 191, 196
Field, Rachel, 162
Fields, Gracie, 113
Films of Bette Davis, The, 337
Finkel, Abem, 123, 134
Fiske, Dwight, 181
Fitzgerald, F. Scott, 38
Fitzgerald, Geraldine, 154, 163,
   171, 198, 342
Flaming Youth, 36
Flavin, Martin, 60
Flirt, The, 74
Flynn, Errol, 128–129, 130, 141,
   153–156, 202
Fog Over Frisco, 93
Fonda, Henry, 37, 129, 134, 136–
   37, 342
Fonda, Jane, 136, 341
Ford, Glenn, 232, 233, 236, 299–
   300
Ford, Wallace, 53, 54
Fox, Sidney, 75
Francis, Kay, 101, 143, 145, 160
Frankenstein, 69, 73
Freedman, Dave, 212–213
Frings, Ketti, 288
Frolick, Ann, 202
Furse, Dudley, 106, 130, 212,
   233

Gable, Clark, 91
Gang, Martin, 100, 104–106
Garbo, Greta, 70, 74, 91, 131,
   139, 143, 147, 162, 166
Gardiner, Gerald, 120
Garfield, John, 195, 214
Garland, Judy, 268
Gaslight, 48
Gaudio, Tony, 169, 204
Gaynor, Janet, 203–204
Gay Sisters, The, 178–179
Geddes, Virgil, 55
Geist, Kenneth L., 260
Gering, Marion, 60–61, 77
Glazer, Benjamin, 138
God's Country and the Woman,
   105–109, 112
Golden Arrow, The, 104
Goldoni Lilia, 340
Goldwyn, Samuel, 62, 134, 170,
   176, 177, 178
Gollings, Franklin, 325, 326, 327
Gone With the Wind, 50, 128
Good Housekeeping, 211
Goshow, C. Horace, 133
Goulding, Edmund, 129, 134,
   144, 145, 149, 152, 170–171,
   172, 191, 201, 202, 203, 204–
   205, 258–259
Graham, Martha, 43–44
Great Lie, The, 10, 170–172, 338
Greene, David, 330
Greenfield, Vik, 339
Greer, Michael, 340
Griffith, Hugh, 288
Guest, Val, 262, 264
Guillermin, John, 340
Guinness, Alec, 291, 292, 294
Gully, Richard, 211
Gunsmoke, 322

Hague, Albert, 331
Haller, Ernest, 145, 264
Hamer, Robert, 292, 293, 294
Hammett, Dashiell, 99, 196
Hancock, Sheila, 323, 324
Hansen, Chuck, 208
Hard Luck Dame, 101
Harewood, Dorian, 332, 333–334
Harlow, Jean, 73, 80, 91
Harrington, Curtis, 330

Harvest Home, 340
Hastings, Sir Patrick, 115–118, 120
Hayden, Sterling, 267
Hayes, Helen, 196, 299
Hays office, 201
Hayward, Susan, 315, 316
Hearst, William Randolph, 88
Heisler, Stuart, 267–268
Hellman, Lillian, 15, 175, 179, 196, 197
Hell's Angels, 138
Hell's House, 78, 89
Henley, Hobart, 75
Henreid, Paul, 163, 194, 241
Hepburn, Katharine, 16, 17, 91, 97, 104, 131, 139, 143, 171, 240, 241, 332
Hill, Arthur, 288
Hitchcock, Alfred, 281
Holliday, Judy, 265
Hollywood Canteen, 195, 199, 223
Hollywood Hotel, 132, 133
Holm, Celeste, 259–260, 342
Holt, Seth, 320
Hopkins, Miriam, 53–54, 126, 127, 133, 142, 152, 153, 170, 176, 178, 203, 204, 205, 206, 207, 208, 209
Hopper, Hedda, 135, 248, 280
Hornblow, Arthur, 43
Howard, Leslie, 93–94, 97–99, 130, 133
Hughes, Howard, 138–140, 142, 144, 145, 184, 185, 262
Human Jungle, The, 278
Hush . . . Hush, Sweet Charlotte, 317, 319–320
Huston, John, 136, 188–189, 190
Huston, Walter, 136
Hyman, Barbara ("B.D.") Sherry, 248, 255, 263, 266, 274, 275, 278, 287, 289, 291, 292, 294, 296, 297, 299, 301, 308, 310, 312, 313, 314, 315, 321, 335
Hyman, Elliot, 313
Hyman, Jeremy, 313, 314, 321, 335

Ibsen, Henrik, 37, 59, 60
If You Knew Elizabeth, 288
I'll Take the Low Road, 113, 114
Inge, William, 268
In This Our Life, 183–184, 186, 188, 192, 202, 308, 319
Israel, Lee, 344
It's Love I'm After, 130, 132, 133, 319
It Takes a Thief, 327, 328
Ivan, Rosalind, 227
Ivory (maid), 321, 339
"Jack Paar Show," 308
Jaffe, Sam, 212
Jane Eyre, 139
Jazz Singer, The, 66
Jezebel, 12, 19, 126–127, 133–138, 141, 142, 146, 150, 151, 192, 284, 341
Jimmy the Gent, 93
John Paul Jones, 291
Jolson, Al, 101
Jones, Ray, 69–70
Jones, Robert Edmond, 43
Jowitt, Sir William, 114–120
Juarez, 147–153
June Bride, 250, 343

Kanner, Alexis, 326
Karloff, Boris, 73
Keighley, William, 174
Kerouac, Jack, 28
Keyes, Homer R., 213–214
Keyes, Levi, 23–24
Kid Galahad, 127–129, 192
Killer Bees, The, 330
Kind Hearts and Coronets, 292
Kinnell, Murray, 78
Kiss of Death, 249
Kitty Foyle, 191
Knight and the Lady, The, 153
Koch, Howard, 168, 202
Koster, Henry, 279
Krasker, Robert, 264
Krasner, Milton, 259

Lady for a Day, 299
Lady from the Sea, 60
Laemmle, Carl, 72
Laemmle, Carl, Jr., 72–73, 76, 77, 79

Laff That Off, 54
Lambert, Gavin, 319
Lange, Hope, 300
Lansbury, Angela, 340
Lantz, Robert, 331, 339
Lasky, Jesse, 207
Lawlor, Andy, 212
Lawrence, Gertrude, 257
Le Gallienne, Eva, 40–42
Leigh, Vivien, 127, 160
Leighton, Margaret, 302, 303
Letter, The, 11, 15, 18–19, 144, 167, 168, 169, 193, 204, 241
Levee, Mike, 98, 105–106, 148
Lewis, David, 144, 162, 166, 167, 188, 211
Lewis, Ralph, 104–106
Library, The, 280
Life of Emile Zola, The, 147
Light, James, 55
Lightman, Herb, 233
Lincoln, Mary Todd, 242, 250
Linsk, Lester, 185
Lissauer, Herman, 154
Little Foxes, The, 15, 18, 175, 179, 181, 284, 291, 306, 320
Litvak, Anatole, 141, 142, 143, 152, 167, 262
Lloyd, Doris, 77
Locke, Katherine, 170
Loder, John, 215
Logan, Joshua, 167, 331, 332, 333, 334, 335
London Palladium, 338
Lonely Life, The, 92, 129, 301, 308, 330, 337
Lonesome, 69
Look Homeward Angel, 288, 289
Lord, Robert, 153
Love Affair, 191
Luciano, Lucky, 123, 126
Lukas, Paul, 197, 198, 215
"Lux Radio Theater," 156
Lynn, Betty, 250, 343
Lynn, Jeffrey, 134

McCarthy, Joe, 280
McClintic, Guthrie, 127
MacCorkindale, Simon, 340
McEwen, Walter, 126, 127, 143
McHugh, Frank, 53

MacKenzie, Aeneas, 149
McPherson, Aimée, 340
MacWilliams, Paul, 219
Madame Sin, 329, 330
Maltese Falcon, The, 99
Mamoulian, Rouben, 62
Mankiewicz, Joseph L., 19, 256, 257, 258–259
Mantz, Paul, 184, 214
Man Who Came Back, The, 54
Man Who Came to Dinner, The, 181–183
Man Who Played God, The, 78–79, 81
Man with the Black Hat, The, 99–102
March, Fredric, 141, 143
Marked Woman, 123, 125, 126, 130, 284
Marquis, Don, 43
Marsh, Billy, 338
Martin, Mary, 331
Marx, Harpo, 183
Mary of Scotland, 97, 107
Mason, James, 240
Mattison, Frank, 218, 219, 220
Maugham, Somerset, 14, 92–94, 97, 161, 168
Mayerling, 142
Mayo, Archie, 94, 99, 130
Meek, Donald, 61
Menace, The, 77, 78
Men Behind, The, 123
Merrill, Gary, 11, 14, 260–269, 273–280, 283, 289–290, 291, 295
Merrill, Margot, 263, 266, 273–280, 286, 289, 344
Merrill, Michael, 266, 273–280, 289
Methot, Mayo, 125
Metro-Goldwyn-Mayer, 258
Mike Douglas Show, The, 322
Mildred Pierce, 224
Miller, Seton I., 123
Milliken, Carl, 70–71
Milne, A. A., 50
Milton, Robert, 42
Milton Berle Show, 322
Miner, Allen, 310
Mines, Harry, 232

358

Miracle, The, 97
Miracle Worker, The, 311
Miss Moffat, 331, 332, 335
Mitchell, Margaret, 9, 129
Moll, Elick, 280
Monroe, Marilyn, 279–280
Montgomery, Douglass, 113
Montgomery, Elizabeth, 299
Montgomery, Robert, 250
Moore, Colleen, 36
Moore, Paul, 213
Moore, Raymond, 50
Morgan, Dennis, 232
Morgan, Helen, 9
Moseley, Roy, 256–257, 337
Mother Goddam, 330, 337
Mountain Justice, 105
Mr. Pim Passes By, 51
Mr. Skeffington, 19, 211–212,
    215–220
Muni, Paul, 43, 94, 123, 147–148,
    149, 152
Murphy, Rosemary, 288
My Sister Eileen, 202

Nanny, The, 320, 321
Nazimova, Alla, 59
Nelson, Harmon ("Ham") O.,
    13, 38–39, 46, 51–52, 74, 83–84,
    85, 86, 92, 96, 101, 111–121,
    123, 124, 130–132, 135, 139–
    140, 144, 162, 212, 226, 240,
    261, 343, 344
New York Herald Tribune, 280
New York World-Telegram, 270
Night of the Iguana, 301, 302,
    320, 332
Night Without Sleep, 324
Niven, David, 289, 340
Novak, Kim, 283
Now, Voyager, 19, 23, 127, 162,
    192, 193, 194, 195, 196, 197,
    241, 315
Now, Voyager (Prouty), 190

O'Brien, Pat, 78
Obringer, Roy, 100, 109, 112,
    133, 156, 252
Of Human Bondage, 14, 92–98,
    103

Of Human Bondage (Maugham),
    14
Old Acquaintance, 14–15, 201,
    208, 209
Old Maid, The, 152, 154
Oliver, W. E., 77
Olivier, Laurence, 154, 155
O'Neal, Patrick, 302
O'Neil, Barbara, 167, 331
One-Way Passage, 141, 160
Orry-Kelly, 147, 154, 155, 188,
    193, 227, 233, 234, 235
O'Sullivan, Maureen, 291
Oswald, Gerd, 328

Page, Anita, 43
Page, Geraldine, 286
Papp, Joseph, 56
Paramount, 258, 316
Parlow, Michael, 314–315
Parsons, Louella, 135, 240, 248
Paula, 290
Payment on Demand, 255, 262
Pelgram, Barbara Davis. See
    Davis, Barbara ("Bobby")
Pelgram, Robert, 173
Perkins, Anthony, 288
"Perry Mason," 308
Petrified Forest, The, 97–101, 119–
Pfeiffer, Dell, 87, 102, 169, 263
Phantom Crown, The, 147, 149
Philadelphia Story, The, 48
Phone Call from a Stranger, 20,
    266
Photoplay, 211, 236–237
Pickford, Mary, 31, 36, 280
Pierce, Jack, 72–73
Pierson, Lelah, 289
Pirandello, Luigi, 59
Pocket Full of Miracles, A, 299,
    301, 302
Pogany, Willy, 43
Polito, Sol, 106, 204, 233, 264
Pollock, Channing, 43
Pollock, Chuck, 339
Porter, Sadie, 25
Powell, William, 160
Price, Bridget, 74, 133, 146, 212
Prince, Don, 7, 17
Private Lives of Elizabeth and

359

Essex, The, 153–156, 159, 212, 278, 280, 319
Prouty, Olive Higgins, 190

Quietly, My Captain Waits, 166
Quo Vadis, 262

Raffles, 62
Rains, Chou-chou, 335
Rains, Claude, 149, 215, 217, 218, 220, 241, 242
Rakoff, Alvin, 323, 324, 325
Rapper, Irving, 127, 128, 193, 194, 227, 228, 229, 230, 231, 241, 243, 248, 264, 265, 331
Redgrave, Michael, 325, 326, 327
Reinhardt, Max, 147
Rich Are Always with Us, The, 81, 194
Richter, Paul, 185
Ripley, Clements, 134
Ritter, Thelma, 257
Robbins, Harold, 315
Robinson, Casey, 130, 143, 146, 153, 167, 194, 338
Robinson, Edward G., 127, 128
Rogers, Ginger, 141, 147, 191
Romeo and Juliet, 130
Romero, Caesar, 43
Roshanara, 39
Ross, Gene, 227
Rossen, Robert, 123
Rowlands, Gena, 341
Rubber, Violla, 320, 325, 339
Runyon, Damon, 299
Russell, Mary Annette Beauchamp ("Elizabeth"), 211
Russell, Rosalind, 202

Sage, Sally, 106, 134, 166, 176, 235
Sandburg, Carl, 92, 295, 297
Sanders, George, 257
Sangster, Jimmy, 323, 324
Satan Met a Lady, 101
Scapegoat, The, 291, 292, 306
Schalbaugh, Rev. Mark, 84
Schallert, Edwin, 105, 112
Schiff, Harold, 339

Seed, 76
Sergeant York, 176
Selznick, David O., 13, 128, 129, 143
Shadow of a Doubt, 281
Shannon, Peggy, 339
Shaw, Frank, 99
Shaw, George Bernard, 59
Shearer, Norma, 51, 191
Sherman, Vincent, 205–208, 212, 215–216, 219, 220
Sherry, Barbara. *See* Hyman, Barbara ("B.D.") Sherry
Sherry, William Grant, 14, 226–227, 232, 236–237, 239, 240, 243, 247, 248–249, 255, 256, 260, 343
Sherwood, Robert, 97
Shining Victory, 192
Showboat, 69
Shumlin, Herman, 196, 197, 198
Sir Walter Raleigh, 278
Sisters, The, 141
Smith, Cecil, 288
Smith, Maggie, 340
Solid South, 62, 63
Springer, John, 337
Squall, The, 54
Stacey, Eric, 227–228, 230
Stahl, John, 76
Stanwyck, Barbara, 179, 262, 280
Star, The, 267–268
Star Is Born, A, 48
State of the Union, 242
Steel, Anthony, 265
Stein, Doris, 196
Stein, Jules, 196, 205, 232
Steiner, Max, 156, 195
Stella Dallas, 190
Sten, Anna, 170
Stewart, Florence, 276
Stine, Whitney, 330
Stolen Life, A, 232–236, 286, 300, 336
Storm Center, 281, 283, 287
Story of a Divorce, The, 255, 262
Story of Louis Pasteur, The, 147
Story of Temple Drake, The, 142

Strangers, 341, 342
Strictly Dishonorable, 63
Strindberg, August, 59
Sturges, Preston, 63
Sullavan, Margaret, 134–135, 203
Sullivan, Barry, 255–256
Sullivan, Jack, 141–142
Swanson, Gloria, 330
Sweet Bird of Youth, 286
Swindell, Larry, 89–90
Sydney, Sylvia, 170

Tallichet, Margaret, 144, 343
Taplinger, Bob, 168, 186
Taradash, Daniel, 280, 281, 282
Tarkington, Booth, 74, 75
Taylor, Robert, 262
Thank Your Lucky Stars, 203, 336
That Certain Woman, 129, 130, 134
That Woman Brown, 161, 165
Thayer, Abbott, 33
They Died with Their Boots On, 202
They Drive by Night, 94
Third Man, The, 264
This Is Your Life, 342
Thompson, Harriet Keyes, 23–24
'Til We Meet Again, 160–161
Time magazine, 268
Toeplitz, Ludovic, 109, 113, 114, 116, 120, 131
Tone, Franchot, 95, 141
Tracy, Spencer, 89–90, 143, 163
Trevor, Claire, 288
Trilling, Steve, 218, 219, 220, 228, 232, 244, 245–246, 247, 249
Trouble in Paradise, 142
Tryon, Thomas, 340
Turney, Catherine, 226, 232, 233, 234, 235, 249
20,000 Years in Sing Sing, 89
Two Mrs. Carrolls, The, 257
Two's Company, 268–270, 273

Ullmann, Liv, 329–330
Up at a Villa, 161

Van Druten, John, 15, 202, 203, 204
Van Fleet, Jo, 289
Vanity Fair, 142
Variety, 307
Victory Through Air Power, 210
Vidor, King, 251–253
Virgin Queen, The, 278, 279
Vreeland, Bob, 230–231

Wagner, Robert, 327, 339
Wagon Train, 294
Wallace, Mike, 225
Wallis, Hal, 15, 79, 80, 98, 105–108, 123–127, 130, 133–136, 137, 144–156, 160, 170, 172, 174, 176, 178, 181, 182, 184, 188, 190, 191, 192, 193, 196, 198, 201, 204, 212, 218, 220
Wallis, Minna, 212
Walsh, Kay, 326
Walsh, Raoul, 189, 190
Ward, Fanny, 211
Warner, Ann, 120
Warner, Harry, 119
Warner, Jack, 79, 98, 100, 101, 104–109, 111–121, 123, 126, 129, 133, 138, 141, 143, 144, 147, 151–154, 157, 159–162, 176, 181, 182, 184, 187, 189, 192, 193, 195, 203, 204, 208–209, 212, 219, 220, 223, 228, 229, 241, 242, 244–247, 248, 250, 251, 253, 306, 328
Wasserman, Lew, 205, 245, 252
Watch on the Rhine, 196, 198
Waterloo Bridge, 76–77
Watkins, Linda, 57
Watson, Lucile, 198
Way Back Home, 78
Werfel, Franz, 147
Wernick, Sidney, 301
Westmore, Perc, 19, 154, 174, 175, 193, 198, 215, 216, 219, 227, 231, 244, 247, 258
Whale, James, 77
Wharton, Edith, 152
What Ever Happened to Baby Jane? 305–308, 311–313, 317
Where Love Has Gone, 315–317
White Mama, 341

361

Whiting, Harry, 34
Whiting, Marjorie, 33–34
Widmark, Richard, 249
Wild Duck, The, 37, 56–59, 78
Wilde, Oscar, 73
Wilk, Jake, 126
William, Warren, 82, 101
Williams, Andy, 308
Williams, Emlyn, 227, 331, 332, 333, 334
Williams, Rhys, 227
Williams, Tennessee, 300, 301, 303
Wilson, Dr., 243, 244
Winchell, Walter, 271
Windust, Bretaigne, 249
Winter Meeting, 249, 250
Winters, Jonathan, 308
Witness to Murder, 277
Wolfe, Thomas, 288
Wonder! A Woman Keeps a Secret, The, 43
Wood, Audrey, 302
Wood, C. J., 161
Wood, Natalie, 268, 327, 339

Wood, Peggy, 201
Wood, Vernon, 106–108, 111, 115, 161
Woodward, Stanley, 40
Woolley, Monty, 182, 183
World of Carl Sandburg, The, 294, 296, 297, 299
Worth, Irene, 257
Wright, Gilbert, 212
Wright, Tenny, 99, 102, 109, 124, 141, 208, 230, 231
Wyler, William, 15, 18, 134–138, 139, 141, 142, 144, 145, 147, 149, 167, 168, 175, 176, 177, 178, 251, 282, 284, 338, 343
Wynters, Charlotte, 53

Yankee Doodle Dandy, 192
Yellow, 54
Young, Gig, 299
Young, Loretta, 15, 147
Yurka, Blanche, 37, 56–57, 59, 78
Zanuck, Darryl F., 79, 256, 262, 266, 278, 280

THE NATIONAL BEST SELLER

Love, Dad

by Evan Hunter

A deeply moving novel about a father and daughter reaching out to each other as changing times and changing values drive them apart. It is so moving, so true, so close to home—that it hurts. For we all have been there.

"Gripping. Moving. Enormously readable. A fine and sensitive novel that deals with an important aspect of the sixties."—Howard Fast, bestselling author of *The Immigrants*

A Dell Book $3.95   (14998-3)

Dell Bestsellers

- [ ] **ELIZABETH TAYLOR:** The Last Star
  by Kitty Kelley.................................$3.95 (12410-7)
- [ ] **THE LEGACY** by Howard Fast.................$3.95 (14719-0)
- [ ] **LUCIANO'S LUCK** by Jack Higgins...........$3.50 (14321-7)
- [ ] **MAZES AND MONSTERS** by Rona Jaffe...$3.50 (15699-8)
- [ ] **TRIPLETS** by Joyce Rebeta-Burditt..........$3.95 (18943-8)
- [ ] **BABY** by Robert Lieberman......................$3.50 (10432-7)
- [ ] **CIRCLES OF TIME** by Phillip Rock...........$3.50 (11320-2)
- [ ] **SWEET WILD WIND** by Joyce Verrette......$3.95 (17634-4)
- [ ] **BREAD UPON THE WATERS**
  by Irwin Shaw.................................$3.95 (10845-4)
- [ ] **STILL MISSING** by Beth Gutcheon $3.50 (17864-9)
- [ ] **NOBLE HOUSE** by James Clavell.............$5.95 (16483-4)
- [ ] **THE BLUE AND THE GRAY**
  by John Leekley.................................$3.50 (10631-1)

LUCIANO'S LUCK

1943. Under cover of night, a strange group parachutes into Nazi occupied Sicily. It includes the overlord of the American Mafia, "Lucky" Luciano. The object? To convince the Sicilian Mafia king to put his power—the power of the Sicilian peasantry—behind the invading American forces. It is a dangerous gamble. If they fail, hundreds of thousands will die on Sicilian soil. If they succeed, American troops will march through Sicily toward a stunning victory on the Italian Front, forever indebted to Mafia king, Lucky Luciano.

A DELL BOOK   14321-7 $3.50

JACK HIGGINS

bestselling author of *Solo*